INTRODUCTION TO BIL

MACMILLAN MODERN LINGUISTICS SERIES

Series Editor

Professor Maggie Tallerman
Newcastle University, UK

Each textbook in the Macmillan Modern Linguistics series is designed to provide an introduction to a topic in contemporary linguistics and allied disciplines, presented in a manner that is accessible and attractive to readers with no previous experience of the topic. The texts are designed to engage the active participation of the reader, and include exercises and suggestions for further reading. As well as an understanding of the basic concepts and issues for each topic, readers will gain an up-to-date knowledge of current debates and questions in the field.

Introduction to Bilingualism

Christina Schelletter

First published 2020 by
RED GLOBE PRESS

Red Globe Press in the UK is an imprint of Springer Nature Limited, registered in England, company number 785998, of 4 Crinan Street, London N1 9XW.

Red Globe Press® is a registered trademark in the United States, the United Kingdom, Europe and other countries.

ISBN 978–1–137–60954–0 paperback

This book is printed on paper suitable for recycling and made from fully managed and sustained forest sources. Logging, pulping and manufacturing processes are expected to conform to the environmental regulations of the country of origin.

A catalogue record for this book is available from the British Library.

A catalog record for this book is available from the Library of Congress.

Contents

Acknowledgements

When Paul Stevens, the then Commissioning Editor for Psychology, Language & Linguistics at Red Globe Press, visited the University of Hertfordshire back in 2013, I was pleased to find that he was very positive towards the idea of a book on the topic of bilingual acquisition which incorporates different approaches to the topic. Thanks to Paul's encouragement and patience, the ideas slowly took shape, and the project progressed to contract stage in 2016. Paul has been supportive throughout the process and so was Helen Caunce who took over from Paul last year.

My thanks also go to my colleagues at the University of Hertfordshire who have been following my progress and encouraged me on a regular basis. In particular, the so-called 'writing retreat' days, organised by the History group at the University campus in Bayfordbury. These days were crucial in the beginning of the writing process as the peaceful atmosphere there helped with the concentration needed to get started. And it was good to share thoughts and difficulties at the beginning and end of the writing days.

I would also like to thank the three anonymous reviewers for their positive comments and helpful suggestions relating to the terminology and the structure of the material across the different chapters.

Some of my final year students in Hertfordshire this year were kind enough to give me feedback on a draft chapter which was relevant for their coursework. Thank you for taking an interest in the book and suggestions to make it more relevant for students who want to study the subject.

A special thank you to my husband John for proofreading the chapters and to my bilingual daughters, Emily and Sonja. Observing their language development first-hand started my interest in this area in the first place and enabled me to gain valuable insight into this fascinating topic.

Introduction

Bilingualism is a much-studied topic area, both by linguists and psychologists. While linguists focus on the language that children produce and draw conclusions about children's language knowledge, psychologists investigate the mental processes that children go through that enable them to produce language.

This textbook introduces you to the study of bilingualism from both points of view. The study of bilingual acquisition makes a distinction whether children hear more than one language from the moment of birth, or whether they become bilingual through the community or school at a later point. This is important as later onset of another language means that the child has already progressed in the acquisition of the first language and it affects the acquisition process.

When looking at mental processes involved in learning a language, the exact point when someone started hearing another language does not seem as crucial. The question is whether learning two languages simultaneously, sequentially or as second language learners makes a difference to the way both languages are processed. For this reason, both simultaneous and sequential learners are considered in this book.

Within the study of language acquisition, the focus has initially been on the question of whether children are able to differentiate the languages they hear. Early case studies looked at evidence in terms of a common or a differentiated system for the two languages. More sophisticated experimental methods were able to show that even young infants distinguish the languages they hear. This means that they are able to make a distinction well before they have even produced any words.

At the point where language differentiation was no longer in doubt, the interaction between the two languages of bilingual children was studied. If children produce forms in one language that are clearly influenced by the system of the other language, this cannot be due to a lack of differentiation. It seems that such cross-linguistic influences occur if particular conditions are fulfilled by the two languages involved.

The more recent focus of bilingual acquisition studies though has been on the amount of input that bilingual children hear in each of their languages. Usage-based theories have highlighted the role of input frequency in the acquisition of language. There is evidence that children learn what they hear most frequently. In the light of such views, bilingual acquisition has been seen as possibly lagging behind monolingual acquisition. There is the assumption that the amount of language that a balanced bilingual child hears must be half of that of a monolingual in each of their languages.

This view is backed up by findings that bilingual children's vocabulary at school age is generally lower than that of monolinguals in at least one of their languages, as well as similar comparisons in relation to their use of inflectional endings. Overall, studies that focus just on the development of language show bilinguals to be at a disadvantage in terms of their language levels, compared to their monolingual peers.

These findings are in contrast to studies that have focused on the cognitive skills of bilingual children. From quite early on, it was shown that bilingual children are more flexible compared to monolinguals when asked to switch words around arbitrarily. This is possibly because they know that speakers of different languages use different words for the same objects.

Further studies investigating the basis for a difference in cognitive skills have revealed that children with a high proficiency in both languages are better than monolingual children in different areas of language awareness, as well as in non-verbal skills relating to the ability to focus on one particular stimulus and switch attention, as well as memory. The non-verbal skills have been found to develop gradually in children with different levels of language proficiency.

The basis for the enhanced cognitive skills lies in the fact that the languages of a bilingual speaker compete during language tasks. Experimental studies with both children and adults have shown that both languages of a bilingual are activated during language tasks. This leads to enhanced executive functions in bilingual speakers.

By investigating both language and cognitive skills in bilingual children, the textbook gives a more complete picture of bilingual language development than texts that only focus on one of these aspects. Studies of bilingual processing show that even where language levels are lower compared to monolinguals, there are generally no differences in the underlying mental processes in bilingual children. Any possible costs need to be seen in relation to the cognitive advantages.

Bilingual Language Development

1

Growing up with more than one language is a common experience for many children. Contrary to what people used to believe, bilingualism does not delay language learning. Even better, growing up as a bilingual speaker has distinct advantages. If one speaks more than one language, one can talk to more people. In addition, speaking more than one language regularly has also been found to enhance brain function. Bilinguals do better than monolinguals on a variety of tasks, both verbal and non-verbal. And in older age, bilingualism helps to keep the brain fit and to delay the onset of dementia.

This book is about children who grow up with two languages. It is remarkable that children seem to be able to pick up two languages so effortlessly when adult learners find it a lot harder to learn another language, particularly the grammar. The author remembers learning the English irregular verbs by heart, something that a speaker who has been exposed to a language from early on does not need to go through.

So, how do bilingual children learn their languages without getting confused? And does it make a difference if both languages are learnt from birth or if one of them is learnt some time after birth? This book will answer some of the questions related to both types of bilingual learners in terms of the acquisition and processing of two languages. In doing so, we shall discuss some of the basic principles in the way children learn language in general. Bilingual language acquisition is not fundamentally different to learning a first language.

In this chapter, we will look at the beginning of research into bilingual language acquisition. While language acquisition in general has been studied since the middle of the nineteenth century, the study of bilingual language development did not start before 1907. Before the invention of recording equipment, studies involved diaries of children's language development and researchers often studied their own children in this way. As a result, early research into bilingual acquisition involved case studies of children recorded by one of their parents.

With the distinction of different bilingual learners in mind, this chapter will give an outline of studies involving children who grew up with two languages from birth (simultaneous bilingual learners) as well as children where exposure to the other language started at a later point (sequential bilingual learners) in order to draw comparisons in the development of both types of bilinguals.

For monolingual acquisition, the emphasis was on the development of English in particular. Bilingual acquisition, on the other hand, always involves at least one other language which might be different from English in different ways. The case studies that are considered here involve a variety of different language combinations; some include English as one of the languages, others a combination of different European languages, and some involve a European and a non-European language.

A common observation for the acquisition of all languages (monolingual and bilingual) has been that a child progresses through particular stages at specific ages, where they produce one word at a time initially (the one-word stage) and later develop the ability to produce two words (the two-word stage) or more (the multiword stage). Individual children differ in the onset of the stages according to their particular circumstances (such as the amount of language spoken to them) and there is also a lot of individual variation in the speed that children go through them.

For bilingual children, there is even more variation, depending on the way both languages are represented (different speakers in the home, different communities), the amount of time the child hears each of the languages (exposure), whether or not speakers of each language make use of features from the other language (mixing), as well as the point in time when the other language is introduced (from birth or at some time later in the child's development). We will discuss these factors in more detail in Chapter 3. Let us start with an example of different pathways in Box 1.1.

Box 1.1: Examples of different bilingual learners

The two different examples of different bilingual learners are personal knowledge. All the children involved learnt both languages.

Example 1

Both my daughters were brought up with two languages at home, where each parent spoke their own language to the children. This means that they were familiar with both languages from birth.

Example 2

Friends of mine, on the other hand, decided to adopt a different strategy. Although both parents had different first languages, they both used the language that was not the official language of the country when speaking to their son. The child first learnt the language spoken by the parents but then heard the language spoken in the country when he started nursery school.

For the two examples given in Box 1.1, the children involved have grown up speaking two languages, yet their early language development was quite different. While both my daughters grew up with both languages in the home environment from birth onwards, my friends' son first only encountered one language in the home environment but was then subsequently exposed to another language, the language of the country, when starting nursery school.

Though all children ended up speaking both languages fluently, their language development is different and this is why we are looking at different learners throughout this book. My daughters grew up with two languages simultaneously (simultaneous bilingualism), whereas my friends' son started out as a monolingual child hearing only one language at home. Once he started having regular contact with people outside the home, he was exposed to another language. As this contact started at nursery age, this was after he had already learnt his first language to some degree and therefore he can be seen as a sequential bilingual learner.

We will now look at definitions of both types of learners and outline different case studies.

Bilingual learners

Simultaneous bilingual learners

de Houwer (1990) defined bilingual learners as 'simultaneous' or 'sequential' depending on the point in time when regular exposure to both languages started. Simultaneous bilingual acquisition involves continuous and regular exposure to two languages from birth or shortly after birth. The point in time was further specified by de Houwer (1995) to be not more than a month after birth. This is quite different from earlier distinctions between the two types of learners, where the cut-off point was thought to be before the onset of the one-word stage, which is around 1 year of age, or even later, before the age of 3 years.

What is the difference between an early or later cut-off point? de Houwer (1990) strongly rejected a later cut-off point on the grounds that any particular specified point of onset of another language between 1 month and 3 years is arbitrary. There is no particular reason for choosing a specific point of development, except that acquisition patterns might be different. Children who are simultaneously exposed to two languages from birth go through the same developmental stages for both languages at the same time. Coming back to the case studies in Box 1.1, the children in example 1 produced some first words in both languages around the same age. The child in case study 2, on the other hand, already put two words together in the parents' language by the time he started nursery. So the question is whether this later onset, at a point when the child has already progressed to a certain point in their development of the first language, makes a difference to the way the second language is learnt and the way both languages are mentally integrated.

On the other hand, by just setting a particular onset point, such as a month after birth, a number of other factors are not taken into account that also affect the course of language development. In the case of the first example, it makes a difference whether one of the languages spoken in the home is the same as the language spoken in the country of residence. If it is, then the child hears one of the languages both at home as well as outside and it is likely that this language will become more dominant than the other. More dominant means that the child knows more words in this language and has a better command of the grammar than in the weaker language.

If the languages that the child hears at home are different from the language of the country, then the child's situation is similar to that of the second example, except that the language at nursery will then be a third language and the child will become trilingual, that is, have a good knowledge of three languages.

In the second example, though there is a later onset of the other language, the exposure to both languages might be more balanced as one language is spoken at home and the other outside the home. And although the child starts a second language from no prior knowledge, the fact that they are immersed in the language can lead to fast learning and result in a similar level to simultaneous bilingual learners after a relatively short time of exposure to the second language.

Sequential bilingual learners

Following on from the definition of simultaneous bilingual learners, according to de Houwer (1990), sequential bilingual learners are children whose regular exposure to two languages starts more than a month after birth. Exposure to another language, for example from the age of 1, will initially result in a larger vocabulary in the language that is learnt first, and possibly in a lag in the development of language structure in the second language.

The later the onset of another language, the greater the difference between the first language learnt (in terms of words and language structures) and the second language, and therefore an inevitable difference arises between the levels in both languages. Again, if we compare the children in the two case studies, the question is how quickly will a sequential bilingual learner catch up with a simultaneous bilingual learner? Does it make a difference whether exposure through nursery starts at 2, 3 or 4 years of age? Will the catch-up time be the same, or become longer with age?

At first, the sequentially bilingual child in example 2 will clearly have a stronger (home) language and a weaker (environment) language, even if the amount of exposure once the child goes to nursery is similar. In the case of the simultaneous bilingual children in example 1, even if the exposure to both languages in the first years is quite even, the children are likely to develop a weaker and a stronger language if there is more exposure to the language spoken in the country from the time they enter nursery or school.

Comparisons have been made between the development of the weaker language and the child learning a second language (child L2 acquisition). The development of a stronger and a weaker language in bilingual acquisition shows that the quantity (and also the quality – see Chapter 3) of the input is at least as important as the point where exposure to both languages begins in the child's development.

Child L2 learners

In general, if the acquisition of a second language begins after the child has a basic command of the first language (after the age of 3–4), the child's language learning is considered to be early child second language acquisition (ECSLA) (Montrul, 2008). In early second language acquisition, the child is exposed to the second language in the environment, but learns the language through exposure in an informal setting, rather than through formal language instruction. When children are taught a second language through formal instruction at primary school, this is considered late child second language acquisition (LCSLA).

While it has become clear that the borderline between simultaneous and sequential bilingual development is not that clearly defined, and different factors need to be considered, the same can also be said for the borderline between bilingual sequential language development on the one hand and early L2 development on the other. Meisel (2007) characterises child L2 acquisition as second language learning where the learner starts the L2 before the age of 10.

The cases outlined in Box 1.2 are both examples of second language acquisition. As the boy in example 1 is only 5 and is exposed to the language of the country at school, he is an early second language learner. On the other hand, the child in the second example is a late second language learner as she is older and she is learning the language through formal instruction.

But the language situation is not always as simple as portrayed in Boxes 1.1 and 1.2. What if the children are growing up in a country where there are two official languages spoken and the children hear both at nursery and school? Depending on the home languages, the children will become bilingual or multilingual.

Box 1.2: Examples of different bilingual strategies

Let us imagine two case studies of children learning another language as second language learners.

Example 1

A boy arrived as a migrant aged 5 with his parents and younger brother 3 months ago. He continues to speak his native language with his parents and brother at home. But after 3 months he is starting to speak the language of the country at school.

Example 2

A monolingual child aged 8 has learnt her first language at home. Her first language is also the language spoken in the country. She has recently started taking lessons in another language at school.

In the next section we shall give an overview of some of the case studies that have been outlined in bilingual acquisition. With the discussion in mind where the cut-off lies between simultaneous, sequential and early L2 language learning, cases are grouped into different learners.

STUDY ACTIVITY 1.1

1. Consider your own language learning. Did you grow up with more than one language yourself? Or did you learn a second language at school? Which term best fits your own situation?
2. Now consider different people you know. Can you find examples for each term discussed in this section?

Simultaneous bilingual children: Case studies

This section will outline stories of children who have grown up with two languages. The people who wrote the stories down were their parents, and they were also language researchers and interested in how the children learnt their languages. Their observations about the course of their children's language development can inform our general understanding of the acquisition process as well as acquisition theories, which we will outline in Chapter 2.

But before outlining the case studies, we should introduce two terms that are important when discussing bilingual language learning. In the last section we looked at an example where a child was exposed to two languages in the home where both parents spoke only their native language to the child.

This is called the **one person one language principle** (OPOL) (Ronjat, 1913). It was thought that by separating the languages by person, the child would be better able to distinguish between the different languages they are learning.

Regardless of whether the languages are separated by person, all bilingual children have been found to 'mix' their two languages at times. **Mixing** means that they include elements from both languages in the same sentence (or utterance for spoken language). This is illustrated in Box 1.3 where a

---

Box 1.3: Language mixing

Child: *Va dans le water* (go in the water gloss)

In this example of mixing, the child substitutes the French noun 'eau' for the English noun 'water'. Substitutions of the noun with the word in the other language were found to be the most frequent cases of mixing for the three children that were studied.

It is not clear what prompts the language switch at this point. One possibility is that the child does not yet know the French word 'eau' and therefore selects the English word. Another view has been that the child does not yet distinguish between the two languages.

child starts a sentence in French, translated as *go in the*, but then switches language from French into English and finishes the sentence in English with *water*.

Mixing that involves the insertion of one or several words from the other language is called 'lexical mixing'. If the child adopts a structure of the other language, although all the words are from the target language, this is called 'syntactic mixing'.

The table in Box 1.4 gives an overview of case studies of simultaneous bilinguals. The table gives information about the languages the child learnt, whether the parents followed the one parent one language principle, and observed mixing of the two languages as well as the language competence of the children in both languages. The cases are discussed in more detail below: Louis, Hildegard, Eve, Lisa and Giulia, Kate, Siri and Tomas, as well as Manuela. When outlining samples of the children, their ages are given in years, followed by months, separated with a semi-colon, so that for instance 3;1 means that the child was 3 years and 1 month old when the sample was taken.

Box 1.4: Overview of cases of simultaneous bilingual acquisition

Case	Name/ Languages	OPOL*	Language mixing	Language competence
Ronjat (1913)	Louis, French/ German	Yes	Little	Similar in both languages
Leopold (1939–49)	Hildegard, German/English	Yes	Some mixing	Similar, English more dominant with contact
Tabouret-Keller (1969)	Eve, French/ Alsatian	No	Some mixing	French dominant
Taeschner (1983)	Lisa and Giulia, German/Italian	Yes	Lexical and syntactic mixing	Similar in both languages
de Houwer (1990)	Kate, English/ Dutch	Yes	Little	Similar in both languages
Lanza (1997)	Siri and Thomas, English/ Norwegian	Yes	Some mixing	More Norwegian than English
Deuchar & Quay (2001)	Manuela, English/ Spanish	Yes, some of the time	Not reported	Similar in both languages

*One parent one language principle.

Case study 1: Louis

Louis was the first study of a bilingual child. Louis was Ronjat's son who was born in 1908. Ronjat and his German wife were living in Paris and followed the OPOL principle at home. Louis heard French from his father and German from his mother and German nanny. The parents also spoke German to each other.

Ronjat reported that Louis rarely mixed languages, he was aware of the differences between the two languages at the age of 3, translated statements from one parent to the other parent and adjusted his language to the speaker. Louis spoke both languages equally well and the bilingualism was found not to delay his language development, nor did it have any negative effect on his intellectual development. Louis still engaged with both languages as a teenager.

Case study 2: Hildegard

Hildegard's case is remarkable because it is an early case and it was so well documented by her father, though it was not the first case study of the development of a bilingual child. Werner Leopold published his observations on the language acquisition of his daughter Hildegard in four volumes (Leopold, 1939, 49). In these books, he gave a detailed account of his daughter's acquisition of German and English up to the age of 12, based purely on diary records.

Werner Leopold was a native German speaker who emigrated to the United States in 1925 and became a professor of Phonetics at Northwestern University in 1927. He and his American wife followed the one parent one language principle from when their daughter was born. Leopold spoke German to Hildegard as well as his wife, and his wife and everyone else spoke American English. An exception was when the family visited Germany. There were two such visits during Hildegard's early life, one when she was 1 year old which lasted for 3 months. The second visit was when the girl was 5 years old and on this occasion the family stayed for 7 months.

Leopold documented different aspects of the child's language development, including her sound development as well as her vocabulary, grammar, and her development of word and sentence meaning. From Leopold's observations, it seems that at an early age, Hildegard did not distinguish between the two languages she was learning and did not respond appropriately to both language speakers. It was not until her third year that she started separating the two languages.

Examples where Hildegard was mixing the languages occurred in different ways. For example, she was using the words *hot* and the German equivalent *heiss* interchangeably until her third year, until she was thought to separate the two languages. She also created a novel word, *Kandl,* in German, as an invention of the translation of the word *candle.* The German word corresponding to the word *candle* in English is *Kerze.* Leopold also reported that Hildegard used German endings on English words, for example *pour-en.* In this case, the form *–en* signals that the verb is used in the infinitive form. In English, in contrast, infinitive verbs occur either in the stem form or together with *to,* as in *to run*. Similarly, the child used the form *month-e*, where a German plural form *-e* was added to the English word *month*.

As Hildegard got older, she had more contact with the outside English world, except for the two visits to Germany. After returning from the second visit, her German had become the dominant language and she spoke English only in brief sentences. Other than this, English was clearly her dominant language and her articulation was influenced by English. English also became dominant in her sentence structures.

It is clear that Hildegard started out as a simultaneous bilingual, similar to the girls in example 1 that we discussed at the beginning of this chapter. Similarly, as English was the language of the country she lived in, it is not surprising that this became the dominant language in the end. However, it is clear that any changes, such as a prolonged stay in one of the countries, can change the status of the two languages quite quickly.

Case study 3: Eve

Eve was a French–Alsatian bilingual living in Alsace. Her development was observed between the ages of 20 months and 3 years by Tabouret-Keller (1969). Her parents used both languages when speaking to Eve but they did not mix the languages within a sentence.

Up to the age of 3, the child's dominant language was French, though her word classes differed according to the languages (adjectives, adverbs, prepositions and pronouns in Alsatian, nouns and verbs in French). She became aware quite late that she was speaking two different languages. This case can clearly be characterised as a simultaneous bilingual due to the fact that exposure started from birth. Nevertheless, French seemed to be the dominant language in the child's early development.

Case study 4: Lisa and Giulia

The case of Lisa and Giulia has been used to argue that bilingual children go through distinct stages of development. Lisa and Giulia are sisters and their mother (Taeschner, 1983) observed their bilingual language development by recording their spontaneous language between the ages of 1;5 and 3;6 for Lisa and 1;2 and 2;6 for Giulia. The girls grew up as simultaneous bilinguals in Rome, Italy. Their mother, a bilingual German–Portuguese speaker, grew up in southern Brazil but spoke only German at home and used German with her daughters. The father is Italian and spoke his native language to the girls. Recordings took place twice a month speaking to a German and an Italian speaker from the time they started producing their first words (11 months for Giulia and 18 months for Lisa).

Taeschner's aim was to compare the vocabulary development of the bilingual children with that of two monolingual Italian children, Claudia and Francesco, who were recorded monthly from a similar age. She looked at verb growth in the four children over a period of 11 months but did not find any differences in the number of verbs acquired per month. Giulia was found to acquire verbs at the fastest rate (9.2 per month), whereas Lisa had the slowest rate (6.6 verbs per month). The monolingual children were in-between these figures.

Giulia and Lisa's general vocabulary consisted of words of both languages. There were more object names than verbs, and the nouns consisted of both German words, such as *Baum* (tree), *Tasche* (pocket) or *Beine* (legs) as well as Italian words, such as *matita* (pencil), *cane* (dog) and *latte* (milk). As we do not know in which language contexts these words were produced, it is difficult to verify the claim that the children did not distinguish between German and Italian words in their two languages. From the words listed there do not seem to be any equivalents (words where the child knows both language forms). Taeschner uses this as evidence to suggest that the children only have one lexicon containing words from both languages up to the age of almost 2 years.

For grammar, she compares the bilinguals with three Italian monolinguals and a group of seven monolingual German children aged between 2 and 4. Her examples of sentences produced by Lisa and Giulia show evidence of language appropriate forms, such as *dove è pappa* (where is daddy) and *das ist Giulia* (this is Giulia) at the age of 1;9 and 1;10 respectively. At the same time, in structures where the two languages differ in the placement of an element, both orders occur in both languages.

For example, German and Italian differ in the placement of the negative element. In German, the negative element *nicht* (not) is placed after the verb, in Italian, *non* (not) is placed before the verb. At 2;6, Giulia produces the correct German structure *Giulia kann nicht anfassen* (Giulia can not touch) but also the incorrect structure given in example 1.1.

Example 1.1

Giulia <u>nicht</u> schläf-t

Giulia <u>not</u>   sleeps-3rd Person SG

'Giulia does not sleep'

In example 1.1 the negative element *nicht* (not) is incorrectly placed before the verb *schläft* (sleeps). At 2;6, she produces the correct order in Italian, outlined in example 1.2, but at 1;9 the incorrect order *tocca no* (touch no) is produced.

Example 1.2

Io <u>non</u> voglio dormire

I <u>not</u> want   to sleep.INFIN

'I don't want to sleep'

Taeschner concludes that although sentence structures are acquired in the same sequence as monolinguals for each language, the children have not analysed the structures. This provides evidence for a 'single' grammatical system, as well as a single early lexicon (single system hypothesis – see Chapter 2).

Case study 5: Kate

The case of Kate is important because in outlining her language development, de Houwer (1990) shows that the languages of the bilingual child studied can develop independently and without the confusion illustrated by Taeschner. Kate learnt Dutch and English simultaneously and was observed between the ages of 2;7 and 3;4. Kate's mother is an American citizen and spoke American English to the child. The father is a Dutch-speaking Belgian citizen. The family was also following the one parent one language principle. The family lived in Antwerp in Belgium at the time. From the age of 2;6, Kate attended an English-speaking pre-school but was looked after by a Dutch-speaking neighbour three mornings a week. Contrary to the studies by both Leopold and Taeschner who found that the children studied did not initially distinguish between the two languages, for Kate the amount of language mixing was found to be quite low (6.5% overall in the data).

The emphasis in the study of Kate was on the grammatical development of the child, in particular, noun and verb phrase development, as well as general syntactic development. First of all, de Houwer (1990) found that Kate's acquisition of both languages was in line with that of English and Dutch monolingual children. The child used language-specific forms such as past tense in English and the present perfect in Dutch to express past reference. This is shown in Examples 1.3 and 1.4. Example 1.3 was produced at 2;9 while referring to a bird.

Example 1.3

Hij is	**niet weg**	**ge-vlog-en**
He is.PRES	not away	flown-PARTICIPLE

'he did not fly away'

In Example 1.3, the present perfect consists of the auxiliary *is* (is) together with the participle form *ge-vlog-en* (flown). The participle form consists of both a prefix where something is added at the beginning of the word, in this case *–ge*, and a suffix, where a form is added to the end of a word, in this case *–en*. Kate's use of the present perfect in Dutch is correct, both in terms of the grammatical forms produced, as well as in terms of the order of the items.

In contrast, in English at 3;0 she produced the utterance *Annick has that and I wanted it*, where she correctly uses the past tense form of the verb *want*, by adding the language-specific ending *–ed* to the end of the verb.

In the following example which was produced at 3;0 Kate shows the ability to translate an utterance appropriately, making use of language-specific endings and word order.

Example 1.4

Ik ga	der	in vall-en
I go.PRES	there in	fall-INFIN

'I'm going to fall in there'

Kate produced the utterance in 1.4 while sitting on the toilet. The use of the verb *ga* (go) in conjunction with the infinitive form *fall-en* (fall) is used to express a future event. Shortly afterwards, she provided the English translation *I'm go-ing to fall in there*. Both the Dutch utterance and the English translation show the appropriate position of the main verb, *fall*, which in Dutch is at the end of the sentence and has the infinitive ending *–en*, whereas in the English utterance the main verb occurs after the verb *going* but before the information on the location *in there*.

Overall, de Houwer found evidence that the child was able to distinguish between the two language systems from quite early on and argued that a bilingual child can separate the two languages earlier than thought by Taeschner (separate development hypothesis – see Chapter 2).

Case study 6: Siri and Thomas

Siri and Thomas were two simultaneous bilingual English–Norwegian children, who grew up in Norway with the mothers speaking American English, and the fathers Norwegian. Conversations between the children and their parents were recorded from 1;7 to 2;7 for Siri and 2;0 to 2;3 for Thomas. Similar to Leopold, Lanza (1997) found evidence of English words being used with Norwegian endings, as well as Norwegian articles used with English nouns, suggesting that Norwegian was the dominant language for both children.

Lanza particularly looked at the discourse strategies between the parents and the children and found differences between the two mothers. Thomas' mother did not encourage him to use more English, resulting in a high proportion of mixing by the child. Siri, on the other hand, used far fewer mixes, which is seen to be due to the mother's strategy to pretend not to understand the message unless it is expressed in the correct language. Lanza concludes that the children show evidence of an early separation of the two language systems.

Case study 7: Manuela

The case study of Manuela covers an earlier time period than Taeschner, as data collection started at 10 months and consisted of recordings as well as diary entries. Manuela is Deuchar's first daughter (Deuchar & Quay, 2001) who grew up in the United Kingdom and was exposed to native English from the mother and native Spanish from the father. The parents spoke Spanish to each other and the mother also spoke Spanish to the child when the father was present. When the father was not present, the mother spoke English to Manuela until the age of 1 when Spanish became the home language exclusively. The child was exposed to English at the crèche which she attended from the age of

4 months, as well as from the maternal grandmother. The focus of the study, which carried on until the child was 2;3, was to study the child's phonological development, the early lexicon, as well as her early syntactic development.

Manuela's lexical development is outlined in Quay (1995). Between the ages of 0;11 and 1;5, Manuela was found to produce nine pairs of equivalents across the two languages. These included pairs like *duck* and *pato* which the child used to refer to the same toy duck, as well as *down* and *bajar* when she wanted to be lifted out of her high chair. The occurrence of language equivalents suggest that young bilingual children might have a choice of words in either languages from earlier on than thought in previous case studies (see Chapter 5).

Regarding early syntax, Deuchar & Quay suggest that the child has two separate systems from the age of 1;11, based on the fact that language-specific inflections are used. For example, she produces the English possessive *Manuela's book* and the Spanish second person singular form *botas* (bounce).

Discussion of simultaneous bilingual children

We have considered seven cases here and found a number of differences between the children. There are similarities in the cases of Hildegard, and Lisa and Giulia though. Their observers say that the children did not distinguish between the two languages they were hearing until the age of 3. Taeschner uses evidence of language mixing as well as the fact that adjectives and negatives appear in different orders in both languages to support her view.

On the other hand, there are the cases of Kate and Manuela where there is evidence that the child does respond to the respective native speakers in the appropriate language and there is little mixing. While the starting point of Kate's case was quite late (2;7), Manuela was observed from early on and showed evidence of language appropriate responses as well as the existence of equivalents between languages before the age of 2.

It is possible that the children studied are different and that some children are able to distinguish between languages earlier than others. However, it is also possible that the early studies missed important information. After all, Leopold's study was based on diary entries. Taeschner did acknowledge language-specific structures in the language of the children but focused more on the influence of the other language. Current views are in line with the observations of Kate and Manuela that children are able to distinguish the languages early, but there is still an influence from either language on the other (see Chapter 2).

STUDY ACTIVITY 1.2

1. Find examples of 'mixing' in the case study data. What form does this take in the early data?
2. What were the first equivalent pairs in Manuela's data? What do they show about bilingual children's knowledge of both languages?

Sequentially bilingual children: Case studies

How does bilingual development differ if the child hears the second language at a later point? In this section we will now consider cases of sequential bilingualism. In the case studies outlined, the onset of another language was between 6 months and 3 years of age.

In relation to simultaneous bilingual children we introduced the term 'language mixing' to describe the tendency of young bilinguals to insert elements from the other language into a sentence. Some of the children considered in this section are older and any insertion of words from the other language might be more deliberate. The ability to switch between two languages within the same sentence without any grammatical violations has been termed **code-switching** (Meisel, 1994, p. 414).

The example of code-switching in Box 1.5 is appropriate in the context, as the people Speaker B had to contact were German and were called *Bürgermeister.* It did not lead to any disruption of the conversation as the speaker knew that the interviewer was fluent in both languages as well. We can assume that the speaker knew the English word but made the decision to switch into German at this point. Such code-switching is possible among bilingual speakers without interrupting the flow of the conversation. We will look at code-switching in more detail in Chapter 3.

Box 1.6 gives an overview of case studies of sequential/L2 bilinguals. The table specifies the age of onset for each of the languages, again given in years and months, separated with a semi-colon. Like before, the table also shows whether mixing of the two languages has occurred and the language competence of the children in both languages. The case studies will be discussed further.

Case study 8: Peter

The language acquisition of Peter is described in the appendix in Stern & Stern (1907). Peter was the oldest son of a German professor (Volz) from

---

Box 1.5: Code-switching

The example of code-switching below shows an adapted conversation with an 81-year-old English second language speaker who came to London as an Austrian–Jewish refugee in the late 1930s. The context of the conversation is that the male speaker talks about his time in the English army and in particular what happened when he was stationed in Germany at the end of the war. One of his jobs was to contact the mayors of the German towns in the area. The conversation is conducted in English, yet at the point when he talks about contacting the German mayors he switches into German.

A: What did you have to do?
B: I had to contact all *die Bürgermeisters* (the mayors).

Box 1.6: Overview of cases of sequential bilingual acquisition

Case	Languages	Onset LI	Onset L2	Language mixing	Language compet-ence
Volz (Stern & Stern, 1907)	Peter, German/ Malaysian	Birth	From 0.9	Syntactic mixing	Similar to German monolin-guals at 4
Pavlo-vitch (1920)	Douchan, Serbian/ French	Birth	From 1;1	Not reported	More Serbian than French words until 21 months
Burling (1959)	Stephen, English/Garo	Birth	From 1;4	Some mixing	Not reported
Vihman (1985)	Raivo, Estonian/ English	Birth	From 0;6	Not reported	More Estonian than English
Bolonyai (1998)	Hanna, Hungarian/ English	Birth	From 1;3	Yes	Not reported

Breslau and was born in 1903. When Peter was 9 months old, the family went to stay in Sumatra where the father carried out geological investigations. Before the family left for Sumatra, Peter had not produced any words but had been in a monolingual German environment. In Sumatra, Peter was looked after full-time by a Malayan nanny. This led to the parents speaking Malay to him as well. Peter's first words were *máma* and *pápa* which are used in both languages, however, a little later he produced specific Malay words such as *ini* (this), *itu* (that), *djatu* (fall) and *burung* (bird). Before his return to Germany he was able to produce sentences such as *tida baik mi* 'not good this' (this is not good) in a situation where he was looking at a book without pictures.

When Peter was 3 years old, the family moved back to Germany. They were accompanied by a Malay servant, Salem, who had replaced the nanny and started learning German. After their return, Peter used both languages adjacently for the first 2 months but he did not mix them. He was aware which language he spoke and even specified the languages: *malayu pisang, deuss banane* (in Malay 'pisang', in German 'Banane').

Salem had learnt more German in the meantime and spoke more and more German with Peter. At the age of 3;3, Peter switched to speaking mainly

German and only referred back occasionally to Malay. At the age of 3;7, Peter spoke mostly German but still used the syntax and word order of Malay and did not find it easy to make himself understood. When he wanted to express how he had seen a peacock while picking flowers he was misunderstood. He angrily said *nein, wenn blumen pflücken gegehn*, 'no, when flowers picking gone' (when I went picking flowers) where he missed out the subject *I* and the tensed verb and produced the regular participle form of the irregular verb *gehen* (go). The parents interacted with him a lot at this stage in German, such that his German was similar to that of monolingual children at the age of 4.

Case study 9: Douchan

An early study was conducted by Pavlovitch (1920) who studied his son up to the age of 2 growing up with Serbian and French in Paris. The child only had exposure to Serbian in the first 13 months when a family friend regularly visited and spoke French to the child. The child started speaking both languages, though Pavlovitch reported that the child produced fewer French words than Serbian words until he was 21 months old. The child's vocalisations were judged to be native-like in both languages and there was little confusion, yet Pavlovitch thought that his son did not realise that he was speaking two different languages.

Case study 10: Stephen

Burling (1959) studied his son's acquisition of English and Garo, a Tibeto–Burman language. The child only heard English up to the age of 16 months when he moved from America to India and subsequently heard more Garo than English. He moved back to America when the child was 34 months. Burling focused on Stephen's phonological development. He noticed that his son replaced English phonemes with those from Garo and that there was assimilation in terms of word order and morphology as well as syntax.

Case study 11: Raivo

Raivo was the second child of American–Estonian parents. He mainly heard Estonian at home from both parents and his sister but attended English day care from the age of 6 months where English was spoken. As he was only regularly exposed to English from the age of 6 months, Raivo is taken to be a sequentially bilingual child in the current context, however, given the language background of family members, he was exposed to some English in the home. Vihman (1985) followed Raivo's development using a diary as well as monthly recordings. She focused on his lexical development from 1;1 to 1;10 as well as his early grammatical development from 1;8 to 2;0.

Most of his first words were Estonian, reflecting the fact that 75% of his input was in this language. At the age of 1;10 he had learnt about 500 words. Of these, 132 (27%) were English words. The first example of an English word where he already had an equivalent in Estonian was the word *hat* (müts) which occurred at 1;6 and this was followed by the word *moon* (kuu). Of the English words acquired at 1;10, there were 60 words with equivalents in Estonian (45%). By the time the child was 2, this proportion increased to 76%. Vihman concludes that the child's lexicon clearly shows a development towards two corresponding lexical systems.

In terms of his early grammatical development, Vihman focuses on the child's development of negation. Monolingual children have been found to go through different stages of negation where they progress from using the negative marker *no* (Stage 1) as a single word, to the use of *no* or *not* in two-word utterances (Stage 2) until they are able to integrate the negative element into a sentence (Stage 3).

In Estonian, the negative marker is *ei* and it is placed before the verb. In English, *not* occurs after an auxiliary or modal as in *he does not come* or *he cannot go*. Raivo started using *ei* from 1;1 and *no* a bit later from 1;5. In his production of negatives in Estonian, the negative element generally is in the right position, yet Vihman cites examples where the order is different from the adult model. For example, at 1;9 Raivo produces the sentence <u>*ei padi kuku*</u>, 'no pillow fall' (the pillow is not falling) where the negative is in the first position in the sentence, yet the expected form is *padi <u>ei</u> kuku*, 'pillow not fall' (the pillow is not falling). This is evidence that Raivo is in Stage 2 of negation development. In English, he produces negation at the same level at the same age when he says <u>*no* more lunch</u>.

For English, Raivo does not use the full English negative form including *not* or *don't* until the age of 2;7 but produces adult Estonian structures with negatives from 1;11. There is little evidence that he uses the same grammatical rule for negatives in both languages.

Vihman (1985) concludes that the child shows evidence of a gradual transition from a single lexicon initially to developing two corresponding vocabulary systems but there is little evidence in this case of a common grammatical system.

Case study 12: Hanna

Hanna is a Hungarian girl who came to the United States at the age of 1;5. She was studied by Bolonyai (1998). Both parents are Hungarian but are bilingual in both Hungarian and English. At home, the parents mainly spoke their native language with Hanna. From the age of 1;8, Hanna attended English nursery school and later school. She has an older brother who spoke mainly Hungarian but he spoke English with his sister. Hanna was observed at the ages of 3;7, 4;2 and 4;10. At the age of 4;3, the family visited Hungary for a period of 2 months.

Bolonyai found that as Hanna started school (at 3;5) and became more immersed in the second language, she made more use of code-switching. As Hungarian was her stronger language, this language provided the language structure in the switches observed. For example, she produced the sentence *mi-t cook-sz* (what are you cooking), where the first Hungarian word, *mi-t*, is the question word *what*, which is marked by *–t* for singular as well as accusative case. The second word *cook*, is a switch to English, yet she still adds the Hungarian ending for second person singular present, *–sz*.

At the age of 4;2, after spending some time at school, it seems that the dominant language for the child has switched to English, as her code-switches are now insertions from Hungarian into English. For example, she produces the sentence *I want you to put this mosó-gép* (washing machine) *somewhere*.

Finally, at the age of 4;10 after Hanna has returned from her visit to Hungary, the pattern is again reversed and her code-switching is much more frequent in Hungarian sentences.

Discussion of sequential bilingual children

All cases discussed here can be described as sequential bilinguals as they were exposed to a second language later than 1 month after birth. In Raivo's case, he started hearing English when he went to day care at the age of 6 months. It is clear from his vocabulary as well as early grammatical development that Estonian is his stronger language. This became more even though as the child was exposed to more English.

Hanna's case is similar as she heard another language from the age of 17 months, which was the language of the community. Even though Hanna did not hear any English before the age of 17 months, once she spent more time in an English-speaking environment, the community language became more dominant, except for the 2-month visit to Hungary.

Peter's case also shows how children adapt to the language that they mainly hear around them. Although Peter had heard only German for the first 9 months of his life, he started speaking Malay and reverted back to German after his return. As his parents did not carry on speaking Malay to him after their return to Germany, Peter stopped speaking Malay after a while and did not maintain his bilingualism.

Comparison of simultaneous and sequential bilingualism

We have outlined case studies of simultaneous and sequential bilingual acquisition. What can these cases tell us about growing up as a bilingual? In most of the cases of simultaneous bilinguals, parents spoke different native languages and generally adopted the OPOL principle. One exception is Manuela, as her mother also spoke Spanish to the child in the presence of the father.

Where the children acquired the two languages in succession, the contact with the other language was mainly due to a move to a different country. The exception was Raivo because in his case, while the parents also had different native languages, they decided to speak only Estonian in the home. He also heard the other language from quite early on (6 months).

Were the children confused by the two languages? The case studies outlined differ quite a lot with regard to this question. For Hildegard and Douchan, it is argued that the children were not aware of the differences between the two languages. Taeschner (1983) held the view that her daughters initially only had one language system. For Louis, Kate, Raivo and Manuela, the data show little confusion, and it is argued that the children had the ability to separate their languages from fairly early on.

Was there a difference in the amount of mixing? Both simultaneous bilinguals as well as sequential bilinguals were found to insert words from the other language into the language that was spoken at the time. Hildegard was found to use words from both languages interchangeably (*heiss* and *hot*) and she was using a novel word by adapting an English word into German (*Kandl* for *candle*). Such insertions from the other language were also reported for Siri and Thomas as well as Hanna. On the other hand, very little mixing was found for Louis and Kate.

Is the language that is learnt first always stronger? In the cases where children grew up with two languages in the home, the reports from the case studies suggest that the children learnt words and structures from both languages and went through the early milestones (one-word stage, two-word stage) at about the same time. For example, Taeschner (1983) reports that the vocabulary of the children contains words from both languages and gives equivalent structures for the children at about the same age in both languages. This suggests that the children's languages were developed at similar levels. However, for both simultaneous and sequential bilingual children it is clear that the stronger language can change due to external circumstances. In some of the cases, this is due to more contact with the community language (Hildegard, Raivo, Hanna). From the cases of Peter, Hildegard and Hanna it also becomes clear that temporary visits to another country and thereby exposure to the community language in that country can change the status of the two languages in bilingual children.

Are bilinguals slower in their language development than monolinguals? We are going to consider this question in the next section.

Monolingual vs bilingual acquisition

One of the questions in looking at the language acquisition of bilingual and monolingual children is whether there are differences and, in particular, whether bilingual children's language acquisition happens at the same rate as that of monolingual children.

Where bilinguals have been compared to monolinguals in the case studies outlined, acquisition has been found to be similar (de Houwer, 1995): bilingual children exposed to two languages from birth have been shown to go through the same stages of language acquisition (babbling, one-word stage, two-word stage, multiword stage) as monolingual children in both their languages. The diary records as well as audio recordings of the simultaneous bilingual cases show that this is the case.

Simultaneous bilingual children also seem to reach these stages at a similar age (Taeschner, 1983). As we saw in the cases of sequentially bilingual children, when exposure to one of the languages starts later, there seems to be an initial lag between the two languages. In the case of Raivo for example, 1 year after he first went to day care, only a quarter of the words he knew were English words.

In terms of word learning, we also need to bear in mind that bilingual children might not hear the same words in the same contexts. This means that the words they know in one language are different to those in the other. This can make it difficult to assess their word knowledge in relation to monolingual children. The words that children know depend on their age and their input in both languages, as well as the languages spoken at home (Gathercole, Thomas & Hughes, 2008).

We have seen that the occurrence of equivalents in both languages has been discussed in the case studies. Equivalents were found between 0;11 and 1;5 by Deuchar & Quay (2001) but much later in the Taeschner data. The occurrence of equivalents is quite important, as young monolingual children have a tendency not to accept new words for the same object if they have already learnt a name (see Chapter 5). If bilingual children are different from monolingual children in this respect, it suggests that words from the two languages are not part of the same lexicon but that children can distinguish them from early on.

How do monolingual and bilingual children compare with regard to grammar learning? In the case studies, children have been reported to use language-specific inflections where the two languages were acquired simultaneously, yet interference from one language on the other has also been found. The amount of parental language input that children are exposed to is seen as an important factor in the acquisition of grammar (see Chapters 3 and 6). As the input in a bilingual child is split between the two languages, it is possible that it takes the child longer to reach a specific **'critical mass'**, that is a point where the child has internalised the particular form and what it represents (Gathercole, 2007). This means that bilingual children lag behind monolingual children in their acquisition of inflections, at least in their weaker language.

One example is Raivo, who acquired the structure for Estonian negation well before adult negation in English. The structures are different though. But even in comparison with English monolingual children, Raivo's acquisition of adult negatives was later than expected. Is this because he had less input in English?

de Houwer (2014) disagrees with the assumption that bilinguals are necessarily exposed to less input in both their languages. She compared the amount of input received by bilingual and matched monolingual children and found differences in the speech rate of mothers in both groups. She concludes that exposure to more than one language does not necessarily result in a lower rate of input in both their languages.

STUDY ACTIVITY 1.3

1.   Describe the effect of a later onset in the case studies of sequentially bilingual children on the development of words and structures.
2.   Does the first language of the child affect the later acquired language and vice versa? Look at the case studies discussed.

Bilingual language corpora

As we saw in the case studies, early methods of studying child language, including bilingual children, consisted of diaries that were kept by parents. Later on they were replaced or supplemented with audio recordings which were transcribed and analysed further. Different researchers tended to use different conventions for their transcriptions. For example, if a researcher was more interested in the sound development of a child, they would add details of the way a child pronounced words, whereas someone who focused on grammatical development would not detail sound development to the same extent.

In 1984, Brian MacWhinney had the idea to set up a database of child language data, the Child Language Data Exchange System (CHILDES). This system not only enabled researchers in the field to look at more data, but it also required a common way of transcribing the data, and a facility to automate the process of data analysis. CHILDES is therefore not just a place where child language data is stored, but the data is transcribed in a common format – Codes for the Human Analysis of Transcripts (CHAT) – and there are analysis programmes – Computerised Language Analysis (CLAN) – which can be used for a variety of measures.

For example, one common measure when analysing child language data is the calculation of the **mean length of utterance** (MLU) (Miller & Chapman, 1981). In order to derive a child's MLU value, you need to count the number of words and inflections. For example, in the utterance *I helped mummy*, if you count every word, the resulting MLU value is 3. This is the MLU in words. However, the child used the verb *help* in the past tense form by adding the morpheme *–ed* to the end of the verb. **Morphemes** are defined as the smallest unit in language that have meaning. In this case, the morpheme marks the verb *help* as regular past tense. The inclusion of this morpheme signals a grammatical property and the morpheme is therefore called **inflectional**. This is in contrast to morphemes like *un–* which change the meaning of a word, for example from *grammatical* to *ungrammatical*. They are called **derivational** morphemes. If we include the inflectional morpheme in the MLU count, the MLU value for the utterance is 4. This is the MLU in morphemes.

In general, MLU is calculated over a number of utterances in a transcript and represents the mean length of the included utterances. Within CLAN, a measure such as MLU can be calculated automatically by specifying the command 'MLU', as well as the transcript that you want to calculate the MLU value for. CLAN then returns an output MLU for the participants in the transcript.

While the measure 'MLU in morphemes' is generally regarded as a good predictor of children's early grammatical development, it can lead to problems when trying to compare values for different languages. As languages differ in terms of the number of inflectional morphemes, a comparison of a child's MLU value across languages can be misleading, such that the child has a higher MLU in the language that has more inflectional morphemes. For this reason, MLU comparisons across languages are generally made in terms of 'MLU in words'.

CHILDES is described and documented in MacWhinney (2000) and accessible from the website http://childes.talkbank.org/.

The CHILDES database includes different types of child data. There are transcripts from individual children who were recorded regularly over a period of time (**longitudinal data**), but there is also data from groups of children who were only recorded once (**cross-sectional data**). An example of a longitudinal study is the Forrester corpus of a monolingual child in the United Kingdom, Ella, who was recorded regularly in her natural environment from the age of 1;0 until she was 3;6. An example of cross-sectional data, on the other hand, is the Fletcher database, also including children from the United Kingdom, but in this case, there are single recordings from 24 individual children at the age levels 3, 5 and 7. For some of the data, audio and video recordings are also available alongside the transcripts.

Longitudinal and cross-sectional data sets are used for different purposes. In this chapter, we have discussed longitudinal case studies. As a child is observed over a particular period of time and in two different languages, the data collected and analysed from a single child can be substantial, but it is possible to observe the development of particular aspects of language, such as vocabulary and grammar. On the other hand, cross-sectional data allow the simultaneous observation of more children at different ages. It is therefore possible to describe the range of particular language measures (such as MLU) within different age groups.

The data in the CHILDES database include a variety of children at different ages, different languages and different sampling methods (free conversational data as well as other methods, including narratives). There are also a number of bilingual language acquisition corpora, among them the de Houwer corpus (Kate) as well as the Deuchar corpus (Manuela).

The different corpora vary in terms of the number of children studied (from studies of just one child to a narrative study including 420 participants) and include combinations of a variety of languages: Arabic, Catalan, Cantonese, Chinese, Danish, Dutch, Farsi, French, German, Hebrew, Hungarian, Italian, Japanese, Mandarin, Polish, Portuguese, Russian, Scottish Gaelic, Spanish and Swedish.

A number of bilingual language case studies include data from simultaneous bilingual speakers, however, there are also data on child L2 immigrant children and narratives from a sequential Arabic–English bilingual learner (Al-Hindawy, 2016). Some of the corpora include bilingual as well as monolingual children in both languages.

Box 1.7 gives an example of a transcript of a bilingual German–Italian child from the CHILDES database (Klammler & Schneider, 2011). The first part is the German data and the second part Italian. The first line of each transcript refers to the corpus (bilingual, Klammler) as well as the language and the transcript number. Lines 1–11 in each transcript refer to general information about the transcript, the language, the situation, the people present as well as their roles, and the age of the child. Each general line is identified with '@' at the beginning.

The so-called 'header information' in the first transcript specifies that the language is German, the people present are the mother, MOT, another person,

Box 1.7: Example of a CHILDES bilingual transcript

a) German data

	@Loc:	Biling/Klammler/germ1.cha
1	@Begin	
2	@Languages:	German
3	@Participants:	CHI Manuel, Target_Child, MOT Doris Mother, INV Astrid Investigator
4	@ID:	deu|Klammler|CHI|1;9.00||||Target_Child|||
5	@ID:	deu|Klammler|MOT|||||Mother|||
6	@ID:	deu|Klammler|INV|||||Investigator|||
7	@Media:	germ1, audio
8	@Date:	26-APR-2006
9	@Location:	Naples, Campania, Italy
10	@Situation:	looking at a child's picture dictionary, making some pictures and looking at a picture album of the family with MOT and INV
11	@Transcriber:	Astrid
12	*MOT:	und was ist das?
	%eng	and what is this?
13	*CHI:	tia.
14	%gls:	Pizza.
15	%eng:	Pizza.
16	*MOT:	die Pizza und was ist das?
17	%eng:	the pizza and what is this?
18	*CHI:	toate.
19	%gls:	Torte
20	%eng:	cake.

b) Italian data

	@Loc:	Biling/Klammler/ital1.cha
1	@Begin	
2	@Languages:	Italian
3	@Participants:	CHI Manuel Target_Child, FAT Gianni Father, INV Astrid Investigator
4	@ID:	ita|Klammler|CHI|1;9.00||||Target_Child|||
5	@ID:	ita|Klammler|FAT|||||Father|||
6	@ID:	ita|Klammler|INV|||||Investigator|||
7	@Date:	26-APR-2006
8	@Location:	Naples, Campania, Italy
9	@Situation:	looking at a child's picture dictionary, playing a card game with picture-cards and free playing with the father
10	@Comment:	Astrid's mother tongue is German and she hardly speaks Italian to MAN, therefore she is just present to register the conversation

11	@Transcriber:	Astrid
12	*FAT:	va bene.
13	%eng:	all right.
14	*CHI:	pitta.
15	%gls:	Pizza
16	%eng:	Pizza
17	*FAT:	pizza, dovè la pizza?
18	%eng:	pizza, where's the pizza?
19	*FAT:	bravo!
20	%eng:	good.

Astrid, who is the investigator, INV, as well as the transcriber (line 11). The child, Manuel, is 1;9 years old. Both recordings took place in Naples, Italy on 26 April 2006. Line 10 in the first transcript and line 9 in the second transcript give more details about the particular situation of the transcript. The actual conversation begins from line 12 in each of the transcripts. Each utterance is identified at the beginning by the particular speaker. In the first transcript, '*MOT:' indicates that the mother is the speaker. This is followed by what the speaker has said. In the second transcript, the father, identified by '*FAT:' is the first speaker, followed by the child, '*CHI:'. If the child produces a word that does not correspond to the adult form, an additional line (starting with %gls) can provide a 'gloss' which specifies the target form. If the language used is different from English, a translation can be provided on a separate line (%eng).

Overall, CHILDES is a useful resource for the study of monolingual and bilingual language acquisition, though the information on the amount of language exposure and language background needs to be taken into account when drawing any conclusions about particular data.

STUDY ACTIVITY 1.4

1. What is the purpose of the CHILDES database? What types of data are included and in what format?
2. Give examples of the way conversational data is transcribed in CHILDES. What are the advantages of such a system?

Mental representation of the two languages of a bilingual

So far, we have looked at the two languages in relation to language comprehension and production. However, when acquiring language, a child is also building up **mental representations** of words and structures. Mental representations are made up of the knowledge that we have about language, the language forms as well as the relations between these forms. This knowledge is stored somewhere in our brain and can be recalled when needed.

In a bilingual, it is not clear whether mental representations are separate for both languages or whether they are shared. Weinreich (1953) was concerned with representations of the meaning of words and their relationships in what he saw as different types of bilinguals: **co-ordinate**, **compound** and **subordinate**. Let's now look at the definitions of these three terms and see when each situation arises in practice.

In co-ordinate bilingualism, the form of a word and its meaning representation are kept separate, meaning that both the word form as well as the meaning representations are different. Hence a child learning the word *duck* in English and the translation equivalent *Ente* in German would keep them separate, both in terms of the word form as well as the meaning. Separate forms and meaning representations suggest that the child could use both forms but would not realise their connection as translation equivalents. The case studies considered earlier clearly show that children who are simultaneously exposed to two languages do use translation equivalents, hence they cannot be classified as co-ordinate bilinguals.

Compound bilinguals, on the other hand, are said to distinguish the different word forms but have a common meaning representation. A common meaning representation suggests that words from both languages are linked, which can explain the early use of translation equivalents by simultaneous bilinguals.

Finally, subordinate bilinguals are said to link the word in the weaker language through the word form of the stronger language and the respective meaning representation. This means that a subordinate bilingual would always first retrieve a word in the stronger, or first, language. This seems to be the case for L2 learners and perhaps initially for sequential bilinguals.

As a child becomes more fluent and reaches native-like status in the other language, there is the question whether the status of the words and meaning representations can change, such that an initially subordinate bilingual becomes a co-ordinate and then a compound bilingual.

Weinreich's classification of bilinguals does not seem to allow for such a change. In addition, it also does not address the possibility that a speaker has common meaning representations for some words but not for others. As not all words in one language necessarily have translation equivalents (which is often a reason for using loanwords), there will be words which only have a representation for one language. In addition, word meanings are not always exactly the same across languages. The classification is therefore not very helpful for the present purpose.

The bilingual advantage

Does being bilingual have any advantages, apart from the obvious one that the bilingual speaker is able to converse in more than one language?

Bialystok (2001, 2009) has shown that bilinguals develop so-called enhanced **metalinguistic awareness**. The term 'meta' is derived from Greek and means 'about'. Hence 'metalinguistic' refers to knowledge about language, though not in terms of word or grammatical knowledge, but rather, abstract knowledge about language.

An example of metalinguistic knowledge is the notion of what constitutes a word (word knowledge task). Karmiloff-Smith et al. (1996) tested 4–5-year-old children with a task where they listened to a story. At certain points, the story was stopped and the child was asked to repeat the last word. Pauses either occurred after **open class** or after **closed class** words.

Open class words include nouns, verbs, adjectives and adverbs. They are called 'open class' because new words can be added. For example, recent additions include the search engine Google and the verb *to google*. Closed class words, on the other hand, refer to words that have a grammatical meaning, including articles (a, the), conjunctions (and, because), pronouns (he, she), auxiliaries (have, do) and prepositions (on, under). They are called closed class because it is not possible to add new words.

The results show that 4-year-olds performed less well with closed class words than open class words, whereas 5-year-olds performed equally well with both. This task requires what Bialystok (1988, p. 563) calls **analysis of knowledge** (see Chapter 8). This relates to knowledge of what constitutes a word and where the boundary is between what is a word and what is not a word.

Younger children clearly restrict this concept to open class words, words that directly relate to objects (nouns), actions (verbs) or attributes of either (adjectives or adverbs). While closed class words have meaning, this is more related to grammar and thereby less transparent to children.

The results of the task show that metalinguistic knowledge still develops at pre-school age, in contrast to language use, as both age groups are able to understand and use both types of words in their own language.

According to Bialystok (2001), the term 'metalinguistic awareness' includes three aspects: abstract knowledge about language, the ability to apply this knowledge in particular tasks (ability), as well as the ability to focus on particular mental representations (awareness). In terms of the task outlined, the children who have developed metalinguistic knowledge about the notion of a word were able to apply this knowledge in the task and repeat both open and closed class words when the story was paused and they were prompted for the last word. The result that there was a difference between the younger and the older children shows that children are in the process of developing metalinguistic skills as they develop both language and cognition.

Bialystok (1986) suggests that metalinguistic awareness is linked to **control of attention** where the child can intentionally consider language in a way that facilitates the solution of a metalinguistic task. An example is the so-called **'sun moon' problem** that was studied by Piaget (1929) and is outlined in Box 1.8. Children are questioned as to whether the names of the sun and the moon can be exchanged through a general agreement. Using the idea of such a name exchange, the child is then asked to engage in a play situation, keeping in mind that labels have been exchanged (Ianco-Worrall, 1972).

> ## Box 1.8: The 'sun moon' problems
>
> Children before the age of 10 differ in the way they reason about changing the names of the sun and moon:
>
> ### First stage
>
> **And could the moon have been called 'sun' and the sun 'moon'?**
> Roc (6;6): No, because the moon must be the moon and not the sun and the sun must be the sun.
> Fert (7): No. Because the sun makes it warm and the moon gives light.
> Zwa (9;6 knows some German): No, because the sun shines brighter than the moon.
> **Could the sun have been given another name?**
> Fran (9): No, because it's nothing else but the sun, it couldn't have another name.
>
> ### Second stage
>
> **If the sun had been called 'moon', would we have known it was wrong?**
> May (10): No, because they would have given the name 'moon' to the 'sun'. They wouldn't have seen any difference.
>
> While Piaget did not think that knowledge of another language made any difference to children's realisation that names can be arbitrary, a study by Ianco-Worrall (1972) showed that bilingual children that were matched with monolinguals in each of their languages were better at expressing the concept that the assignment of names to objects is arbitrary. There was no difference though in the ability to use interchanged names in a play situation.

The ability to consider an exchange of names for the sun and the moon and to label them correctly requires control of attention. This ability develops in particular when the child acquires literacy as they need to switch between forms, such as **phonemes** and **graphemes** (the written representations of phonemes).

In what way do bilingual children have an advantage when it comes to metalinguistic awareness tasks? Remember that the subject in the Deuchar & Quay (2001) study was found to use translation equivalents such as *duck* and *pato* quite early. This suggests that bilingual children have an early awareness of the arbitrariness of object names and should therefore be better at meta-linguistic awareness tasks, particularly where control of attention is required.

Bialystok (1986) carried out a study with a group of 119 children aged 5–9 where half of the children were bilingual and the other half were monolingual English. The children were given a grammaticality judgement task including sentences that differed in terms of grammaticality and meaningfulness. The children were asked to correct a puppet when the sentence was ungrammatical, but not when it was not meaningful. For example, the sentence *I have two pencil* is ungrammatical as the word *two* indicates that there is more than one pencil. The children were expected to correct this sentence to *I have two pencils*. On the other hand, the sentence *apples grow on noses* is grammatically correct but not meaningful. In this case, the children were expected to accept the sentence.

Both groups of children were found to perform equally well for sentences that were ungrammatical but meaningful. Bilingual children were better at responding correctly to (i.e. not correcting) grammatical sentences that were not meaningful. These results can be explained in terms of metalinguistic awareness skills. Making a grammaticality judgement requires metalinguistic knowledge. Not surprisingly, older children were better at the task, similar to the children in Karmiloff-Smith et al.'s (1996) study on words, as metalinguistic knowledge develops with age.

On the other hand, the fact that bilingual children were found to be better at responding to grammatical sentences that were not meaningful, shows that they have a better control of attention. In order to judge sentences correctly, children need to separate the form and the meaning and make a choice to correct the grammatical form where needed but to leave the meaning, regardless of whether or not this makes sense.

Bialystok (2001) points out that metalinguistic awareness is of particular importance for second language learning. As the learner already has knowledge of the structure of a language, this knowledge can be applied to the new language and can thereby facilitate second language learning, at least from the point where metalinguistic knowledge about language has sufficiently developed. The studies on bilinguals showing a greater control of attention demonstrate that this type of metalinguistic awareness develops early and is due to exposure to different language forms.

In the context of simultaneous and sequential bilingual learners, there is the question as to whether the type of bilingualism makes a difference to the degree of metalinguistic awareness observed. Bialystok (1988) included monolinguals, fluent bilinguals and less fluent bilinguals in tasks that required either control of attention or analysis of knowledge. She found that in terms of control of attention, both bilingual groups were similar and outperformed the monolinguals. In terms of analysis of knowledge, there was no difference between the partially bilinguals and the monolinguals.

These results show that contact with another language increases the ability to control attention, yet it is only through prolonged contact that other aspects of metalinguistic awareness, such as analysis of knowledge, are affected.

STUDY ACTIVITY 1.5

1. Distinguish between the terms 'analysis of knowledge' and 'control of attention'. Give examples for both.
2. Explain what is meant by the term 'bilingual advantage'. Give an example of a particular skill where bilinguals have been found to perform better than monolinguals.

SUMMARY

This chapter has discussed the terminology relevant to different bilingual learners. In particular, we have discussed simultaneous versus sequential bilingual acquisition, and where the cut-off lies between the two types of bilinguals. We have also looked at different case studies of bilingual acquisition from the point of view of this distinction. It is clear that learners who are exposed to two languages from birth are more likely to have a similar proficiency in both languages. However, in the case of learners where exposure to another language started before the age of 3, it seems that children are still able to attain native-like proficiency, though it is clear that the languages did not initially develop exactly at the same time.

The cases considered make clear that bilingual acquisition proceeds in a similar way to monolingual acquisition, though the amount of input in both languages as well as the point of onset of the second language have an impact on a child's proficiency, thereby resulting in possible lags in comparison to monolinguals.

We also considered Weinreich's (1953) classification of bilinguals into co-ordinate, compound and subordinate bilinguals, though from the point of view of the types of bilingual learners considered here, both could be classed as compound bilinguals.

Bilingualism has been seen as an advantage in that it leads to the development of an enhanced metalinguistic awareness. Bialystok (2001) divides metalinguistic awareness into three components: knowledge about language, ability and control of attention. Bilinguals have been shown to be better at control of attention due to the fact that speakers have learnt two different word forms linked to the same mental representation.

FURTHER READING

For the original discussion of the cut-off point between simultaneous and sequential bilinguals see McLaughlin (1978) and also Meisel (2004) for a later view. Children's use of items from the other language has generally been seen as mixing, yet more proficient child learners are regarded as being able to use code-switching. For a discussion of mixing and code-switching in child bilinguals see Cantone (2007). A summary of the use of CHILDES for the study of bilinguals is given in Yip, Mai & Matthews (2018). For further details on bilingual children's metalinguistic awareness skills see Bialystok (2001).

Theories
of Bilingual
Development

2

In this chapter we shall look at the theoretical debates relating to bilingual development as well as early second language acquisition. The first question in bilingual acquisition was concerned with the status of the two languages for the child. We saw that in the case studies in Chapter 1 observations of children growing up bilingually led to different views on whether the child treats the two languages as one system or is able to separate the languages from early on. While this particular issue was resolved in the light of evidence showing an early distinction between the two, there are other debates relating to bilingual acquisition that will be outlined.

The early debates highlighted the fact that the languages of the bilingual child interact to some degree. More recent research focused on such cross-linguistic influences of one language on the other and what underlies these influences. Does the stronger language always have an influence on the weaker language? What aspects of language are affected? Are cross-linguistic influences more likely to occur if the child's input in the other language started at a later point than shortly after birth?

We shall also look at theoretical approaches in child language acquisition in general. For a long time, views that assume innate linguistic knowledge in children (nativism) have dominated the discussion about language acquisition, and these approaches have also been applied to bilingual language learning. More recent studies are based on views such as constructivism and the Usage-based theory to see whether these views can make particular predictions about bilingual language development.

Single system and separate development hypotheses

The two views, the single system and the separate development hypothesis, both make assumptions about the way children perceive the languages they hear and access the words and grammar of both systems. The focus of both views has been on word learning as well as early grammar. Volterra & Taeschner (1978) suggested that the bilingual child develops from a so-called 'fused' system up until the age of 1;11 where they only have one lexicon and grammar, to a stage where they have a separated lexicon but a common grammatical system between 2;5 and 3;3, and finally two separate language systems at the ages of 2;9–3;11. The alternative and nowadays accepted view is that the two language systems develop as separate systems from the start. We will discuss both views in relation to word learning and grammar.

Note that both views have developed on the basis of observations of particular children – the case studies that we have outlined in Chapter 1. This is an **inductive** or **bottom-up** approach as a researcher first looks at specific occurrences and then makes more general assumptions on this basis. The general assumptions can then be tested by investigating a new case. This way of reasoning is different from the **deductive** or **top-down** approach where the researcher starts with a set of assumptions or a theory and derives specific predictions that can be verified when looking at a set of data.

Bilingual word learning: One or two lexicons?

How do bilingual children learn the words of their two languages? We shall talk about word learning in more detail in Chapter 5. However, in the context of the single system hypothesis, the assumption was that bilingual children at first treat the words of both languages as part of the same lexicon and do not separate them according to language. This was based on observations of children's word use and lack of language equivalents in the case study of Lisa and Giulia (case study 4) which were outlined in Chapter 1. Yet the examples given of word productions in both languages are not related to the language context where they were produced.

In contrast, Genesee, Nicoladis & Paradis (1995) investigated the language choice of five French–English bilingual children between the one- and two-word stage interacting with their parents. Two of the children were also observed interacting with strangers speaking either English or French.

Box 2.1 gives an example of a conversation between one of the children investigated and a stranger. The stranger is a monolingual English speaker.

Box 2.1: Conversation with a monolingual English stranger

A train passes outside the house and the child goes to look

    *CHI: choo-choo train!
    *CHI: he parti.
    %eng: he's gone.
    *STR: I'm sorry, I didn't understand.
    *STR: it's a what?
    *CHI: parti.
    %eng: gone.
    *STR: you can't see it?
    *CHI: this is a choo-choo [points to a picture of a train].

The child uses one French word during the conversation, *parti* (gone), otherwise the child's utterances are language-appropriate.

In their study, it was found that all children were able to use their languages selectively with the parents, even in the case of the non-dominant language. The two children who were observed with a stranger were both found to be able to respond in the appropriate language. This shows that bilingual children do not use their two languages randomly but they have control over their language choice.

What about the claim that children do not have equivalents in their early lexicon? From the list of words produced by Lisa and Giulia at 1;6 and 1;11, there were some where the child produced both language forms. Lisa used both forms of *biscuit* (*Keks* in German and *biscotto* in Italian) as well as *water* (*Wasser* in German and *acqua* in Italian). Her sister Giulia produced both forms for *thank you* (*danke* in German and *grazie* in Italian). Volterra & Taeschner (1978) also report that Hildegard used both forms for *snow* (*Schnee* in German and *neve* in Italian).

This finding clearly goes against their claim, however, they suggest that the children have not made the connection between the two language forms. This means that they have picked up both words in specific contexts but have not connected them as alternatives of the same object. They describe how Lisa starts connecting equivalents at the age of 2;5 for the word *glasses*. Her mother produces the German word in relation to a picture, yet Lisa uses the Italian word *occiali* when referring to the father's glasses, even when talking to the mother. During the conversation she seems to suddenly start connecting the two words. This is seen as evidence for the start of the next stage where children have separated their lexicons but still use one grammatical system.

Language equivalents have been reported since then from quite an early age. We have seen that Manuela (see case study 7, Chapter 1) was able to link some English and Spanish equivalents as early as 0;11. Therefore, the evidence from children's appropriate language use, as well as the early occurrences of language equivalents, suggest that young bilingual children are able to distinguish the two lexicons of the languages they hear from early on.

Bilingual grammar

At the second stage of bilingual acquisition, Volterra & Taeschner (1978) suggested that children have separated the lexicons of the two languages but use the same grammar rules for both languages. They give examples where Lisa seems to use the same rules for possessives, adjective-noun combinations, as well as negatives in both languages. An overview of these structures is given in Box 2.2.

Take, for example, possessives. In German, possessives are formed by adding an 's' to the noun that is the possessor (genitive): *Lisas Katze*, 'Lisa's cat', or by using the preposition *von* as in *die Katze von Lisa*, 'the cat of Lisa' (Lisa's cat). In Italian, the preposition *di* specifies the role of possessor: *il gatto di Lisa*, 'the cat of Lisa' (Lisa's cat). In Lisa's early language, the order of the head noun and possessor is mostly in accordance with the German order possessor-possessed

		Box 2.2: Early grammar in Lisa and Giulia	
		Example	**Translation**
I. Possessives:	Italian:	1;8 *la cucu di mamma.*	the cuckoo of mum (mum's cuckoo)
		2;4 **Lisa bibicletta.*	Lisa bicycle (Lisa's bicycle)
	German:	1;9 **Giulia Buch.*	Giulia book (Giulia's book)
		2;2 die Strasse von Giulia.	the street of Giulia (Giulia's street)
2. Adjectives:	Italian:	2;4 *bambino piccolo.*	child little (little child)
		2;9 **nero capello.*	black hair
	German:	2;3 *schöne Blume.*	nice flower
		3;6 **Schuhe dunkelbraun.*	shoes dark brown (dark brown shoes)
3. Negatives:	Italian:	1;9 *lo non vuole.*	I not want (I don't want to)
		2;4 **quetto parla non.*	this speaks not (this does not speak)
	German:	3;2 *noch nicht gekommen.*	yet not come (not come yet)
		3;6 **nein, ich nicht will.*	no, I not want (no, I don't want to)

* indicates non-target structures.

for both languages, just the genitive marker 's' is missing. Giulia, on the other hand, uses the correct order for Italian with *di* inserted before the noun from the age of 1;8.

For the other two structures, German and Italian are also different: while in German attributive adjectives occur before the noun, in Italian they are placed after the noun. For example, in the phrase *schöne Blume* (nice flower), the adjective *schön* (nice) occurs before the noun. In the Italian phrase *riso buono,* 'rice good' (good rice), the adjective is placed after the noun. In Lisa's language, both constructions occur in both languages.

A third structure where Italian and German differ is in the placement of the negative. This difference between German and Italian in the placement of the negative element either after or before the main verb was already discussed as part of case study 4 (Chapter 1). For example, in the German sentence *Er kommt nicht,* 'he comes not' (he is not coming), the negative marker occurs after the main verb, whereas in the Italian translation, *lui non viene*, 'he not comes' (he is not coming) the negative element occurs before the verb. Again, both orders occur in both languages, as illustrated by the examples in Box 2.2.

Overall, it is not clear from the examples cited in Volterra & Taeschner (1978) how frequently non-target structures occurred. It could be argued that if the majority of constructions are language-appropriate, this suggests language separation. In addition, there is evidence that monolingual children learning languages where the negative element is placed after the verb, still go through stages where pre-verbal placement occurs, hence the examples cited are not necessarily due to a mixing of the grammatical rules.

The single system hypothesis was challenged first by Meisel (1989), who criticised the vagueness of the stages in Volterra & Taeschner's outline as well as the claim that the children were using the same syntactic rules in both languages. He provided evidence from two French–German children aged 1;0 to 4 that children use language-appropriate word order patterns as soon as they produce multiword utterances and they also start learning inflectional endings at this point. For example, in German, the children produced verbs in the correct position and marked the verb correctly as first person plural, the same as the infinitive ending *–en* as in *jetzt spiel-en wir*, 'now play we' (now we're playing), whereas in French the equivalent short form *on joue*, 'one plays' (let us play) occurs (Schlyter, 1990).

The view that the languages of a bilingual develop separately from early on was outlined as the 'separate development hypothesis' by de Houwer (1990). Her study of Kate (case study 5, Chapter 1) focuses on the child's word order and inflections in both languages. As described before, Kate's development of English and Dutch was studied between the ages of 2;7 and 3;4. de Houwer emphasises that similar and distinct forms across languages need to be distinguished.

Separate development can only be confirmed if the child shows different but language-appropriate knowledge of the structures in both languages. One area that de Houwer (1990) focused on was her use of **bound** morphemes in the two languages. Bound morphemes are forms that cannot stand on their own. For English, the investigation includes the use of plural (*book-s*), possessive (*John-'s book*) as well as third person *–s* (*he read-s*) and past tense (*she arriv-ed*). For Dutch, it includes gender marking, plural, possessives, person marking and past tense. Gender in Dutch is marked by the definite determiner *de* (the) for masculine and feminine nouns, *het* (the) for neuter nouns as well as the indefinite determiner *een* (a) for all three genders. Plural is marked either by the ending *–en* in *boek-en* (books) or the ending *–s* in *tafel-s* (tables). The possessive is marked by the ending *–s* in *Toms auto* (Tom's car). Person marking includes different endings to the stem of the verb. For example, for the verb *komen* (come) the stem form *kom* is used for the first and second person singular (*ik kom*, I come), the ending *–t* as in *kom-t* marks the third person singular (*hij kom-t*, he comes) and the ending *–en* as in *kom-en* marks the plural forms of the verb (*we/jij/ze kom-en*, we/you/they come). Events in the past are expressed in Dutch by using the present perfect. This is formed by the auxiliary *zijn* (be) or *hebben* (have) in conjunction with the participle form of the main verb (*hij is gekomen,* he has come).

In general, she found that language-specific bound morphemes were used in both languages. For example, at 2;10 Kate produces the utterance *hij gaat nu,* 'he's going now' where she adds the correct third person singular ending *–t* on the Dutch verb *gaan.* At the same age she produces the sentence *I am not going to go to Amsterdam* where she uses the language-appropriate present progressive *–ing.*

The other area where de Houwer (1990) compared acquisition patterns, was word order. In English, the order of constituents usually follows the pattern subject, verb, object, as in *Mary has read the book,* where *Mary* is the subject, *has read* the verb and *the book* is the object. Dutch, on the other hand, has a different word order pattern. The sentence translates as example 2.1.

Example 2.1

Mary   heef-t   het boek ge-lez-en

Mary   has-3rd SG   the book read-PARTICIPLE

'Mary has read the book'

In example 2.1, the object *book* occurs between the auxiliary *heeft* (has) and the main verb *gelezen* (read). If there is another element in the first position of the sentence, the verb occurs in second position. This is shown in example 2.2.

Example 2.2

Het boek   heef-t   Mary   ge-lez-en

The book   has-3rd SG   Mary   read-PARTICIPLE

'The book Mary has read'

Kate observes the placement of the verb in Dutch at the age of 2;10 in her sentence *twee vingers heb ik,* 'two fingers have I' (I've got two fingers) and in English at the same time when she says *then I do this* where the verb occurs after the subject in the third position in the sentence.

Taking all the evidence together, the fact that children were found to respond appropriately to the person they were talking to, were able to link equivalents in the two languages from quite early on, and acquired the structure and bound morphemes in a language-appropriate way, shows that bilingual children are able to separate their two languages from quite early on.

In the discussion of the two positions, we have seen how observations from children's language productions (empirical data) have led to theoretical assumptions, though the focus of these observations has differed. While the single system hypothesis emphasised the occurrence of forms from both languages as well as the occurrence of structures that were clearly influenced by the other language, researchers advocating separate development differentiated the observations by language context and the frequency of forms that did not conform to the target language. This shows possible shortcomings of the inductive approach, as empirical data is open to different interpretations.

More evidence for separate development

We have seen that the amount of language mixing in bilingual children was found to vary quite a lot. Volterra & Taeschner (1978) reported that Lisa and Giulia were mixing languages in about 33% of their utterances. In Kate's data, on the other hand, de Houwer (1990) found that language mixing was much lower (under 5%). Low rates of mixing can be seen as further evidence that the child is able to use language appropriately for the language context and thereby support the separate development hypothesis.

One reason for the difference of mixing rates in different studies is the degree of mixing in the parents, as well as language dominance in the child, that is, the child is more likely to use words from the other language if this is more dominant.

Parents mix languages to a certain degree, even if they interact just with their child, particularly where there is no equivalent or no suitable equivalent for a word in the other language. Paradis & Genesee (1996) suggested that children's mixing can also be interpreted as 'borrowing' from the other language where the child has a lexical gap. In this way, children's mixing is not fundamentally different from language mixing in adults (see Chapter 3) and rather than showing confusion between languages, it shows that children can make use of the resources available in both their languages.

The studies considered here focus on children from the time they start producing language, however, we know that children understand language before they start producing their first word. In Chapter 4 we will be concerned with bilingual children's speech perception and phonological development, and the question whether there is evidence that bilingual infants can distinguish between the languages they hear from a very early age.

Single system vs separate development in relation to sequential bilingualism

The two views that we have discussed so far both relate to simultaneous bilingual acquisition. The case studies are all children who heard both languages from birth. If simultaneous bilinguals can distinguish between their languages from early on, can we assume that this is also the case for sequentially bilingual children?

Given that these children have had a certain amount of exposure to their first language already, does this mean that they notice differences more clearly when they start hearing another language? For case study 9, it was reported that the child did not realise that he spoke two languages (Serbian and French – see Chapter 1) after hearing the other language from the age of 13 months.

On the other hand, the boy in case study 11 was found to develop separate lexicons in Estonian and English after starting to hear English in day care from 6 months. Similarly, the child in case study 8, Peter, who had been exposed to Malay only between the ages of 0;9 and 3;1, was found not to mix Malay and German after his return to Germany. He was also able to express which word was from which language (see Chapter 1). This suggests that both children were clearly able to distinguish the languages. Yet at the same time, Peter used the word order from Malay in his German sentences.

One of the main differences between simultaneous and sequential bilingual acquisition is the age at which the language is heard. Age, in turn, is related to cognitive development, the increasing ability to store, process and manipulate information. As Peter is the oldest child among the case studies considered here, he can also be assumed to be the most 'cognitively mature'. Peter is not only aware of the different languages, he is also able to express this knowledge verbally by explicitly saying what the equivalents in the languages are.

At the same time, it is clear that his dominant language, Malay, has an influence on the word order used in the non-dominant language, German. The ability to distinguish between the two languages on the one hand and cross-linguistic influences of one language on the other, clearly do not exclude each other. Given the evidence presented in support of separate development in bilingual children who hear the languages from birth, as well as the case studies of sequentially bilingual children, separate development can be assumed for both, simultaneous and sequentially bilingual children.

STUDY ACTIVITY 2.1

1. What particular language productions by bilingual children have led to the assumption that children initially only have one language system?
2. Which findings suggest that bilingual children distinguish their languages from early on?

Universal Grammar and cross-linguistic influences

In this section we shall be considering a deductive theoretical approach to bilingual language acquisition that is based on 'nativism', the idea that the child has innate linguistic knowledge available when starting the process of language acquisition. This idea was put forward by the linguist Noam Chomsky in his critique of Skinner's (1957) view that the child learns language through imitation and reinforcement by the parents (behaviourism). Chomsky did not arrive at this assumption by observing empirical language data, as was the case in the previous sections, though he did consider facts about child language, such as the relatively short time that it takes children to learn their language.

What kind of linguistic knowledge could be innate? Chomsky (1965) argues that humans have genetically encoded knowledge about language. This knowledge is applicable to all languages and includes basic word categories (such as nouns and verbs), principles that apply when words in a sentence are moved around, as well as a set of so-called **parameters** that can account for differences in the structure of different languages. Taken together, this knowledge is captured by the term '**Universal Grammar**' (UG).

In principle, a child has the same innate linguistic knowledge as an adult but in order to learn a particular language, they need to hear that language in order to discover the particular principles that apply and to set the parameters in a particular way.

Note that the basic assumptions of this theory cannot be verified through data observations, but on the other hand, specific cases such as bilingual children can possibly provide us with more insight of how children might apply innate linguistic knowledge to two different languages in their environment.

Universal Grammar

How does this work? The UG perspective is a view that holds for language acquisition in general and is not specific to bilingual language acquisition. However, taking a more general theoretical perspective and applying it to bilingual development might lead to specific insights or predictions about language development in general.

The innate linguistic knowledge that children are equipped with is called **Language Acquisition Device** (LAD). It consists of the basic principles of grammar, for example, the principle that sentences in all languages have a subject, even if this is encoded in the verb inflection and is not overtly present, as in *amo*, 'I love', where the *–o* ending of the verb marks the first person, *I*. In addition, the parameters determine language-specific characteristics, for example whether the verb is placed before or after the object (see Box 2.3).

Box 2.3: Parameter setting

Chomsky suggested that first language acquisition involves the setting of a number of parameters. A parameter is a two-way option, similar to a switch. The parameter is either set in one direction or the other. One suggested parameter is word order.

Languages differ in terms of their order of the object noun (O) and the verb (V). The parameter can either be set as VO or OV. VO languages are characterised by the object following the verb, as is the case in English:

He (subject) eats (verb) an apple (object).

The other setting is OV. This is the setting for languages that place the verb at the end of the sentences, as for example in Japanese:

Mari-ga	**Jon-o**	**sasotta**
Mary-Subject	John-Object	invited
'Mary invited John'		

A child learning English as well as Japanese will hear both VO and OV sentences. If we assume that the child differentiates the languages from early on, it is possible to set the parameters differently for both languages.

In order for the child to acquire the grammar of a particular language, they have to set parameters (Chomsky, 1981; Hyams, 1986) based on the patterns that they hear in the input. But if children have the same innate knowledge as adults, why do they only say one word at a time when they start speaking? One explanation put forward by Radford (1990) was that the child has to first go through a process of maturation. In particular, he suggested that this process was necessary before children could learn words and word endings that carry grammatical information.

We introduced the distinction between open and closed class words back in Chapter 1. Within the grammatical framework described here, a similar distinction is made between **lexical** and **functional categories**. Lexical categories (in English) include open class words like nouns, verbs, adjectives and adverbs. Functional categories, on the other hand, include not only closed class words such as determiners, pronouns, auxiliaries and conjunctions, but also inflectional endings.

Let us look at these categories in the context of child language. At the one-word stage, children produce mainly open class words, such as *dinner, daddy, bye*, as well as words like *allgone* which children use as a single unit. On this basis, Radford (1990) suggests that children's early language consists of a set of just lexical categories.

Functional categories develop around the age of 24 months. When children are able to produce multiword utterances, their utterances contain pronouns and inflections, for example *I like Teletubbies*, where the subject consists of the pronoun *I*, or *monkey like-s (ba)nana* where the verb *like* has the ending *–s* to mark the third person singular subject *monkey*. Determiners and negation are also evidence of the child's use of functional categories, for example *I go in the sofa*, where the child uses the definite determiner *the* and *don't like soft*, where the verb is negated.

Within the framework of UG, functional categories also include extensions of a category to a phrase. For example, the phrase *the old man* is the extension of the category 'determiner' and is called a Determiner Phrase (DP). Within the phrase, the determiner acts as the head of the phrase. Similarly, all other functional categories can also be extended. We can therefore say that functional categories include closed class words, inflections and negation, as well as the expanded categories Determiner Phrase (DP), Complementiser Phrase (CP), Negation Phrase (NegP) and Inflection Phrase (IP).

If children only start learning functional categories after they have gone through a process of maturation, a process that affects their cognitive development, then a bilingual child should start using functional categories in both their languages because a child cannot be at different cognitive stages at the same time. If there are differences in the onset of functional categories, these can be seen in relation to specific language characteristics and reflect the structural characteristics or the degree of transparency of the category in a particular language. Looking at the emergence of functional categories in bilingual acquisition can therefore give an insight into the interplay between the principles of UG and the specific languages to be learnt.

Paradis & Genesee (1997) investigated the acquisition of the categories IP and DP in two bilingual children between the ages of 2 and 3 who were acquiring English and Canadian French simultaneously. The children were recorded for an hour with both parents alone and together on several occasions. In the analysis, Paradis & Genesee (1997) included occasions when the children were using elements belonging to both categories. For DP, this included the frequency and use of determiners before a noun. For IP, this included the frequency and use of verbs that carry tense (finite verbs).

They found that both children used definite and indefinite determiners in both French and English at a similar age. As the determiners occurred with different nouns, they can be assumed to have been used productively, rather than memorised. For example, the first child produced the definite determiner in the phrase *le loup* (the wolf) at the age of 1;11 and the indefinite determiner in English at the same age as in *a book*. Examples of the indefinite determiner in French occurred at the age of 2;3 in *un oiseau* (a bird) and the definite determiner in English at 2;3 in *the ball*.

For the category IP there were some differences between the languages, such that sentences with finite verbs occurred earlier in Canadian–French than English and were more frequent. For example, at 2;1, one of the children produced the sentence *daddy pousse* (dad is pushing), in French, where the verb form agrees with the third person singular form of the verb *pousser* (pushing). The English third person singular form of the verb occurs at 2;11 in the sentence *goes crash*.

The differences in the timing of sentences with finite verbs in the two languages cannot be due to different maturational stages, as they involve the same child. But the languages differ in terms of inflectional endings. While the singular verb forms sound identical, as in *je chante* (I sing), *tu chantes* (you sing), *il chante* (he sings), the plural forms differ: *nous chantons* (we sing), *vous chantez* (you sing) and *ils chantent* (they sing). In English, on the other hand, all forms of a regular verb are identical, except for the third person singular, *he/she/it sings*. We can therefore say that Canadian–French has a richer morphological system compared to English, where most forms are the same as the stem of the verb. For a child learning the language, a richer system seems to provide more opportunities to learn that verb endings can change, depending on the subject.

Cross-linguistic influences in bilingual development

We will now turn to influences from one language on the other. As we saw earlier, bilingual children at times not only use words from the other language, but also 'mix' word order where these are different in both languages. For example, we saw that Lisa and Giulia initially used word orders such as 'adjective noun' and 'noun adjective' in German and Italian. Volterra & Taeschner (1978) argued that such cross-linguistic influences show that the children are 'confusing' the two languages. Supporters of the separate development hypothesis successfully showed that the majority of children's structures are language-appropriate from very early on. But apart from the explanation of 'borrowing' at the lexical level, little was said about any patterns that clearly show contact between the two languages. They were dismissed as 'performance errors' (Paradis & Genesee, 1996), yet their occurrence shows some form of contact between the two languages of the child.

Box 2.4 gives some examples of cross-linguistic structures. They involve elements from both languages, either inflectional marking from one language in conjunction with words from the other language or adopting the word order of a structure from one language in the other language.

Children's use of cross-linguistic structures can be seen as a form of 'mixing' in that they involve both language systems (and possibly words or forms from both languages). But instead of seeing them as evidence of 'confusion', it is possible to see them either as a form of borrowing, as competition or as an ambiguous interpretation of the language structures they hear in both languages. We shall illustrate this with an example from the adjective order in Italian and German.

We said that attributive adjectives in Italian are generally placed after the noun. However, it is possible for adjectives to occur before the noun, but if they do they express a different meaning. For example, while the sentence *un*

Box 2.4: Cross-linguistic structures

Cross-linguistic structures are structures produced by bilingual children that contain elements from both languages, either inflections from one language in conjunction with words from the other language or the adoption of a structure from the other language. Examples are given below:

a) **German–English, verb morphology**

kiwis, oh …	du hast	*gebuy(d/t)	them?
kiwis,	you have.2nd SG	buy.PARTICIPLE	them?
	'kiwis, have you bought them'?		

In this case, the English verb *buy* occurs with German participle inflection added.

b) **English–German, verb placement**

Ich möchte	*essen	das.
I want.1st SG	eat.INF	this.
'I want to eat this'		

The non-finite verb *essen* (*eat*), should be placed at the end of the sentence.

c) **Cantonese–English, wh movement**

this on the *what?
'what is this on'?

The wh-word should occur in sentence-initial position in English.

amico vecchio (an old friend) refers to a friend that is old in age, the sentence *un vecchio amico* (an old friend) is also possible, but here the adjective *vecchio* (old) refers to a friend that the speaker has known for a long time. Similarly, while in German adjectives are generally placed before the noun, there are instances where the adjective occurs after the noun. An example is given in example 2.3.

Example 2.3

Du   sieh-st   deiner Mutter ähnlich

You   look-2nd SG   your   mother similar.ADJ

'You look similar to your mother'

It is therefore possible that the child has analysed the grammar of both languages in such a way that both orders are possible.

In the examples b) and c) in Box 2.4, the word order of the other language has 'intruded' into the structure of the utterance, even though there is no lexical mixing. Döpke (1998) interprets these examples as evidence that there is a competition between the structures of the two languages during the stage of sentence formulation. A competition at this level would suggest that a bilingual cannot just switch off the other language system, or at least children are not as efficient in selecting just one of the languages.

Example a) in Box 2.4 is different though because there is a switch to the other language such that the main verb and object are expressed in English. Gawlitzek-Maiwald & Tracy (2005) describe the language background of this particular child as being stronger in German and her English not showing any use of auxiliaries, tense or agreement. The child's switch to English and, at the same time, use of German morphological marking, is seen as a bridge to fill a structural gap, which they call 'bilingual bootstrapping'.

Döpke (2000) points out that while the occurrence of cross-linguistic structures in children is low, their occurrence suggests that the child has analysed the language structures in a particular non-adult-like way. It seems that the occurrence of these structures is dependent on the particular language combination that the child is exposed to, the amount of input in each language, the amount of language overlap as well as the particular language level.

Cross-linguistic influence at the interface between two language modules

We have seen different possible explanations for the occurrence of cross-linguistic structures in bilingual children. One explanation is that the overlap between languages might lead children to analyse the structure in a non-adult way. If this is the case, then the question arises as to whether cross-linguistic structures can be predicted for particular language combinations, based on the structural properties of the language systems involved.

Hulk & Müller (2000) suggest that the transfer from one language to another constitutes a kind of shortcut where the child comes across particular problems in the grammar of one of the languages and solves the problem by referring to the grammar of the other language. What kinds of problems would this involve? Could these be predicted by the particular language combinations that the child is learning?

Language acquisition is often studied separately for different areas of language, for example vocabulary, morphology and grammar. But these levels also integrate with each other and with other domains, such as cognitive or pragmatic skills (the ability to interpret language in context). The integration between two areas of language or cognition is called an **interface**. It has been found that a delay in the development of one area can lead to delays at interface levels. An example is autism where the lack of ability to read the intentions of others also affects their language skills. We can therefore say that interface levels, the point where different types of information integrate, are particularly vulnerable to delays.

This is important for bilingual acquisition as well, because it has been argued that it is at the interface between syntax and pragmatics where bilinguals are more likely to take shortcuts that result in cross-linguistic structures.

We will illustrate this with an example from Italian and German. Italian is a language where pronouns do not need to be included in the sentence (**pro-drop**) if the referent can be inferred grammatically or from the context (pragmatics). For example, in a context where a particular person has been introduced, it is possible to say *mangia una mela* (eats an apple) without explicitly referring to the person eating the apple.

German, on the other hand, is not a pro-drop language. This means that utterances need to overtly specify the subject of an action, though there are some exceptions in spoken language. A bilingual child learning both Italian and German might therefore draw the same conclusions about both languages allowing pronoun dropping.

Let us look at an example from both languages. Box 2.5 shows a conversation between an Italian–German bilingual child and his father about having a birthday party for a turtle.

Box 2.5: Conversation with a bilingual Italian–German male child, aged 2;11, Italian

1. *FAT: allora a chi   facciamo   la   festa?
       %eng: now for whom   make.1st PL   the party?
                'now, for whom do we have the party?'

2. *CHI: a   della, a   dessa tataruga.
       %gls: a   quella, a   questa tartaruga.
       %eng: for this,   for this   turtle.

3. *FAT: a   questa tartaruga.
       %eng: for this   turtle.

4. *FAT: e   quanti   anni <u>ha</u>?
       %eng: and how many   years has.3rd SG
                'and how old is it'?

---

5. *CHI: datto.
    %gls: quattro.
    %eng: four.

6. *FAT: quattro anni   ha   la   tartaruga.
    %eng: four   years has.3rd SG   the turtle.
              'The turtle is four years old'.

7. *FAT: <u>e</u>   più   grande di   te.
    %eng: is.3rd SG much bigger   than you.
              'It is much bigger than you'.

In the conversation, the father says in utterance 4, *e quanti anni ha*, 'how old is it', where the referent, the turtle, is not spelled out. The form of the verb, *ha*, indicates that the referent is in the third person, which excludes the speakers. Also, in utterance 7, the father says *e più grande di te*, 'is much bigger than you', excluding the same referent, the turtle, as this is encoded in the third person form of the verb, <u>e</u>. The information that the child gets from the Italian input therefore is that subjects need not be spelled out if the referent is clear from the context. This affects the interface between pragmatics and syntax, as it involves a syntactic phenomenon (the presence or absence of a subject) which is affected by the context of the conversation.

What information does the child get from the other language, in this case German? Box 2.6 shows a conversation between the same bilingual child and his German mother.

Box 2.6: Conversation with a bilingual Italian–German male child, aged 2;9, German

1. *CHI: will   Tommy haben.
    %eng: want.1stSG   Tommy have.INF
              '(I)want to have Tommy'.

2. *MOT: du möchtes   den Tommy   haben?
    %eng: you want.2nd SG   the Tommy   have.INF?
              'you want to have Tommy'?

3. *CHI: ja.
    %eng: yes.

4. *MOT: wo   is(t)   der Tommy?
    %eng: where is.3rd SG   the Tommy?
              'where is Tommy'?

5. *CHI: hab   Tommy mit   genommen.
    %eng: have.1st SG Tommy along taken.PARTICIPLE
              '(I) have taken Tommy along'.

6. *MOT: du hast   den Tommy mit   genommen ja.
    %eng: you have.2nd SG the Tommy along taken.PARTICIPLE, yes.
              'yes, you have taken Tommy along'.

While the mother addresses the child using the second person pronoun, *du*, the child drops the first person pronoun in utterance 1 as well as in utterance 5. In the same transcript, the mother produces the utterance *willst einmal Manuel schreiben?* (do you want to write to Manuel?), where the second person pronoun *du* is omitted, but can be understood from the context, as the mother is addressing the child.

Dropping subjects is quite common for young monolingual English children as well, even though subject dropping is not grammatical in English. The difference between monolingual and bilingual children is the extent and the length of time they produce utterances without subjects.

In order for cross-linguistic transfer to occur, Müller & Hulk (2001) suggest the following conditions:

1. Cross-linguistic structures occur at the interface between syntax and pragmatics.

2. One language allows the possibility for different grammatical analyses.

3. The other language provides significant support for this analysis.

Are these conditions fulfilled for subject dropping for Italian and German? Subjects can be dropped in Italian, and at times in German, when the referents are clear from the context. Subject dropping therefore involves the interface between syntax and pragmatics. Secondly, subjects can be dropped in Italian and in certain situations in German and English as well. In German, commands often occur in negative sentences, as for example in *nicht aus dem Fenster lehnen* (do not lean out of the window), a command that is often found in trains. While in English, the verb *do* is used in the imperative form, in German the verb is not inflected and occurs in the infinitive form.

It is clear then that German allows the possibility for different grammatical analyses regarding the dropping of subjects, yet this is not generally the case. Italian, on the other hand, provides significant support for subject dropping, such that subject dropping is one of the areas vulnerable for cross-linguistic structures.

Universal Grammar and cross-linguistic influences in sequential bilingual development

Most of what we have said about the UG approach and cross-linguistic structures so far applies to simultaneous bilingual children. In the context of sequential bilingual development, there are a number of questions relating to the application of the same principles at a later point. The ability to set parameters and thereby acquire the grammar of another language is possible until puberty (see Chapter 3). Although the acquisition of the second language is delayed compared to the first language, parameter setting can occur based on the evidence in the input of the second language.

In terms of the emergence of functional categories, a delay in the later learnt language is likely, simply because the child has to build up their lexicon in the second language. This does not mean that they are at different cognitive stages in relation to both languages. Given the delay in the onset of a second language, this language is likely to have the status of a 'weaker' language (Meisel, 2007) until the point when the child has 'caught up'.

Are sequential children equally likely to produce cross-linguistic structures compared to simultaneous bilinguals? It is likely that children have already adopted a particular analysis for the first language and possible that they might temporarily adopt this analysis for the second language as well.

STUDY ACTIVITY 2.2

1. What does the term 'parameter' mean? Explain in relation to word order and subject dropping in different languages.
2. Does the Italian–German child in Boxes 2.5 and 2.6 show evidence of cross-linguistic transfer from Italian to German?

The Constructivist account and the Usage-based theory

In the last section we introduced the UG theory and looked at the way bilingual acquisition can be viewed from this perspective. More recently, claims of innate linguistic knowledge have been rejected in favour of the view that children build up structures gradually from the language they hear. In these views, known as Usage-based accounts, experience with language leads to a mental representation of language structure. Further experience results in more abstract representations, yet these are still based on usage. In order to build up representations, children use a general ability to learn, rather than innate linguistic knowledge and the process is guided by particular mechanisms.

Two theories are outlined in the following sections, the Constructivist account and the Usage-based theory. While the two overlap, the former was developed with specifically bilingual children in mind, whereas the Usage-based theory is based on children's language acquisition in general.

The Constructivist account

The Constructivist account was put forward by Gathercole (2007). This account of language development has been applied to monolingual as well as bilingual children's acquisition of morpho-syntax. In this view, two major components drive the language acquisition process in children. One of these is increasing general knowledge/understanding, including cognitive knowledge, the other is linguistic input.

Language development based on these components is characterised by a number of principles. The first one is (A) **piecemeal acquisition**. 'Piecemeal' means that a particular category is not acquired as a whole, but initially only for particular occurrences. For example, when children start acquiring the inflectional system of verbs in an inflected language, they do not acquire all possible inflections (all person endings), but initially pick up on the most frequent forms. One of these is the third person singular on the verb, as in the English phrase *he stops* (see Chapter 6). Piecemeal acquisition is quite different from parameter setting, which was discussed earlier, as parameter setting assumes that the child has acquired a category as a whole and would therefore be expected to use all forms that belong to the category.

The second principle is (B) **acquisition in context**. Children can work out the meaning of a word from the context that the word occurs in. If the child is offered an apple to eat and the verbal utterance includes the word 'apple', the child can link the word with the object. But the child does not know what other types of fruit can be called 'apple'. This can lead to differences between the child and the adult categories (see Chapter 5).

Another principle is (C) **emergence from accumulated knowledge**. This refers to children's ability to draw on patterns that they have observed in different contexts. For example, when children have learnt the name of an object, they often use the same name for objects that have the same shape (shape bias), that is, they might call all fruit that have a round shape 'apple' (see Chapter 5).

The next principle, (D) **structure affecting timing of acquisition**, highlights that the structure of the language to be learnt can affect the timing as to when a particular structure is learnt. For example, it has been observed that children learning English initially learn words for objects, that is nouns and only a few verbs. This is different in languages such as Japanese or Korean where the verb occurs in sentence-final position and stands out more for the child, as it has been found children learning these languages have more verbs in their early lexicon.

The last principle, (E) **amount of exposure affects timing of development**, highlights that the amount of language children hear has an impact on their language development. Hart & Risley (1995) showed that children's language development was different as a result of the amount of language they heard (see Chapter 3).

Applying these principles to bilingual language development, the application of the first two principles, (A) piecemeal acquisition and (B) acquisition in context, should result in the acquisition of both languages in different contexts and thereby minimal overlap between the structures of both languages. So, even if a particular routine (such as bath time) is alternated by two caretakers, they are still different contexts if both caretakers speak different languages.

The third principle, (C) emergence of structure from accumulated knowledge, suggests that a child is able to extract the patterns once a 'critical mass of data' (see Chapter 3) has been accumulated. In addition, principle (E) suggests that acquisition is affected by the amount of exposure.

The question in relation to bilingual acquisition is whether the extraction of patterns is necessarily language-specific. If it is, then there is a possibility that a bilingual child takes longer to collect the necessary critical mass, due to less exposure in each of the languages compared to monolingual children (see Chapter 6 for a discussion of this point). Another possibility is that the extraction of patterns is across both languages. Where these concern object words, the child might take contexts from both languages into account. So, for example, if a child uses 'apple' to apply to all round fruit, the equivalent of this word in another language might also be applied to all round fruit. If further words are learnt in one language and the class of 'round fruit' is divided into 'apples', 'oranges' and 'peaches', the child might then divide this class in the other language as well.

If the patterns to be learnt relate to particular language structures, it is possible that both contexts are taken into account for structures that are similar, resulting in an emergence of the structure at a similar time. If structures are different, then according to principle (D), the language structure itself can affect the timing of acquisition. This is in line with previous findings and can result in the kind of lead-lag pattern observed earlier (Paradis & Genesee (1997), Garman, Schelletter & Sinka (1999)).

Finally, principles (A), (B) and (C) together predict that bilingual development follows similar stages to monolingual development (even if the timing is different) and results in the acquisition of linguistic structures that are qualitatively similar to those of monolinguals. Evidence for the account and the components that are outlined comes from two distinct bilingual corpora, the Miami data and the Welsh data (Gathercole, 2007). We shall only outline the study relating to the Miami data in the next section.

The Miami data were collected as part of a large-scale study to evaluate the effects of bilingualism in children of school age (Oller & Eilers, 2002). Miami was a good setting because it has a large Hispanic population that includes a balance of socio-economic backgrounds and also well-established bilingual education programmes. These include English immersion schools, where only English is spoken, or two-way programmes where both languages are spoken at school (with a split of about 60% English and 40% Spanish).

The overall study included 704 Spanish–English bilinguals as well as 248 monolingual English children. In order to compare children's morpho-syntactic skills, 311 Spanish–English bilinguals in grades 2 and 5 were grouped by language at home: only Spanish, only English, both English and Spanish. They were compared with the monolingual English children, as well as with a group of monolingual Spanish-speaking children from Lima, Peru.

For the study, English and Spanish were contrasted in terms of three structures where English and Spanish differ. They were: the gender of nouns, the count/mass distinction and complex questions as in *Who do you think kissed Mary?* In Spanish, these questions require the conjunction *that* after the first verb, yet in English this is ungrammatical, even though it can occur in sentences like *I think (that) John kissed Mary.*

Box 2.7 gives examples of the three structures in both languages. In contrast to English, Spanish has grammatical gender. This means that every noun is either masculine or feminine, even if it does not have a 'natural' gender. The gender of a noun determines the form of the article. In Spanish, *el* is the article for masculine singular nouns and *la* that for feminine singular nouns. The gender of the noun also affects the endings of the adjectives occurring with the noun, such that the *−a* ending is the feminine form and the ending *−o*

Box 2.7: Examples in support of the Constructivist account

Miami data Spanish–English		
Examples:		
English	**Spanish**	
1. Gender		
the open door. It … .	*la puerta abierta.* the door open *'the open door'* *puerto abierto.* port open *open port*	feminine masculine
2. Mass/Noun distinction		
much coffee. Mass a lot of dirt. Count many chairs.	*mucho* *polvo.* a lot of/much dirt *muchas sillas.* many chairs	Mass/Count Count
3. Complex questions		

Who do you think has
green eyes?
 	
*Who do you think
that has green eyes?
	*¿Quién piensas tiene ojos verdes?
	   Who think.2nd SG has.3rd SG eyes green
	   'Who do you think has green eyes?'
	
	¿Quién piensas que tiene ojos verdes?
	   Who think.2nd SG that has.3rd SG eyes green
	   * *'Who do you think that has green eyes?'*	

is associated with the masculine form. In contrast, English only has natural gender. This means that the pronouns *he* and *she* are used in accordance with the natural gender of a referent, but other nouns that do not have a gender are referred to as *it*.

The second structure where Spanish and English contrast is the count/mass distinction. In English, different quantifiers are used for count and mass nouns, namely *much* and *many*. Mass nouns occur with *much*, as in *much coffee*, whereas *a lot of* or *many* can only be used for countable nouns such as *many chairs*. In Spanish, on the other hand, the use of the quantifier *muchas* (much or many) is related to the properties of the referent and can be used for either count or mass nouns. The form varies, depending on whether the noun is feminine or masculine, therefore it is either *mucho* (masculine) or *muchas* (feminine).

The third structure also differs between English and Spanish. While the equivalent of the conjunction *that*, the word *que* in Spanish, can occur in the example in 3) in Box 2.7, this is ungrammatical in English.

In order to investigate bilingual children's knowledge of the structures in both English and Spanish, they were given both grammatical and ungrammatical structures for gender in Spanish, count and mass nouns in English, and complex questions in both Spanish and English. The children had to say whether the sentences sounded acceptable and if they were not, children had to suggest how they would say them.

For the first structure, gender, bilinguals were compared to monolingual Spanish speakers. It was found that the Spanish monolinguals were better at the grammaticality judgements than the bilingual children. However, differences between the bilingual groups were also found, particularly in the younger age groups (grade 2). The bilinguals who heard the most Spanish were better at ungrammatical gender sentences than the bilinguals with less Spanish.

For the count/mass distinction, bilingual children were compared with monolingual English children. Again, the monolingual children were better than the bilinguals. But there was a difference between the bilingual children, as the ones attending immersion schools were better than children attending two-way programmes. These differences can again be related to the amount of English that children heard.

For the last structure, bilingual children were tested in both languages and compared to monolingual speakers in each language. For both languages, the monolingual group performed better than the bilinguals, regardless of the bilingual school programme.

Overall, the findings of the Miami corpus confirm the predictions of the Constructivist account: the amount of input predicts the sequence of development until a critical mass is reached. The complexity of a structure, as well as its opacity or transparency, affect the order of development. Bilingual development parallels that of monolingual acquisition.

The Usage-based theory

The Usage-based theory is a view of child language acquisition which was put forward by Tomasello (2003, 2009). The essence of the Usage-based theory is that structure emerges from the use of language. No specific innate language knowledge is necessary for language acquisition to occur. Instead, children make use of a general ability to learn and in particular two mechanisms which are particularly useful for learning language, namely 'intention reading' and 'pattern finding'.

The first of these, 'intention reading', is a mechanism that infants make use of from early on when interacting with their caretakers and includes 'joint attention'. Children acquire the communicative function of language from early on and make use of gestures such as pointing. Gestures like these are important, particularly at the stage of word learning where the child often uses pointing as a request for the adult to supply a particular word for an object.

The second mechanism, 'pattern finding', is essential for grammar learning, as children go beyond a particular utterance to create abstract schemas and patterns to build the grammar rules of the language they learn. Based on the observations of his daughter's language acquisition, Tomasello (1992) has shown that children's acquisition of language structure is organised around individual verbs, and that the structures the first verbs can occur in are learnt on an individual basis.

Intention reading and pattern finding are cognitive mechanisms which interact with each other when the child is faced with particular acquisition tasks, resulting in four different processes which together guide the language acquisition process (Tomasello, 2009, p. 86): (A) Intention Reading and Cultural Learning, (B) Schematisation and Analogy, (C) Entrenchment and Pre-emption, and (D) Functionally Based Distributional Analysis.

Young children are increasingly able to read the intentions of the people around them and to understand that people carry out actions in order to achieve specific goals. One of the ways children learn is by adopting the same goals, that is by imitating the adult. This leads to an understanding of the reasons behind the actions, hence cultural learning. One area of language learning where intention reading is important, is in the use of phrases such as *thank you*, as children have to understand the communicative function underlying the use of these phrases.

Schematisation and Analogy refers to the way structures are learnt. Children tend to learn a basic structure and use it repeatedly with only minor variations. This suggests that they have formed a schema. Analogy refers to the ability to compare across different contexts. Matthews & Tomasello (2009) give the examples of two sentences, *I kicked the ball* and *Daddy threw it*, which differ in terms of sentence length as well as in the words used; yet both are examples of transitive verbs, where there is an object following the verb. On this level, the sentences follow the same pattern.

We know that children produce utterances that are not in line with the adult grammar. In the sentence *he falled me down*, the child uses a verb transitively, as well as treating an irregular verb *fall* like a regular verb and adding the past tense *–ed*. Tomasello believes that children imitate a lot of the language that they hear. The more often they hear a verb like *fall* in a construction without a direct object (intransitive), the more likely it is that the structure and the irregular past tense form become entrenched, and the likelihood of non-adult structures is reduced (pre-emption).

How do children come to understand different word classes and larger syntactic categories? Matthews & Tomasello believe that children can identify words as well as groups of words that have the same communicative function and link them through a process that he calls 'functionally based distributional analysis' (Matthews & Tomasello, 2009, p. 202). As this process is applied to word classes as well as to larger units, it forms the basis of how children build up their grammar.

In the framework of Usage-based grammar, the frequency of occurrence of particular words or structures is important for the acquisition process. The frequency of a particular class of words or structures (type frequency) allows the child to draw comparisons (analogy), while the frequency of particular items (token frequency) facilitates their acquisition.

Comparing the Constructivist account and the Usage-based theory

Remember that the driving processes of acquisition in the Constructivist account are (a) increasing general knowledge/understanding and (b) linguistic input. On the other hand, the main drivers in the Usage-based theory are intention reading and pattern finding. While there is some overlap, the focus of both theories is different. The Usage-based theory takes a pragmatic perspective, emphasises social learning and thereby accounts for language learning from the earliest stages. The Constructivist account, on the other hand, focuses on the interplay between knowledge and structure in the acquisition of morpho-syntax. The Constructivist account emphasises the learner's interaction with the input. However, the processes derived from the principles in each view are actually not that different.

The first process in the Constructivist account, 'piecemeal acquisition', is in line with Tomasello's (1992) observation that verbs are learnt on an individual basis. Tomasello (2009) states that early syntactic marking is 'local' and thereby item-specific. This explains why children can produce the adult form of a particular structure, such as *how do you,* but a non-adult form for a similar structure, as in *what you can.* The explanation would be that a structure with the word 'how', and others with the word 'what', are separate, both involving an 'item-specific' structure. In the Constructivist account these structures demonstrate 'piecemeal acquisition'.

The idea that structures emerge from accumulated knowledge corresponds to entrenchment and pre-emption. In the Constructivist account, structures need to get to a 'critical mass' before they are acquired, in the Usage-based theory this seems to happen more gradually, yet both assume that frequency of occurrence drives acquisition. This is specifically stated in principle (E) of the Constructivist account, namely that the amount of exposure affects the timing of development.

The only principle that does not seem to show equivalence is principle (D) of the Constructivist account, namely that the transparency of the language structure itself can affect the timing of acquisition. Presumably, the transparency of a structure could affect the process of schematisation and analogy, yet this is not explicitly stated.

The Constructivist account and Usage-based theory in simultaneous and sequential bilingual acquisition

The Usage-based theory has not generally been applied to the study of bilingual acquisition. However, similar to the Constructivist account, its emphasis on input frequency predicts that bilingual children develop at a slower rate initially in each language due to the lower rate of input in each language. Depending on the input, simultaneous bilingual children should reach the critical mass for a particular structure in each of their languages earlier than sequentially bilingual children in their second language.

Paradis, Nicoladis, Crago & Genesee (2011) compared monolingual and bilingual English–French children's regular and irregular past tense productions in an elicitation task based on the predictions of the Usage-based theory.

The bilingual children were grouped according to the information parents gave in a questionnaire about their home language, similar to the Miami study. They tested 23 French–English bilingual children and 21 monolingual French children aged 4 years who were living in Edmonton in Canada. The children were given a past tense elicitation task (TEGI – see Chapter 6) in both languages, where they were prompted to produce a past tense verb. The verbs either followed a regular pattern, as in *he wash<u>ed</u> his hands*, or an irregular pattern, as in *the ball <u>fell</u> down*. The bilingual children were compared to the monolingual French children as well as monolingual children that were used as the normative sample for the test for English.

They found that the monolingual children produced more correct past tense forms than the bilingual children in both languages, and all children produced more correct regular past tense forms than irregulars. The bilingual children's past tense forms were in line with their dominant home language, showing that they produced more past tense forms in the language that they heard more often. This is in line with the predictions of the Usage-based theory.

However, the findings did not show a difference between monolinguals and bilinguals in French regular past tense. Given the difference of exposure in the input, the Usage-based theory would have predicted the bilingual children to have a lower proportion of correct French regular past tense forms. Also, there were cross-linguistic differences which cannot be accounted for by the frequency of regular and irregular verbs in English and French. It is possible that the Usage-based theory underestimates the role of transparency in acquisition, particularly when input frequency is reduced, as in the case of bilingual acquisition.

The Constructivist account has been applied to the acquisition of different bilingual speakers. In the Miami data (Gathercole, 2007), children were grouped according to home language. While the study did not focus on the starting point of the other language, it is likely that the children who only heard one language at home (particularly if that language corresponded to the dominant language in the community) were initially only exposed to one language.

The study also makes clear that the amount of ongoing language input (regardless of particular starting point in the first years) determines the language competence of bilingual children in each of their languages. While it confirms the exposure of a particular critical mass of input for a particular structure, it also shows that the interaction between a structure and its degree of transparency affects acquisition. Moreover, the findings of the study suggest that the difference between different learners disappears once the critical mass is reached.

STUDY ACTIVITY 2.3

1. What is the role of frequency of grammatical structures in monolingual and bilingual acquisition?
2. In what aspects do the Constructivist account and the Usage-based theory differ? Is this important for bilingual acquisition?

SUMMARY

This chapter has given an overview of the theoretical background on which studies in bilingual acquisition have been based. The discussion of the single system vs separate development hypotheses, as well as the occurrence of cross-linguistic structures, was specific to bilingual acquisition, and in particular, simultaneous bilingual acquisition. On the other hand, acquisition theories such as UG, the Constructivist account and the Usage-based theory are general theories of first language acquisition, including both monolingual and bilinguals.

The study of bilingual acquisition based on these views has allowed the testing of particular hypotheses. Within the framework of UG, there was the question as to whether any maturational processes would apply to both languages at the same time. The occurrence of cross-linguistic structures has attracted particular interest, as it can give an insight into the way the two systems interact in the bilingual context, and can lead to particular predictions concerning difficulties arising in particular language combinations.

Within the Constructivist account and the Usage-based theory, the emphasis on frequency of exposure has led to assumptions that bilingual children are at a disadvantage, as their language exposure is divided between two languages. We shall come back to this point in the next chapter.

FURTHER READING

For more details of cross-linguistic structures in different language combinations see Döpke (2000). For more details on bilingual bootstrapping see Gawlitzek-Maiwald & Tracy (2005). For more details on the Syntax-Pragmatics interface in relation to different languages see Serratrice (2005) and Schmitz, Patuto & Müller (2012). In the context of this chapter, we have only described the Miami study here. For an outline of the Wales study see Gathercole (2007).

Characteristics of the Bilingual Learner

3

In this chapter we shall look at characteristics of bilingual children that make them different from monolingual learners. Apart from the fact that their language input is in two languages, rather than just one, different home language strategies can have an influence on the way the languages are learnt. We have already heard about the one parent one language (OPOL) strategy. This is common in parents with different native languages but is not the only strategy that can be employed.

The status of the languages in the community also has a significant influence on a bilingual child's language development, particularly when they have more contact with the community at nursery or school age. This is different in countries where the community has two official languages, such as Belgium, Switzerland, Canada, South Africa or India, where children will hear both languages in the community and at school.

The age when children start learning a language matters, both in first and second language learning. We know from the study of children who have either grown up with animals or who were neglected by their parents (feral children) that lack of language exposure until puberty leads to the situation where the child is no longer able to acquire a first language. The period from birth to puberty is generally regarded as the **critical period** for first language acquisition (Lenneberg, 1967). It is the maturational stage where learners are particularly sensitive to language input.

Critical periods in development are accompanied by a sharp decline in the ability to develop particular skills once the critical period is reached. In relation to second language learning, the decline in the capacity to learn another language seems to be more gradual. For this reason, the term **sensitive period** is used in this context. Sensitive periods can differ for different aspects of language; hence it seems that there are sensitive periods for pronunciation and lexical knowledge as well as grammar.

We are also going to look more closely at those factors that are important in language learning in both types of bilinguals. The languages that children hear, how often they interact with their caretaker, and how caretakers speak to them, are all part of children's input, which in turn predicts the language level of the child at a given stage of development. In both monolingual and bilingual children, the amount of language (quantity), as well as the way it is structured and expressed (quality), can vary and has a significant influence on the children's language. There has recently been an intense interest in input by researchers, particularly those who are concerned with bilingual development. The type and quality of input matters, in particular in light of recent acquisition theories which place input at the centre of language learning (see Chapter 2).

Parents also have different strategies in relation to language mixing. If they are able to speak both languages, they might be code-switching themselves and accept mixing and responses in the other language by the child.

Code-switching is one of the characteristics of bilinguals, showing that they are able to use both languages as a resource, and might at times do so in various situations in order to achieve communication objectives. Whether children's use of both languages in the same utterance can always be seen as 'mixing', or to what extent this is on a par with adult code-switching, is another point of discussion in this chapter.

Finally, we shall also discuss the question whether ultimately, speakers who grow up with two languages reach native speaker levels of language and thereby 'catch up' with monolinguals in relation to different language levels, including vocabulary and grammar.

Home and community language

The age of onset alone cannot explain differences in the way the languages develop in the long term. So, let's look more closely at the relationship between the home and community languages. We can certainly verify from the case studies considered in Chapter 1 that the majority of children growing up with two languages simultaneously do so in the context of the home. Children who acquire their languages sequentially tend to acquire the first language at home and the subsequent language outside the home. Before we discuss the differences between the two, let us first look more closely at both settings.

Home language strategies

In most of the case studies of children who are described as simultaneous bilinguals, the child was exposed to both languages in the home with parents with different native languages following the OPOL principle (see Chapter 1). But this is not the only possible strategy. Romaine (1999) distinguishes between six different types of early childhood bilingualism which are outlined in Box 3.1. In the outline, for each pattern, home and community language are specified, as well as the specific strategy that is adopted by the parents.

The first pattern, the OPOL principle, involves each parent speaking their own language to the child. In addition, the community language is the same as the language of one of the parents. This means that the two languages that the child is exposed to do not have an equal status but represent the majority

Box 3.1: Types of early childhood bilingualism

Romaine classified early childhood bilingualism into six patterns of language choice, depending on the language spoken by the parents, the community language and the strategy adopted by the parents:

1. **The one person one language (OPOL) principle**

    Parents: Each parent speaks their own native language to the child from birth.
    Community: The community language is one of the parents' languages.
    Strategy: One parent one language at all times.
    Case studies: Most studies of simultaneous bilingualism outlined in Chapter 1.

2. **Non-dominant home language/one language one environment**

    Parents: Parents have different native languages but speak the same language to the child according to context.
    Community: The community language is one of the parents' languages.
    Strategy: Parents speak the non-dominant language at home and the dominant language outside the home.
    Case study: Fantini (1985).

3. **Non-dominant home language without community support**

    Parents: Both parents have the same native language.
    Community: The community language is different from the language of the parents.
    Strategy: The parents only speak their own language to the child.
    Case studies: Most cases of sequential bilingualism discussed in Chapter 1.

4. **Double non-dominant home language without community support**

    Parents: Parents speak different native languages.
    Community: The dominant language is different from the language of either parent.
    Strategy: The parents speak their own language to the child.
    Case study: Hoffmann (1985).

5. **Non-native parents**

    Parents: Parents speak the same native language.
    Community: The dominant language is the same as the parents' language.
    Strategy: One of the parents always speaks a non-native language to the child.
    Case study: Döpke (1992).

6. **Mixed languages**

Parents: The parents are bilingual.
Community: Parts of the community are also bilingual.
Strategy: Parents switch between languages.
Case study: Tabouret-Keller (1969).

and a minority language. In case studies 1 and 2 (see Chapter 1), both fathers spoke the majority language and the mothers the minority language. In order to further support the minority language, both Leopold and Ronjat made a conscious decision to support the development of the child's minority language and spoke German to their wives. While the development of both bilingual children was similar in many respects, Louis maintained both languages quite well, whereas for Hildegard, English became the dominant language.

In the fourth strategy, 'double non-dominant home language' the child also hears two languages from native parents, similar to the first strategy. However, the difference is that the community language is different from either of the parental languages. This is a strategy for 'trilingual' language development where the child hears three languages. We have not discussed any cases of trilingual language development in this context but Hoffmann (1985) describes the development of her children, who grew up with German and Spanish as home languages, and English as the community language.

Another common strategy is listed as strategy 3, 'non-dominant home language without community support', where the parents speak the same native language in the home (the minority language) and the community language is the majority language. This is the situation of migrant parents who maintain their native language when speaking to the child, but the children come into contact with the majority language at pre-school or school. In the majority of cases described as sequential bilingualism in Chapter 1, the subsequent language was introduced and spoken by people outside the immediate family.

A variant is the 'non-native parents' strategy (5), where one of the parents speaks a non-native language to the child, as well as 'non-dominant home language/one language one environment' (2) where parents use the non-dominant language in the home environment and the dominant language outside the home. Finally, the strategy of 'mixed' languages occurs when the parents are bilingual and live in a bilingual community. This was the case of Eve (Tabouret-Keller, 1969) who grew up in a French–German community in Alsace and whose parents were using both languages with the child, although they did not use both languages within the same sentence.

Discussion

We have seen that the home language strategies adopted with most simultaneous bilingual speakers are different to the strategies found with sequential bilingual learners. Therefore, the acquisition process between both types of bilinguals does not just differ in terms of the age at which exposure to both languages started.

On the other hand, both types of bilingualism are similar in that the languages are learnt in a naturalistic context, rather than through a process of formal instruction, as is the case with later L2 acquisition. From the case studies discussed earlier, it seems that a relatively early onset of another language in early childhood (between the ages of 1 and 3 years) still results in a native-like level of language competence.

While the outlined home pattern strategies are quite clear, their implementation might not always be as straightforward. Döpke (1992, pp. 63–67) discusses different techniques by parents following the OPOL principle to respond to children who use the other language in a first language context. Parents' strategies ranged from either translating but acknowledging children's utterances, pretending not to understand what was said, or requesting the child to use the other language.

Responding to the child's use of the other language can become more challenging later on when the child attends school, has more contact with the community language and does not want to be 'the odd one out'. This can lead to a shift in the status of the languages of a bilingual. At this point, parents' use of home language patterns might change as a result.

The home language patterns outlined in the previous section also do not take account of the language used by other speakers in the home environment. Lanza (2008) points out that the language that parents speak to each other, and the language spoken among siblings, as well as the amount of code-switching by the parents, can make a difference to the child's input in both languages, and thereby to their language learning. Parents who follow the one language one environment pattern are providing consistent input at home, whereas parents following the OPOL principle generally use one of the languages to communicate with each other.

Home language has been found to affect bilingual children's vocabulary levels from the age of 2. Gathercole et al. (2008) investigated lexical skills in children in Wales and found that these skills were in line with the language(s) spoken at home (either English, Welsh or both – see Chapter 5).

STUDY ACTIVITY 3.1

1. Outline the home language strategies adopted by the parents in case study 7. What prompted a change in this case?
2. Compare the OPOL principle to the one language one environment strategy. Can you think of advantages and disadvantages for both?

Age of onset

We know that a lot of developmental changes happen to a child between birth and puberty, changes that go together with neurological developments in the brain. It is therefore possible that there are a number of different sensitive periods relating to different aspects of language? A crucial difference between simultaneous and sequential bilinguals is in the point when another language is regularly heard (age of onset). If they are at different points of cognitive development, this could affect the way the languages are learnt, as well as the attainment in the later learnt language.

How can bilingual learners be compared? One criterion that has been applied is the extent to which a later learner can achieve the level of a native speaker, both in terms of the way they sound, and also in their knowledge of words and grammar.

We know that when a second language is learnt in adulthood, the person can have quite a good command of the language, but they will speak with a non-native accent. What is the cut-off point for sounding native-like? Does the same cut-off apply to both vocabulary and grammar? We will consider each of these levels next.

Sensitive period for pronunciation

In order to answer these questions, Granena & Long (2012) investigated the language of a group of 65 speakers of native Chinese living as long-term residents in Spain. The people who took part in the study had started learning Spanish between 3 and 29 years of age. This means that the subjects who started learning Spanish from an early age can be considered sequential bilingual learners, the older ones are clearly second language learners.

The participants were recruited through advertisements and were required to have lived in Spain for around 10 years as well as have a high level of Spanish. The subjects were divided into different groups depending on the age when they started to live in Spain: 3–6 years, 7–15 years or 16–29 years. All participants were tested for pronunciation, vocabulary, grammar and morphology. They were compared to a group of 12 Spanish native speakers of a similar age.

The first question to be investigated was native-like pronunciation. In order to assess pronunciation, subjects were asked to read a paragraph which contained sounds that are particularly difficult for Chinese learners of Spanish. For example, Chinese does not have an equivalent of the /r/ sound; that is why Chinese learners tend to replace this sound with the sound that is closest to the /r/ sound, which is the /l/ sound. The text of the passage is given in Box 3.2.

The recordings of the reading were then judged by 12 native speakers of Spanish using a 9-point scale where a rating of 1 indicated a 'very strong accent' whereas a rating of 9 indicated 'no accent'. The chart in Box 3.2 gives the group percentage ratings for each group. It is clear that ratings of pronunciation were highest for native speakers and lower the later the group started learning Spanish.

Among the non-native speakers, the group that started learning Spanish between the ages of 3 and 6 had the highest ratings compared to the other two groups. However, even then, there were differences among the 20 participants in this group. Subjects who had started hearing Spanish from the age of 3–5 had higher pronunciation ratings than those who started learning Spanish

Box 3.2: Performance on pronunciation

Percentage

a) Task

In order to assess participants' native pronunciation, they were asked to read the following passage:

Hace años me encantaba observar a los conductores del antiguo ferrocarril de vía estrecha. Me emocionaba verles girar la palanca de freno con precisión hasta que-salían chispas de las ruedas. Era una auténtica maravilla.

Many years ago I used to enjoy looking at the drivers of the old narrow-railtrain. I used to get excited when I was seeing them turn the brake with precision until sparks were coming out from the wheels. It was a real wonder.

b) Results

Group percentage ratings

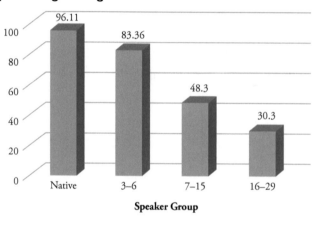

at the age of 6. Among the subjects in the 3–5 group there were differences, where some subjects sounded more native-like than others.

This suggests that there are other factors contributing to perceptions of whether someone sounds like a native. But, on the whole, the findings confirm the existence of a sensitive period for phonology, which can be assumed to be up to the age of 5 years. This means that children who start hearing another language later than 5 years of age are less likely to sound like a native speaker.

Sensitive period for lexical knowledge

Can we assume that there is a sensitive period for lexical knowledge as well? If there is such a sensitive period, it would be expected that speakers who started hearing a language later will have less knowledge about words than a native speaker, particularly which words go together frequently (**collocation**), as well as set expressions. Granena & Long (2012) assessed the knowledge of lexis and collocation of the same participants. The tasks and the results are outlined in Box 3.3.

In the first task, participants had to complete the second noun in a string of two nouns (compounds). While the participants are likely to know each of

---

Box 3.3: Performance of word knowledge

a) Tasks

Compound completion: *cubre (cama)* – bed(spread).

String completion: *sano y (salvo)* – safe and (sound).

Error detection:
  en un abrir y cerrar de <u>boca</u> (ojos) – in the twinkling of a <u>mouth</u> (eye).

Prepositions after verbs:
  los pájaros se alimentan <u>de</u> semillas – birds feed <u>on</u> seeds.

Judging words or combinations: *abrellaves (abrelatas)* – (can opener).

Collocational judgement: *ser tarta (pan) comido* – to be cake (bread) eaten,
                                                          a piece of cake.

b) Results

Group percentage ratings

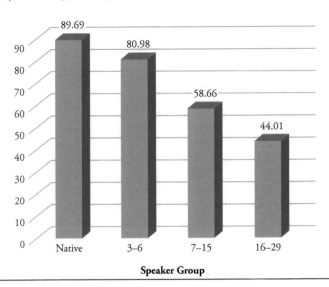

the nouns involved separately, they might not know how the words combine. In the example, the nouns *bed* and *spread* combine to refer to *cloth covering a bed*. While the word *spread* combines with *bed*, it cannot combine with table. To express a similar meaning, the combinations *table cover* and *table cloth* are used.

For the second task, subjects had to complete a string of words. For this, they needed to know which words combine to express the same meaning in both languages. In the case of one example, *sano* literally translates as *healthy* and *salvo* as *safe*, whereas in English it is the words *safe* and *sound* that combine to express the meaning of a safe arrival, for example.

The error detection task requires participants to notice that one of the words in a given expression does not fit and to detect which word is out of place. In the given expression 'in the twinkling of a mouth' the wrong part of the face is used.

Prepositions after verbs are often difficult to learn for a second language as they often do not translate in the same way for the same context. In the preposition task, the Spanish preposition *de* translates as *from*, yet in English the preposition *on* is used in conjunction with *feed*.

In the word judgement task, subjects were asked to judge whether a word or a combination of words is a real string in the language. The Spanish word *abrellaves* is not a real word but it is similar to the real word *abrelatas*, which translates as *can opener*. The final task involved judging collocations.

In order to compare the different groups with regard to their lexical and collocational knowledge, the scores for all tasks were combined into one score. As before for pronunciation, it was found that the native speakers had the highest group score, and that scores were lower for groups that had started hearing English later. In the case of the 3–6 group, the majority of speakers were judged to be on a par with native speakers, and even in the 7–15 group there were some individuals who had achieved native-like performance. The results again suggest a sensitive period, yet the cut-off point for lexical knowledge was judged to be around the age of 9.

Sensitive period for morpho-syntax

Finally, participants were also tested on grammar and morphology. The tasks included an online grammaticality judgement task, oral retelling of a video clip from a comedy TV programme – *Mr Bean* – two word-order preference tasks and a gender assignment task. The results are outlined in Box 3.4.

The results again show a negative relationship between the age when learners started Spanish and the test scores achieved in the grammar and morphology task. The decline for grammar and morpho-syntax was less steep, compared to phonology and lexical knowledge. The results again show a sensitive period where the cut-off point can be assumed to be around 12 years of age.

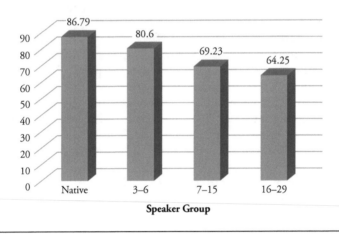

Box 3.4: Performance on morpho-syntax

a) Tasks

Grammaticality judgement of Spanish structures that are difficult for non-Romance speakers including gender agreement, prepositions and different verb types.

b) Results

Group percentage scores

From these results it seems that the age when children start to hear another language is an important factor in bilingual acquisition, particularly in relation to the different sensitive periods specified for different aspects of language.

STUDY ACTIVITY 3.2

1. What is the cut-off point for each of the different sensitive periods in the Granena & Long (2012) study?
2. How have the different language skills (pronunciation, lexical knowledge and morpho-syntax) been assessed?

Input and exposure

We know that children need to hear language in order to learn. They also learn the particular language they hear in their environment. So how do they pick up language from what they hear? Does it matter how much caretakers speak to their children and the way they speak?

The language or languages that are spoken in the environment of the child is generally described as **input**. On the other hand, the term **exposure** refers more specifically to the caretaker language at a particular time and in a particular context. It is measurable, for example by recoding the conversation and subsequently analysing the caretaker's language. The precise nature of the input, its quantity, how children learn from exposure and whether this is the only source of evidence they have, are all discussions that have carried on for some time in child language acquisition research.

Within the Usage-based theory of acquisition (see Chapter 2), input and exposure alone are thought to determine a child's level of language proficiency. This means that the child is dependent on what they hear and in particular how often a particular string occurs because the words and strings that occur more frequently will be learnt earlier.

An example of a study looking at input and output frequencies in monolingual children is given in Box 3.5, showing that there is a relationship between input and output frequency for verbs. In the context of bilingual acquisition, we can assume that exposure still determines what is learnt, however, children's input is divided between two different languages. As we have already seen, the point of onset as well as the frequency of exposure might differ between the languages. In addition, there is the question whether exposure to the equivalent lexical item or grammatical feature facilitates acquisition or possibly even delays it.

Box 3.5: Verb input and output

In a study of verb input and output, Naigles & Hoff-Ginsberg (1998) analysed videotapes of 57 mothers and their children who were at the beginning of the two-word stage at two points in time, 10 months apart. In the first recording, the verbs used by the mothers, and their frequency, were analysed. In the second recording, the children's verbs and their frequencies were analysed. The most and least frequently used verbs by the mothers and the children were compared.

The verbs go and put were the most frequent verbs for the mothers and children. Similarly, both want and see were frequent verbs for both, mothers and children. When looking at the least frequent verbs used by the mothers, for example run, it was found that this verb only occurred once in the children's data. Therefore, there is evidence that children learn what is used frequently in the language that is addressed to them as well as the children 10 months later, though the overall frequencies differed.

The only exception to this pattern was found for the verb 'think'. This occurred frequently in the input data but was taken up only twice in the child data. One explanation for this discrepancy is that thinking is a verb that does not describe a visible action and it is therefore not clear for the children what 'thinking' involves.

For example, if a bilingual child hears the lexical item *dog* and the French translation equivalent *chien*, does the fact that the same lexical item occurs in the input make it more likely that both are acquired, or does the fact that the same referent is labelled differently in different language contexts delay the acquisition of the items as well as its translation equivalent, given that the overall frequency of exposure for each is perhaps lower, compared to the input of the same item in the case of a monolingual child?

Exposure to the language to be learnt is clearly important, however, Carroll (2017), in a recent keynote article, expresses scepticism that input and exposure alone can explain levels of language proficiency, particularly in the context of bilingual language acquisition.

While an analysis of the input language can determine what words or structures are frequent, it does not explain how exposure leads the child to learn from the input, except when a word or string is memorised. There are other learning mechanisms that the child can make use of, for example 'learning by analogy' and 'rule learning'. Learning by analogy involves a comparison between a new item, say the verb *sink*, to an already familiar item, such as *sing*, and to apply what is already known about *sing* to the new item. If the child has learnt that the past tense of *sing* is *sang*, this knowledge can be applied to the analogous word, *sink*, resulting in the past form *sank*. In the case of 'rule learning', an already acquired rule, such as 'add *–ed* to a verb to form the past tense' is applied to a new verb, thereby forming another regular past tense of a new verb.

Carroll also emphasises the role of cognitive maturation in the language-learning process. She refers to Meisel (2011) who argues that children go through changes in brain development between 3 and 3;6 which affect the way language is processed. In particular, the changes affect the role of the left hemisphere in language learning, such that language is increasingly processed in the right hemisphere.

Based on the evidence of cognitive maturation, simultaneous and sequential bilingual learners differ not only in the age of onset of each of their languages, but possibly also in terms of the level of cognitive maturation. If sequential language learners, at the point of starting another language, are already skilled in the application of some learning mechanisms through exposure to their first language, this knowledge can facilitate the process of learning a different language.

Finally, Carroll (2017) also argues that frequent exposure might be more important in affecting the size of children's vocabulary rather than grammar acquisition. A word is learnt from a number of exposures, either in the same or similar contexts. Morpho-syntax, on the other hand, requires the application of different learning mechanisms and more exposure for the patterns to be extracted.

Input frequency

But how much do parents talk to their children? Can one really say that a bilingual is exposed to only half of the input in either of their languages?

In an investigation of the language experience of 42 monolingual American–English children between 10 and 36 months, Hart & Risley (1995, pp. 64–66) measured the speech rate of parents with different backgrounds over a period of four months. There were three groups of parents: welfare parents, working-class parents and professional parents. They found that, on average, parents interacted 28 minutes per hour with their child, producing 341 utterances and 1,440 words.

However, there was considerable variation according to the socio-economic status of the parents, ranging from just 7 minutes of interaction per hour (178 utterances, 930 words) for welfare parents to 48 minutes' interaction per hour (487 utterances, 2,671 words) for professional parents. Parents' speech rate increased to some extent as children got older.

Does the amount of interaction have an effect on children's learning? They found that children who were exposed to a higher speech rate produced more words themselves. Also, when measuring children's vocabulary at the ages of 3 and 9, they found that children's scores related to the amount of exposure they had, such that children of professional parents had a larger vocabulary size at ages 3 and 9 compared to working-class and welfare parents.

This finding is important in that it shows that the rate of exposure to language is not absolute but varies for different parents. Obviously, this is also the case for bilingual children. It would be useful to compare speech rates for monolingual and bilingual children for one language, to see whether there are differences.

Such a comparison was carried out by de Houwer (2014) for 46 middle to upper middle class families in Belgium. She included 30 families who only spoke Dutch at home and 16 bilingual families with children simultaneously exposed to both Dutch and French. In the bilingual families, all mothers spoke Dutch to their children and the fathers spoke French from the time the children were born. In the study, the speech rate of Dutch mothers to their monolingual and bilingual children was measured and compared when the children were 13 and 20 months old, an age comparable to that in the Hart & Risley study.

de Houwer found that the number of words per hour produced by the mothers was 2,715 for the bilingual children and 2,673 for the monolingual children. This is comparable to the rate of words produced by professional parents in the Hart & Risley study. de Houwer found that there was variation in the number of words produced within each group, yet there was no difference in the speech rate of both groups of mothers.

The findings are interesting because they suggest that the rate of speech of mothers with the same socio-economic background is comparable between monolingual and bilingual children, at least as far as the exposure to the language of the primary caretaker is concerned.

Quality of input

We have so far looked at the frequency of exposure to language for both monolingual and bilingual children. The language that the child hears can also differ in terms of quality. The way parents talk to their children at an early age is different to that of a later age and the language of both caretakers can also differ.

We will demonstrate this with an example, which is given in Box 3.6. The child language is taken from male twins. Both are growing up bilingually with English and Spanish. We consider the parents' languages at different ages, starting with the English mother's language to the children at age 1 and age 4.

Box 3.6 shows how the mother's language is different when the children are 1;1 compared to when they are 4;5 years old. At the earlier age, the mother's utterances are shorter (2 to 5 words), and the mother repeats the animal noise associated with a cow, *moo*. She also tries to get the children to produce the noise associated with a dog, *woof*. The children do not produce much language at this early stage and utterances consist of just one word. At the later age, 4;7, the mother's language is more elaborate (between 3 and 10 words) and includes quite specific questions. The children also produce longer utterances, though there are still some phonological substitutions, as the last utterances show, where the alveolar approximant /r/ is substituted by the labio-velar approximant /w/.

Box 3.6: Input at different ages, English

English Data

a) **Input at 1;1**

1	*MOT:	where's the cow ?
2	*CHI:	moo@o .
3	*MOT:	moo@o !
4	*CHI:	moo@o .
5	*MOT:	oh, the doggie !
6	*MOT:	where's the doggie ?
7	*MOT:	what does the doggie say ?
8	*CHI:	hm@i .
9	*MOT:	woof@o woof@o woof@o.

b) **Input at 4;5**

10	*MOT:	ok lets see so next time you can get the clues .
11	*MOT:	see the tail spike ?
12	*MOT:	what does he use that tail spike for ?
13	*CHI:	to defend hi(m)self .
14	*MOT:	uhhuh@i from whom do you think he defends himself ?
15	*CHI:	from dis [: this] one .
16	*MOT:	what's this one ?
17	*CHI:	fwom [: from] da [: the] tywanasowus [: tyrannosaurus] wex [: rex] .

Box 3.7 gives an overview of the father's language at the same ages.

The father's language does not seem to differ as significantly as that of the mother at the same ages. The length of the father's utterances varies from three to five words in the earlier transcripts and from three to seven words in the later transcript. In both transcripts, different questions are put to the child. We cannot draw any specific conclusions from such a short data sample though. The father might have modified his language more on different occasions that were not taped. However, studies that have investigated the language of different caretakers have found some differences between mothers and fathers in the language to their children.

In general, the early form of communication where parents modify their language when talking to the child has been characterised as child directed speech (CDS) (Richards, 1994). CDS has been characterised by a higher pitch, more repetition, a more limited vocabulary, simplified syntax and limited

---

Box 3.7: Input at different ages, Spanish

Spanish Data

a) Input at 1;1

1	*FAT:	qué es esto , un papel ?
	%eng:	what is this, a paper ?
2	*FAT:	pero qué es esto ?
	%eng:	but what is this ?
3	*FAT:	es un papel ?
	%eng:	is (it) a paper ?
4	*CHI:	aaah@i !
5	*FAT:	qué hay ahí detrás ?
	%eng:	what is there behind ?
		'what is behind there' ?

b) Input at 4;5

6	*FAT:	qué es lo que tienes ahí L ?
	%eng	what is it that (you) have there L ?
		'what have you got there L' ?
7	*FAT:	xxx pelotitas ?
	%eng	xxx balls ?
8	*FAT:	les has contado cuántas tienes ?
	%eng	them (you) have told how many (you) have ?
		'have you told them how many you have' ?
9	*FAT:	cuántas tenías L ?
	%eng	How many (you) had L ?
		'How many did you have L' ?
10	*CHI:	[after other adult utterances] dinosaurio.
	%eng	dinosaur.

communicative intents (Snow, 1995). These features are said to help children to identify strings in the speech stream and to memorise words.

CDS is associated primarily with the primary caretaker, the mother. It was suggested that in the traditional family, fathers modify their language to the child less than mothers do, yet more than strangers. In this way, fathers' language was seen as a 'bridge' to the outside world (Bridge Hypothesis, Gleason, 1975).

While for the monolingual child, the conversational styles of both mothers and fathers complement each other, this is not the case for bilingual acquisition. Where the parents follow the OPOL principle, the extent to which both parents engage in CDS can affect the quality of the input in both languages as each caretaker is the main provider of the input for the given language (Pierce et al., 2015).

Other factors that affect the quality of input include the amount of contextual information provided by the caretakers, as well as the parental speech rate, as discussed earlier.

The 'critical mass' hypothesis

We started out considering the view that children's language development is determined by the exposure and the frequency of elements within the input. While the meaning of a particular word can be learnt after a few occurrences, a particular grammatical pattern, such as the regular past tense for example, will need a certain amount of exposure before the pattern is said to have been acquired. The amount of required exposure needed is the 'critical mass'.

The term was first introduced by Marchman & Bates (1994) in relation to the acquisition of irregular and regular past tense inflections. Children initially produce uninflected verb forms, such as *go* in a past tense context or learn the past tense form for individual verbs, such as *went*. On the basis of computer modelling, it seemed that the size of vocabulary predicted when a pattern was learnt. Their study tested whether this was also the case with young children.

They conducted a large-scale study including 1,130 English-speaking children between the ages of 1;4 and 2;6. Parents were asked to make a judgement about the size of their children's vocabulary by completing the MacArthur Communicative Development Inventory (Fenson et al., 1994) which is outlined in Chapter 5. In the context of regular and irregular past tense, they were particularly interested in the list of verbs understood and produced by the children, as well as children's production of past tense verb forms.

It was found that verb vocabulary size was the strongest predictor of the number of both correct and overregularised verb forms. Correct irregular forms occurred when the vocabulary size was small but there were no overregularisations, hence no pattern was applied. Overregularisations occurred when the verb vocabulary reached a particular size. These findings show that there is a continuity between the development of verbs on the one hand and the development of grammar on the other. Patterns are acquired when a 'critical mass' of exposure has been reached.

In the context of bilingual development, this finding is important as it suggests that differences in vocabulary size can affect the morpho-syntactic development of both languages. If the vocabulary size is lower in a bilingual in comparison with that of a monolingual child, the grammatical development might be slower. Similarly, if there is a difference between languages, this might lead to a pattern where the child's grammatical development is more advanced in one of the languages compared to the other. This will be explored further in Chapter 6.

Discussion

We have discussed different aspects of the language that monolingual and bilingual children are exposed to when going through the language acquisition process. We have looked at the role of the input in terms of the only available evidence that children have to learn about language but also Carroll's objections to explanations that are solely based on input and exposure.

Carroll's view is based on the framework of generative linguistics which assumes that children have innate linguistic knowledge that helps them to learn the grammar of the language they are exposed to (see Chapter 2). Rather than building up structures just from the input, children extract patterns in line with their innate knowledge.

STUDY ACTIVITY 3.3

1. Does the language input to monolingual and bilingual children differ? Distinguish between input frequency, speech rate and quality.
2. How does children's vocabulary size affect grammatical development in both monolingual and bilingual acquisition?

Language contact: Code-switching and mixing

One of the characteristics of bilingual learners is that they are able to use resources from both languages. We have seen that in early bilingual child language acquisition, mixing languages was seen as evidence that the child is not distinguishing languages; yet in adults, code-switching is a strategy that is used when bilinguals converse with other bilinguals. In this section we shall look at parental mixing in the home, child mixing, and the difference between mixing and code-switching.

Bilinguals can switch modes and either function in a monolingual or bilingual mode. According to Grosjean (2008), bilinguals can be in different language modes, depending on the context and the situation they find themselves in. When communicating with monolinguals of either of their languages, they switch to the monolingual mode where the required language is activated and the other language is deactivated. On the other hand, when communicating with other bilinguals, both languages are activated. As for the conversation, mainly one of the languages is used; this language is more activated than the other language. The activated language is the **matrix language** and the less activated language the **embedded language**.

Code-switching and borrowing occur when a bilingual is in the bilingual language mode. The matrix language is the default language in the situation, therefore this language determines the position of the elements in the sentence. In general, code-switching would be expected to involve a switch from the matrix language to the embedded language, either between utterances (inter-sentential) or within an utterance (intra-sentential). In the case of a borrowed word, the word from the other language would be inserted into a particular position in the sentence and inherit any inflections from the other language.

Box 3.8 gives examples of different kinds of code-switching from the Bangor Miami Corpus in Talkbank, one of the databases that can be accessed via the CHILDES database. (https://talkbank.org/access/BilingBank/Bangor/Miami.html)

In the transcripts, switches between utterances are indicated by '[-spa]', where 'spa' refers to the language that the speaker switches into, in this case Spanish. Switches within the same utterance are indicated by '@s'.

In the first example, the matrix language is English. The speaker, *LAU, talks about an experience when making a doctor's appointment. At the end

---

Box 3.8: Code-switching

1. **Inter-sentential code-switching**
   - *LAU: well I had to make an appointment.
   - *LAU: and then I had to say that I was taking doctor's appointments and everything.
   - *LAU: (be)cause I had to go.
   - *LAU: <I wa(s)> [/] I was two hours in line.
   - ***LAU: [- spa] lo que pasa   es   un relajo.**
   - %eng: it that happens.3rd SG   is.3rd SG   a   joke.
                        'What happens is a joke'

2. **Intra-sentential code-switching**
   - *CHL: she's just above us.
   - *LAU: okay.
   - ***CHL: she has like una@s mala@s fama@s.**
   - %eng: she has like a   bad   reputation.

3. **Borrowing**
   - *TOM: sólo viene   a pasar   el **spring_break@s y+...**
   - %eng: only comes.3rd SG spend.INFIN the spring break   and
             'he's only coming to spend the spring break here and ...' .

she produces a Spanish sentence. This is an example of inter-sentential code-switching as the switch occurs between utterances.

In the second example, two Spanish–English bilinguals talk in English as the matrix language. In this case, the speaker, *CHL, switches within an utterance from English to Spanish, hence this is a case of intra-sentential code-switching.

The third example is a case of borrowing. The matrix language in this case is Spanish. Within the utterance the speaker, *TOM, uses the English phrase 'spring break', presumably because there is no suitable translation equivalent of this word in Spanish, therefore the word is borrowed from the embedded language.

Parental mixing

In the beginning of this chapter we have considered different parental language strategies when communicating with their children. One of these strategies is mixing. What effect does mixing by the parents have on children's development? Advocates of the OPOL principle specifically avoid mixing languages so that the children can distinguish between the two. Given the close relationship between the child's input and their language proficiency, as outlined in the previous section, what effect does parental mixing have on children's language development?

Byers-Heinlein (2013) investigated the rates of mixing in bilingual parents in relation to vocabulary development in bilingual children. A sample of 181 parents living in the Vancouver area of Canada and who had a child aged 1;5 was included in the study. They all spoke English as one of their languages, but a variety of other languages in addition to English. Parental mixing was investigated via a questionnaire where parents answered questions about their language behaviour when interacting with their children. In particular, the questionnaire asked whether parents were switching from one language to the other during a sentence, and also the order of the languages. In addition, they were asked about borrowing a word from English when speaking another language, or the other way round: borrowing a word from another language when speaking English.

The results of the parental questionnaire showed that most parents were switching between languages, such that English was spoken about 40% of the time and the other language was spoken about 60% of the time, though this varied by context. However, even when they were alone with the child, they still reported mixing languages to some degree. One of the reasons for switching languages was to borrow a word from the other language. This often occurred when they were teaching a new word. This also occurred the other way around: they reported that they were likely to use an English word when speaking their other language because there was either no translation equivalent, or a 'poor' translation equivalent in the other language.

Children's comprehension and production of words at the age of 1;5 was assessed, using the MacArthur Bates Communicative Development Inventory (see Chapter 5). In this test, parents judge for a range of words whether the child knows the word and whether the child can say the word. For children aged 2 only their production of words was tested. It was found that mixing by the parents predicted that children knew fewer words at the age of 1;5 and were able to produce slightly fewer words at the age of 2.

Child mixing versus code-switching

In Chapter 1 we introduced the terms 'mixing' as well as 'code-switching'. We return to these terms at this point in order to discuss both in relation to child bilinguals. Young bilingual children mix their languages. This is what is reported by most studies of bilingual acquisition. Yet bilingual adults who use elements from both languages code-switch. So, what is the difference between early child mixing on the one hand and later child or adult mixing on the other?

Young children's sentences are, of course, shorter than adult sentences and do not contain as many elements. In the early stages, children produce only one word at a time (one-word stage). The only way these productions can be considered as 'mixing' is if they occur in the wrong context. For example, a child who produces the Italian word *palla* (ball) when talking to the non-Italian speaker is said to mix languages (Cantone, 2007, p. 115). In the two-word stage, a mixed utterance contains one word from each of the languages. For example, the utterance *nein, balena* (no, whale) consists of a word in German, *nein* (no) and one word in Italian, *balena* (whale). Regardless of whether the language context is German or Italian, this can be considered a mixed utterance.

Cantone (2007) looked at the mixing of five German–Italian children between the ages of 1 and 5. All children were born in Germany and had German fathers. The parents of four out of the five children followed the OPOL principle. The remaining child grew up with Italian as the home language, spoken by the mother and the brother but he heard more German when he went to nursery at the age of 3;4. All children were recorded every two weeks for about 30 minutes in both languages.

The children's recordings were transcribed and were analysed in two stages: the early stage was from about 1;7 to 2;4, and the later stage from 2;4 to 5;5. For each language context, mixes were analysed for each child for each observation across the observation period.

The results for the early stage show that, overall, children produced words and two-word combinations that were appropriate for the language context. The amount of mixing varied among the children, and also according to language context, but got less as the children got older. The child that was exposed to more Italian in the home environment seemed to produce more mixes in the Italian context, but this was mainly due to him using the words *yes* and *no* in German. These words can be classed as 'function words' (*yes, no, this, that, here, there* and *more*). In the case study of Raivo, which we discussed in Chapter 1, Vihman (1985) found that the child's mixes involved mainly function words. This was also confirmed for the other children in the Cantone study.

Box 3.9: Children's code-switching

Children's code-switching

1. **Compound:** *Himbeer* *odore.*
   Child 4;9 <u>raspberry</u> (German) scent (Italian).

2. **Intra-sentential:** et *puis Patti a* <u>*sein arm gebrochen.*</u>
   Child 3;7 and then Patti has (Italian) <u>his arm broken</u> (German).

3. **Borrowing:** *adesso è pronto il* <u>*Nachtisch.*</u>
   Child 3;4 now is ready the (Italian) <u>dessert</u> (German).

So, how does early mixing compare to adult code-switching? We saw in Box 3.8 that the adults either switch to produce a whole utterance, part of an utterance or a content word (these include nouns, verbs, adjectives and adverbs). Child mixing in the early stages involves mainly function words. Cantone (2007) argues that early mixes are a sign that the child is not as practised in picking words from the lexicon of a specific language context but are not fundamentally different from adult mixing.

Box 3.9 gives examples of child code-switching from the later stage. In example 1, the child switches within a noun compound, a combination of two nouns. While the combination of the two nouns *raspberry* and *scent* is possible in German, it is a novel compound in Italian. Even where similar compounds are possible in two languages, the particular nouns that combine can be different. For example, the English compound *light house* translates into German as *Leuchtturm* (shining tower), giving rise to novel compounds in German–English bilinguals, such as *Lichthaus* (light house). Example 2 is an intra-sentential switch from Italian into German, and example 3 shows the insertion of a German noun, *Nachtisch* (dessert) into the Italian context.

The difference between children and adults mixing was seen in the extent to which grammatical rules were applied when mixing languages. Children's mixing seemed less constrained than adult mixing. Cantone (2007) argues that most of children's mixes adhere to similar rules and can be treated in the same way as adult mixing.

STUDY ACTIVITY 3.4

1. Think of reasons why adult bilinguals use different types of code-switching in conversation.
2. In what ways does early child mixing differ from the way adults code-switch?

Final attainment

One of the questions concerning bilingual acquisition concerns the final outcome, that is, what language level is ultimately achieved by a bilingual speaker who has been exposed to both languages from birth.

Is it possible for a simultaneous bilingual to be on a par with monolingual speakers at all levels and in both of their languages? This would indeed mean that a bilingual is 'two monolinguals in one'. Given what we said earlier about sensitive phases as well as the amount of input affecting the development of both languages, the question is how likely it is that a bilingual speaker will achieve a similar language level to a monolingual speaker in both of their languages.

Let us consider two scenarios here. In the first scenario, there is only one language in the community and the bilingual child either hears both languages at home or is exposed to a language at home that is not spoken in the community. This language is called a **heritage language** (Hager & Müller, 2015). In either case, when the child starts to have contact with the community language, this is likely to become the more dominant language. According to Montrul (2008), heritage speakers can show similar patterns of incomplete acquisition in their heritage language. Incomplete acquisition means that speakers make some errors that also occur in second language learners and they are not on the same level as native speakers on different language measures. In the case of bilingual learners, the lower language level in the weaker language is not due to the age of onset but can be related to a lower level of input, particularly from the point where exposure to the community language outside the home began.

In the second scenario, there are two community languages, and the child either hears both languages in the home or is only exposed to one of those languages. This is the case in parts of Canada, and also in Wales in the United Kingdom. In Wales, all children are taught Welsh at school, yet their home language differs. At home, children speak either Welsh, English or both. Depending on the home language, their language levels in both languages differ. Children who only hear English at home or both English and Welsh tend to have lower vocabulary and grammar levels at early school level compared to children who only speak Welsh at home (see Chapter 6).

The presence of both languages in the community enables speakers to improve their language levels well into the teenage years and there is some evidence that bilingual children can 'catch up' with monolinguals (see Chapter 9).

When trying to assess the final language attainment of a bilingual speaker, home language background as well as the community status of both languages need to be taken into consideration.

STUDY ACTIVITY 3.5

1. In what way does the community language affect the language development of a bilingual speaker's languages?
2. Do simultaneous bilinguals achieve 'native-like' language levels in both their languages?

SUMMARY

In this chapter we have looked at different factors that characterise bilingual learners. One important factor is the home language pattern they grew up with. There is no specific reason why two languages in the home would be a better option than a strategy where languages are chosen according to the context, provided exposure to the other language starts from fairly early on. In fact, given the likelihood that the community language will become more dominant, a focus on the heritage language early on might be a more preferable option.

A second and important characteristic of bilingual learners is the point at which exposure to each of the languages begins. This is particularly important in relation to sensitive phases in the course of the child's development. We have seen that later onset, as in second language acquisition, leads to a lower level of language in the area of phonology and lexical knowledge as well as in grammar.

The quality and quantity of the input in both languages is an important factor in bilingual acquisition that determines the language proficiency of the language learner (both monolingual and bilingual). While differences between monolingual and bilingual acquisition patterns can be linked to frequency in the input, one has to be careful with any assumption that growing up with two languages in the home automatically means that the input in each of the languages is half the input of a monolingual child.

A typical characteristic of a bilingual speaker is that they can make use of the resources given by both languages, particularly when talking to other bilingual speakers. Code-switching is a language strategy that has been observed in both adults and children who speak two languages. While children's use of two languages has been seen as more unsystematic and a sign that they have not differentiated between languages, this does not seem justified.

Finally, we have considered the final language level of bilingual speakers in two scenarios. The so-called heritage language of a bilingual speaker is more in danger of incomplete acquisition, whereas in dual language communities there is more opportunity for both simultaneous and sequential bilinguals to catch up with monolingual learners.

FURTHER READING

In this chapter we have considered different sensitive phases for different aspects of language. For a more detailed outline of the evidence of such phases see Meisel (2011). For a more detailed account of the relationship between input and the acquisition of two languages see Grüter & Paradis (2014). For a further account of mixing in bilingual children see Müller & Cantone (2009).

Bilingual Speech Perception and Sound Development

4

This chapter addresses the question of bilingual speech perception and sound development. Speech perception refers to the ability of babies to distinguish between different speech sounds that they hear, even when these sounds are not part of their native language. In addition, babies can distinguish between a familiar language, namely the language they hear in their environment, and an unfamiliar language.

If babies have such remarkable abilities to discriminate speech sounds, does this mean that bilingual infants should be able to distinguish between both the languages they hear from a very early age? Given that babies only have limited ways of responding, on what basis can we draw any conclusions about the way they perceive speech sounds?

When young children start producing their first sounds, they do not yet produce words, but they 'babble' from the age of about 6 months. Do bilingual babies babble differently from monolingual infants? Is there a relationship between the sounds that young children produce as part of their babble and the sounds that make up their first words? Do bilingual babies have a different sound repertoire in their babbling compared to monolingual children?

As children progress from babbling to the linguistic stage, they develop different phonological systems. The language combination they are exposed to means they have to learn different sounds for the different languages, though there is generally an overlap for a certain number of sounds. How do bilinguals compare to monolinguals in terms of the sound development for each of their languages?

As we look at both simultaneous and sequentially bilingual children in this context, we shall consider the effect of age of onset of another language on the ability to discriminate and produce different speech sounds. Does a later onset of a second language mean that the child does not perceive the speech sounds of the new language as accurately as the sounds of the first language?

What effect does this have on the development of speech sounds? We know from studies considered in Chapter 3 that there seems to be a sensitive period of sound development up to the age of 5 years.

Infant speech perception

Before outlining the speech perception and sound development of infants growing up with two languages, let us first look at methodologies that have been used, particularly when investigating pre-linguistic infants. As their ability to react to particular stimuli is limited at this age, certain methods of investigation were developed. For more details on the methodologies see Jusczyk (1997).

Research methodologies

The first methodology makes use of the sucking reflex, something that babies are born with. This reflex is important for feeding, and therefore sustaining life. The methodology developed involves measuring the baby's rate of sucking with a specifically adapted dummy. Babies start sucking faster when they are hungry, but also when they are excited by something. When they are no longer hungry, bored or falling asleep, the sucking rate slows down.

In the **High Amplitude Sucking** paradigm, infants' sucking rate is measured when they hear different sounds. It relies on the idea that hearing a new sound will excite the baby and result in a higher rate of sucking, initially. Once babies get used to the sound, the sucking rate becomes slower until a new sound is introduced. If the new sound is perceived to be different, the rate is expected to go up again. If not, it will stay the same or become even slower.

For example, babies initially hear the sound /b/ which is found in the beginning of words like *bath*. The introduction of this sound results initially in a higher sucking rate which then slows down. When they then hear a new sound, the sucking rate goes up again. The sucking rate therefore provides a good measure of the speech perception abilities of newborn babies and very young children. However, this method requires the baby to be fairly awake during the procedure, otherwise no change in sucking rate can be measured.

Alternatives to measuring infants' sucking rate include monitoring an infant's heart rate (**cardiac deceleration**). The principle for this method is the same as for the High Amplitude Sucking paradigm. When a new stimulus is perceived, the heart rate increases, otherwise it stays at a similar rate or will go down if the baby gets bored.

Another method used to investigate young children's perception of sounds is the **conditioned head turn** procedure. This can be used for older infants between the ages of 6 and 10 months. This method is outlined in Box 4.1.

A more recent method that can be used with newborn babies is to measure brain and facial muscle activity while infants are exposed to sounds and air puffs to the eyelid. This methodology was developed by Fifer et al. (2010). When newborn babies were exposed to different speech sounds, it was found

---

Box 4.1: Conditioned head turn procedure

The conditioned head turn procedure is a method designed to test children's knowledge of sounds and language. The child is placed on the mother's lap opposite an experimental assistant. The child is taught to turn their head towards a plexiglass box which lights up and shows animated toy animals when the head turn response is correct.

During the trial, both the mother and the assistant wear headphones so that they cannot hear the stimulus and inadvertently give cues to the child. A computer generates either an experimental trial which involves a sound change or a control trial, where there is no such change.

During the control trial, no head turn by the child is expected, as the sound does not change. During the experimental trial, the head turn is expected at the point where the sound change occurs.

---

that there was a measurable brain reaction, even when babies were asleep. This suggests that there is some awareness of external stimuli even when a newborn is asleep.

The different research methodologies have allowed some conclusions about newborn babies' abilities to perceive the sounds of different languages, which is summarised in the following section. Their ability to react to differences in sounds and different sound patterns does not mean though that they understand the language that they hear at this stage.

Perception of sound contrasts, voices and languages

The early research conducted into the speech perception abilities of newborn monolingual infants has shown that language acquisition does indeed begin from day one, or even before children are born.

In the early research (Eimas et al., 1971) infants' sucking rate was measured when they heard a particular sound. It was then observed whether or not the sucking rate changed when they heard a slightly different sound. In particular, they tested whether infants were able to discriminate voiced and voiceless stop consonants (e.g. /b/ and /p/) that were produced by a synthetic voice. Stop consonants are produced when particular parts of the mouth come together and prevent the airstream from flowing out. For example, the consonants /b/ and /p/ are both produced by a closure of the lips (bilabial stop). One difference between them is that the vocal cords which vibrate during speech production, set in later for the voiceless sound /p/ and earlier for the voiced sound /b/. The onset of vocal cord vibration is called the **Voice Onset Time** (VOT).

In the experiment, the release of the closure of the articulators and the onset of voicing was varied to produce different varieties of /b/ and /p/. It was found that 1- and 4-month-old infants perceived the sound contrast between /b/ and /p/ in a similar way to adults. Using the High Amplitude Sucking paradigm, babies' sucking rate was measured during the time they heard a bilabial stop consonant, followed by a similar sound with a 20-millisecond later VOT. When the change was from 0 to 20 milliseconds or from 60 to 80 milliseconds, babies did not suck at a higher rate. However, a change of the onset of voicing from 20 to 40 milliseconds resulted in an increase in the sucking for both age groups. This is in line with the way adults perceive the difference in both speech sounds.

Using the same paradigm, it was also possible to show that infants not only distinguish between sound contrasts in their native language, but they are also sensitive to non-native contrasts. Non-native contrasts are given by two different sounds that make a meaning distinction in another language but not the child's native language.

Words that differ in just one sound are called **minimal pairs**. For example, the English words *ship*/ʃɪp/ and *sip*/sɪp/ differ in their initial phoneme and express different meanings. This suggests that they are minimal pairs and that the phonemes /ʃ/ and /s/ form a contrast. Babies learning English as their first language will perceive this contrast from birth. As it is native, there will be no decline in English babies' perceptions when they get older. Now let us look at the same contrast in Korean. Both sounds occur in words in the language, as in /ʃɪ/ (poem) and /so/ (cow), however, there are no minimal pairs where the exchange of both sounds results in a difference in meaning. Both sounds can occur at the beginning of a word but the /ʃ/ sound occurs before the vowel /ɪ/, whereas the /s/ sound occurs before the vowel /o/. This means that the two sounds do not represent different phonemes, instead, they are variations of the same phoneme (allophones).

This means that Korean babies will be able to distinguish the contrast between /ʃ/ and /s/ at birth together with native Korean contrasts, however, as it is non-native, the perception of the contrast will decline. It was generally found that non-native contrasts decline between 6 and 12 months as infants have more exposure to their native language.

Babies have also been found to react to the sound of their mother's voice in contrast to that of strangers. But this was only the case if the mothers were speaking normally, as if they were addressing the baby. One-month-old babies preferred the sound of the mother's voice only if she spoke normally but did not distinguish between the voices if the mother's voice lacked intonation.

Finally, using the same methodologies, infants have been found to distinguish between the sound of their 'native' over a non-native language (Mehler et al., 1988). This ability increased with age. Newborns were found to be able to distinguish between languages from different language families, such as English and Japanese, but not between English and German. The ability to distinguish more similar languages was found in older babies from the age of 4 months.

Bilingual speech perception

The research on infant speech perception has shown that newborns already have remarkable abilities that enable them to tune into the language around them. In the context of bilingual development, the question is whether infants who hear two languages in their environment perceive both as 'native' and thereby different from 'non-native' languages. At the same time, at what stage are they able to distinguish between the two native languages?

The research methodologies used to investigate these questions are the same as those outlined in the beginning. A study by Byers-Heinlein et al. (2010) comparing monolingual and simultaneous bilingual children is outlined in Box 4.2.

Does the result of the study described in Box 4.2 suggest that newborn bilingual infants can actually distinguish between the two languages they hear? As was discussed in Chapter 3, if bilinguals get less input in both of their languages, it could be that the bilingual infants had insufficient experience with either language and were therefore unable to discriminate between the two.

A second study (Byers-Heinlein, Burns & Werker, 2010) was designed to investigate this question, using the same 30 infants. They first heard one of the languages (English or Tagalog), then after a while the other language was introduced. While listening to the first language, infants' sucking rate went down as they got bored with the same stimulus. When there was a language switch, the sucking rate of both monolingual and bilingual infants increased, suggesting that they interpreted the switch as a new stimulus. For the monolingual infants, the result clearly shows that they distinguished between their native and non-native language. Given that English and Tagalog are from different language families, this result is in line with similar findings from monolingual infants that were discussed earlier.

For the bilinguals, on the other hand, the increase suggests that they were able to distinguish between their two native languages. This means that the exposure they had in utero was sufficient. In line with monolingual babies, the ability to distinguish between two similar native languages was found in bilingual babies at the age of 4 months.

In the last section, we discussed infants' initial ability to perceive native and non-native sound contrasts. Across languages, sound contrasts can differ.

Box 4.2: Bilingual speech perception

The High Amplitude Sucking paradigm was used to compare the sucking rate of 30 newborn infants between 0 and 5 days old. Half of them were only exposed to English and the other half heard English as well as Tagalog, a language spoken in the Philippines. In the experiment, all infants were exposed to both languages alternatively for 1 minute and the number of sucks were compared by language.

The English infants were found to suck at a higher rate when they listened to English. These results show that they have a clear preference for English over Tagalog. The bilingual infants, on the other hand, sucked at a similar rate when they heard English and Tagalog. This suggests that they recognised both languages as 'native'.

> ### Box 4.3: Non-native contrasts in sequential bilinguals
>
> A variation of the conditioned head turn procedure was used to test the perception of the sound contrast /d-ð/ in English in comparison with the contrast /b-v/ which occurs in both English and French. The study included 12 simultaneous bilingual adults and 36 children aged 4–5. There were 12 monolingual English children learning French, 12 monolingual French children learning English and 12 simultaneous bilingual children. The participants heard sounds and had to press a button when they detected a sound change.
>
> The groups showed differences in their perception of the English /d-ð/ contrast. The monolingual English 4-year-olds were better than the monolingual French and bilingual children. In the adult group, the bilinguals were not different in their perception of the contrast from a group of monolingual English adults. These differences suggest that experience with the contrast over time improves perception.

We discussed the example of the sounds /ʃ/ and /s/ which contrast in English but not in Korean. Differences can also arise in the VOT interval where speakers assign the sound to a particular voiced or voiceless consonant.

The results from different studies (Byers-Heinlein, 2018) suggest that while monolingual infants' ability to perceive non-native sound contrasts declines, bilingual children retain the contrasts in both their native languages. There is also some evidence to suggest that bilinguals discriminate some non-native contrasts better than monolinguals.

The decline of non-native contrasts in infants during their first year suggests that sequential bilingual learners might have difficulties perceiving sound contrasts that are not native to their first language if they start learning another language after the age of 1 year. The results on pronunciation by sequential bilingual learners (see Chapter 3) suggested a sensitive period for phonology up to the age of 5.

An example of a study of sequentially bilingual children's perception of non-native sound contrasts is given in Box 4.3.

The results of different studies suggest that sequential learners are able to perceive different contrasts in their non-native language and that some contrasts might be learned very quickly. Overall, exposure to the non-native contrasts helps to discriminate them as different sounds.

STUDY ACTIVITY 4.1

1. How has the High Amplitude Sucking paradigm been used to investigate the speech perception of monolingual and bilingual infants?
2. What effects does a bilingual environment have on the speech perception skills of a newborn baby?

Bilingual phonological development

Before children produce their first words, they go through different stages of phonological development. One significant milestone in the course of phonological development is babbling, the time when children start producing combinations of **consonant** and **vowel** sounds. We described consonants earlier in the context of speech perception. They generally involve closure, or partial closure, of the articulators. Consonants can be 'voiced' or 'voiceless', depending on whether the vocal cords start to vibrate at some point during the production of the sound (Voice Onset). Vowel sounds, on the other hand, do not involve any closure of the articulators but vary in the position of the tongue in relation to the roof of the mouth, as well as the position of the lips (rounded, spread).

Regarding the babbling stage, there have been different views on whether babies just practise sounds during this stage of development, or whether babbling is related to the sounds in their native language. As there are differences in the sounds used in different languages, babbling might be language-specific. This means that bilingual babies might have a different sound repertoire, and that they might produce different sounds for different language contexts.

At the point where children produce their first words, phonological development is not yet complete. They can produce a range of sounds but are still in the process of acquiring others that are more complex, as well as consonant combinations. For example, sounds like /f/ or /s/ that involve friction between articulators are generally acquired later than bilabial stops such as /b/ and /p/. At this stage, young children also make some particular errors in pronunciation. For example, they tend to simplify the production of two consonant sounds following each other, as in the word *tree*/triː/ to just one phoneme, as in /tiː/. As these errors occur systematically, they are not really errors but so-called **phonological processes** which are applied while learning the adult phonology of a language. Fewer phonological processes are used as children get older and they disappear in normal development around the age of 5. Some typical phonological processes are listed in Box 4.5. Phonological processes are shared across a number of different languages.

We have seen earlier that children mix their two languages. To what extent does this also apply to the two phonological systems that the child is in the process of acquiring? Is there a transfer from the sound system of one language to the other? Does it make a difference if the child is a simultaneous or a sequential bilingual?

Bilingual babbling

All babies go through a stage of babbling, starting from about 6 months. During this time, they produce sequences that consist of consonant-vowel sequences, for example *ba ba ba*. It was thought that babies initially repeat consonant-vowel sequences in babbling (reduplicated babbling) and later progress to a variation of different consonant-vowel sequences, as in *ba da ga* (variegated babbling). However, studies have shown that variegated babbling can occur from the beginning of the babbling stage (Davis & MacNeilage, 1995).

Do bilingual babies babble differently from monolingual babies? Not many studies have investigated the sounds bilingual babies produce during the babbling stage. But we know from the last section that infants are sensitive to sound contrasts and stress patterns in their native languages.

Poulin-Dubois & Goodz (2001) analysed the consonants produced in the recorded babble of 13 French–English babies aged 12 months in both French and English contexts, and compared the percentage of produced consonant types to results from monolingual babies in both languages. The distribution of different consonant types in the babbling and early words of babies from 9 months until they produced 25 words is outlined in Box 4.4 for English, French and Japanese.

Box 4.4: Sounds in babbling and first words across languages

The consonant sounds used by 20 babies while babbling and producing their first words was investigated in different languages. The chart gives the means for three consonant types and three of the four languages investigated.

Means

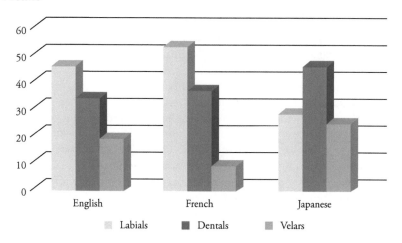

The results are summarised by the place of articulation of the sounds. Labials involve a closure of the lips and include stop consonants such as /b/ and /p/ as well as the nasal /m/. These sounds were the most frequently produced in both English and French, but not in Japanese. French babies produced more labials than English babies.

Dentals, on the other hand, involve a closure of the tongue and the front teeth and include the consonants /t/ and /d/ as well as the nasal /n/. These sounds were the most frequently produced in Japanese and occurred with similar frequency in English and French.

Velars include sounds that are produced when the back of the tongue closes against the soft palate. Examples are sounds like /k/ and /g/. They were more frequent in Japanese and English compared to French.

Given that young monolingual children show differences in the distribution of consonants across languages, how do bilingual babies compare? In the research of French–English bilingual babies, no difference was found in the frequency of labials, dentals and velars across language context.

When the bilingual babies were compared to the monolinguals outlined in Box 4.4, some differences emerged: the bilingual English–French babies produced more labials than the monolingual English toddlers, but fewer than the monolingual French babies. They also produced more velars than either of the monolingual groups. The consonants that were observed for the infants overall though were more in line with the repertoire of French monolingual toddlers. Most of the mothers of the bilingual children were French speakers. The results suggest that the children's distribution of consonants reflected the language of the mother more than that of other caretakers.

It is possible that for the bilingual babies, French was the dominant language, though there was no evidence that the children heard more French than English. Overall, the results on bilingual children's sound production in babbling provide some support for the view that bilingual babies are sensitive to differences in sound distribution in the languages they are exposed to.

Separate phonological systems

We have seen that there can be some differences in sound production at the babbling stage between children learning different languages as well as between monolingual and bilingual children. The question is whether babies develop two separate sound systems, or whether there is an overlap between the two. A separate sound system involves the acquisition of the different consonant and vowel sounds for both languages, as well as the acquisition of language-specific stress patterns. In addition, we know that young children tend to simplify word segments and sound combinations as they still learn to co-ordinate the different speech articulators to produce specific sounds.

These speech error patterns or phonological processes occur in different languages and some are outlined in Box 4.5. The application of these processes in different languages is similar, yet some processes can differ. For example, the process of 'weak syllable deletion' is applied to words consisting of several syllables. The syllables that are truncated in words with a similar phonological form can vary across languages, as different stress patterns result in different weak syllables in the word. In English, word stress generally follows a pattern where stressed syllables alternate with unstressed syllables. For example, the first syllable of the English word 'e-le-ˌphant, 'e, carries the main stress of the word and the final syllable, ˌphant, carries secondary stress. Young children tend to omit unstressed syllables and reduce the word to fewer syllables, such as *efant*. For the word ˌba-'na-na, the main stress is on the second syllable 'na-na. Weak syllable deletion therefore truncates the word to *nana*.

In a language like French, on the other hand, word stress is predominantly on the final syllable. The word *telephone* is similar in English and French. However, the main word stress differs. In English, the main stress is on the first syllable, 'te-le-phone, whereas in French it is on the last syllable as in

> ## Box 4.5: Some typical phonological processes
>
> Children between the ages of 3 and 5 show error patterns in their speech productions that follow a number of patterns:
>
> | Process | Explanation | Example |
> | --- | --- | --- |
> | **Final consonant deletion** | Omission of final consonant. | boat = bow |
> | **Weak syllable deletion** | Omission of a weak syllable. | elephant = efant |
> | **Reduplication** | The initial sound sequence is repeated. | daddy = dada |
> | **Consonant cluster reduction** | One of the consonants in a cluster is deleted. | slug = lug |
> | **Assimilation** | One consonant becomes similar in sound to another consonant. | yellow = lellow |
> | **Stopping** | A non-stop consonant is replaced with a stop consonant. | van = ban |

te-le-'phone. This leads to possible differences in the way phonological processes are applied, resulting in different truncations in both languages.

Children's phonological patterns while learning two languages with different stress patterns can therefore tell us something about their underlying phonological system. Paradis (2001) examined the sound development of a group of 17 French–English simultaneously bilingual children aged 29 months. The bilinguals were compared with a group of 18 monolingual English and 18 monolingual French children. In order to investigate children's phonological processes, examiners interacted with a child and introduced names for toys and animals in picture books, then asked the child to repeat the name. The nonsense words in each language were constructed in line with language-specific stress and syllable patterns, and were four syllables long. While the monolingual children only repeated syllables in their native language, the bilinguals were tested on both English and French nonsense words. Their word repetitions were recorded, phonetically transcribed and syllable preservations were analysed.

The results showed that the bilingual and monolingual French children were similar in their tendency to preserve the final stressed syllable for nonsense words introduced in the French context. In the English context, the bilingual children had mostly similar syllable preservation patterns, suggesting that bilingual children develop separate phonological systems. However, there were differences between the bilinguals and the monolingual English children in that the bilinguals preserved initial stressed syllables less than the monolinguals. This result shows that there is a cross-linguistic influence in the application of phonological processes.

Phoneme inventories of monolingual vs bilingual children

Do bilingual children acquire sounds in the same way as monolinguals in each of the same languages involved? Does the language combination affect acquisition? Unfortunately, at the moment there are not enough studies covering different language combinations to answer this question in full. Studies that have been conducted focus on Spanish and English.

In the light of what we said in Chapter 3 about input quantity and quality, there is the possibility that bilinguals take longer to acquire both sound systems, and in particular the sounds that do not overlap in the two languages. Fabiano-Smith & Goldstein (2010) compared the phonological acquisition of eight bilingual Spanish–English children aged 3–4 with that of monolingual Spanish and English children. Children's inventory of speech sounds was determined on the basis of speech samples consisting of single words and connected speech.

English and Spanish share a number of sounds, in particular consonants such as /b/, /p/, /m/, /t/, /d/, /n/, /k/ and /g/. They also share fricatives, such as /f/ and /s/. Spanish has fewer vowel sounds than English and the vowels differ in quality. On the other hand, both languages include sounds that do not occur in the other. For example, in the English word *lava*, the phoneme /v/ is described as a *labiodental fricative*. It is produced with the lower lip against the upper teeth and involves friction resulting from the outgoing airstream. In Spanish, on the other hand, the /v/ sound is described as a *bilabial fricative*, which is produced by friction between the partial closure of both lips.

Another sound that differs between the languages is the /r/ sound. While in English the sound is produced with the oral cavity fairly open and the air flowing round the sides of the tongue, the equivalent sound in Spanish is a so-called *trill* where the front of the tongue is made to vibrate as a result of the airstream.

These differences often lead to transfer in second language acquisition, where speakers use sounds from their native language to replace the non-native sounds. In the study, the bilingual 3–4-year-olds were not often found to transfer sounds from one language to the other in their word productions. This shows that the phonological systems of simultaneously bilingual children develop separately.

Overall, the range of sounds that were produced by the bilingual children was in line with their chronological age. However, compared to the monolingual Spanish children, the bilinguals did not produce a number of Spanish-specific sounds. Compared with English monolinguals, neither group produced sounds which occur in the beginning of words like *this* and at the end of words like *bath*. This, together with the finding that the bilingual children were less accurate at sound productions in both languages, suggests that there is a delay in the acquisition of sound development in bilingual children.

Let us come back to the question of frequency of input. If any delay in the development of sounds in both languages is due to a lower rate of frequency of language-specific sounds, shared sounds between languages should not be affected as the frequency should be similar in the input for monolingual and bilingual children. Such a relationship has indeed been found in some studies, yet no such link was found by Fabiano-Smith & Goldstein (2010) for the acquisition of English and Spanish.

Sound development in sequentially bilingual children

How does the sound development of a second language child differ from that of the first language if the onset happens before the sound development of the first language is complete? Does the sound development of a second language affect the further development of the first language?

In order to investigate phonological development in sequential bilinguals, Morrow et al. (2014) observed 19 learners of English over 2 years. The children were aged 4 to 7 at the beginning of the study and had different first languages. Their exposure to English began between the ages of 3;3 and 5. They were recorded every 6 months in free-play and semi-structured play sessions with an experimenter. For every participant, 60 words were analysed.

The children's phonological skills were measured in terms of accuracy of both consonants and vowels as well as their use of phonological processes. It was found that children's vowel accuracy was over 90% throughout the observation period. Consonant accuracy increased from over 88% at the beginning of the observation period to 91% at the end, though there were differences between consonant types. Fricatives in particular had the lowest accuracy rating.

In terms of phonological processes, consonant cluster reduction as well as stopping (see Box 4.5) were the most frequently used throughout the observation period. In monolingual children, both patterns are no longer applied after the age of 4.

Overall, the study shows that sequential bilingual learners progress well in their phonological development, though their skills are not identical to those of native speakers at the same age. There was a significant correlation between age of onset of the second language and phonological skills, such that the children who were exposed to English earlier achieved higher accuracy ratings on particular consonants and showed lower rates of phonological processes such as cluster reduction and stopping.

While some differences were found between monolingual and bilingual phonological development, there is evidence of an influence from the L1 on L2 production up until a certain point when native-like production is achieved.

STUDY ACTIVITY 4.2

1. Do bilingual babies babble differently from monolingual babies? What evidence do we have that this is the case?
2. Which aspects of sound development can be affected by learning another language from birth and sequentially?

SUMMARY

In this chapter we have considered bilingual infants' speech perception skills as well as their phonological development. The research considered has shown that infants have very good speech perception skills and that babies who have been exposed to two languages in their environment are able to make specific distinctions in line with the view that they are able to separate the languages in terms of sound patterns as well as specific contrasts.

In terms of phonological development, there is evidence that the two phonological systems develop separately, though there is some transfer from one system to the other. Sequentially bilingual children are able to develop phonological skills in a second language, though their progress is related to the age of onset.

FURTHER READING

For a more detailed outline of the research methods used in Speech Perception studies, see Jusczyk (1997). For findings of speech perception in infants that have been exposed to two languages see Fennell, Tsui & Hudon (2016) as well as Byers-Heinlein (2018). Vihman (2016) explores the question of separate phonological systems in terms of templates. For more details on transfer in simultaneous and sequentially bilingual children see also Goldstein & Bunta (2012) and McCarthy et al. (2014).

Bilingual Lexical Development

5

This chapter looks into the way children learn words. Words are the building blocks of language. Children start talking by producing single words. We will consider children's word learning in general but specifically children who grow up with two first languages simultaneously and those who learn a second language within the first three years of their lives. In order to outline the task of word learning, we will first consider different aspects of word knowledge. A more detailed outline of different relationships between words and the organisation of the bilingual mental lexicon is given in Chapter 7.

In general, we can say that word learning involves linking a string of sounds to a particular meaning. This sounds easy enough, but there is a lot more to it. First of all, children need to identify the string of sounds that a word is made up of in the speech stream. Secondly, when linking a word with a particular object, how do we know which aspects of the object the word signifies? When considering the word for the object *cup*, how do we know that the word does not refer to the handle of the cup, for example? And when linking words to objects, how do we know which object would be classed as *cup* and which one as *mug*?

We can say that words are labels that can be used for a group of similar entities. A word does not label only one particular item, but a group of items that are similar. Take the word *dog* for example. Dogs come in different shapes, colours and sizes, and yet they are all labelled *dog*. This means that despite their differences, there are commonalities between all animals that can be classed as *dog*, such as the fact that they produce similar sounding noises (barks) or that they have fur, four legs, etc.

The mental representations of these categories of similar entities is what psychologists call **concepts**. So, we have a concept of *dog*, *cat*, etc. This means we can make a decision what category a particular object belongs to, we can list attributes of the objects and we also have an idea of what a typical object within the particular category looks like (**prototype**). The prototypical member of a category is the one that can be recognised quite easily as belonging to this category. Less typical ones might be situated more at the boundary of the category and share some characteristics with a neighbouring concept.

In terms of the category *dog*, a prototypical member of this category would be a medium-sized dog with fairly short fur.

While bilingual children learn words as such in a similar way to monolinguals, their lexical development differs as bilingual children will need to realise that concepts have different word forms in the two languages. The emergence of so-called **translation equivalents** has been seen as evidence that children separate the languages, but they also show that children have linked the two to the same concept.

Bilingual children's lexical knowledge has been assessed in relation to monolingual children in each of their languages to see whether there are differences between the two groups. Differences in the amount of input can affect children's vocabulary size in particular and a number of studies have documented a disadvantage in bilingual lexical development.

The task of word learning in monolingual and bilingual children

Word learning is closely related to the development of conceptual representations. Children do not just have to identify sound sequences and relate them to particular meanings, they also have to learn to assign the word to a particular category.

Learning a word can therefore be assumed to have three different components (Hoff & Naigles, 2002): (1) children need to identify a particular sound sequence in the input, (2) they need to relate the sequence to a particular referent, for instance a 'thing' in the real world, and (3) they need to complete the knowledge of the word concept through repeated exposure.

In order to identify a particular string of sounds in the speech stream, children need to be able to identify boundaries between words. This is not easy in fluent speech so in order to break this down into identifiable units, they need to have some knowledge of what sound sequences are possible in the language and also be aware of the stress patterns in the input. Once they have identified a particular string, they need to relate it to a particular meaning, such as a particular referent in a given context. Say, for example, you identify the string /dog/ in the input and you try to relate it to different possible referents that are present. If you already know the names of the other referents, you might conclude that the identified string can be applied to the unknown referent.

The process of identifying the referent for a word can be quite straightforward if there are only limited possibilities but more difficult if there are a number of different possible referents present. If you have encountered the same string before, you might have partially memorised it already and be able to associate the string with the referent on the second occurrence. The mental process that enables us to learn a word after a minimal number of exposures is called 'fast mapping' (Gershkoff-Stowe & Hahn, 2007). During fast mapping, a link between the word and the referent is established. However, the knowledge of the concept that the word represents is still incomplete.

In the third suggested component of word learning, also termed 'slow mapping' (ibid.: 683), knowledge of the word concept can be completed through repeated encounters of the word in different meanings. This also involves linking the word at the right level to other, related words. For example, if the child learns the word for a new animal, say *badger*, the word concept needs to be included in the larger category *animal* but it is at the same level of *cat* or *dog*, rather than a type of either category.

Children who grow up with more than one language essentially learn words in the same way as monolingual children, however, if children are regularly exposed to two languages, they will be aware of differences in sounds, sound sequences and stress patterns in the two languages (see Chapter 4). At the point at which they understand words and form concepts, they will become aware that the same concepts have different lexical forms in both languages.

This is illustrated by an example from the author's own experience, outlined in Box 5.1. The fact that the child was able to explicitly express the fact that the parents used different words for the same item clearly shows that the child has linked the two-word forms at this age.

The example illustrates that young bilingual children do not learn words in both languages in isolation. It also does not seem accidental that her first word, *teddy*, is a loan word in German and is used as the same form in both languages. The similarity of form suggests that she will have heard the word in both language contexts. The observation that the child was able to give both translation equivalents for a particular concept and link it correctly to the native language of both parents shows that the child has conscious access to this knowledge as she is able to verbalise it. This is in line with the view of the separate development hypothesis discussed in Chapter 2 and the generally accepted view that bilingual children distinguish both their languages from early on.

Box 5.1: Case study of a German–English bilingual child

E is the first-born daughter of German–English parents in the United Kingdom. She was exposed to both English and German from birth and her parents followed the one parent one language principle. Her first word was 'teddy' at the age of 10 months. This was followed by different words in both languages.

At the age of 12 months she moved with her parents to Germany where she had an English childminder. At the age of 2, she was able to point out words that had a different form across her two languages.

Example

E (pointing to a toy car): daddy says **car** and mummy says **Auto**.
(*Auto* is the translation equivalent of *car*)

Early lexical development in monolingual children

Children's first words emerge between 8 and 14 months. By that time, they can already understand quite a number of words. The development of children's productive vocabulary is initially quite slow. When children have acquired about 50 words, lexical development accelerates. This is what is known as the **vocabulary spurt** and occurs between 18 and 24 months (Goldfield & Reznick, 1990). While some form of acceleration occurs in most children's vocabulary learning, not all children adhere to the particular criteria of the spurt. By the age of 2, children know about 300 words and this goes up to 60,000 by the time the child is 18. A number of reasons have been suggested for the accelerated word learning. One such reason is the 'naming insight' (Ganger & Brent, 2004, p. 621), the realisation on the part of the child that all things have names. Young children at this stage often want parents to give them a name for every object they point to. As parents supply the names, the child is able to increase the number of words more quickly.

A different explanation for the spurt is that children become aware that names stand for a group of objects, hence they are beginning to form concepts. At this time, children also have an increased ability to sort objects into groups and increased word segmentation abilities. Some evidence suggests that children's processing becomes more efficient between the ages of 1 and 2 (Gershkoff-Stowe & Hahn, 2007), which could also be another possible reason for the spurt.

Constraints. The evidence from early infant speech perception seems to suggest that young bilinguals can distinguish the languages in the input from quite early on. By identifying sound sequences in each of the languages and mapping them onto particular referents, bilingual children get to a point where the same referent is identified in each language context, that is, *book* is represented as *book* in English but *livre* in French.

This is not a problem as such, however, it has been suggested that children's word learning is facilitated by a number of mechanisms or constraints. These are the **Whole Object Constraint**, the **Taxonomic Constraint** and **Mutual Exclusivity** (Markman, 1990, p. 57). The constraints are outlined in Box 5.2.

The Whole Object Constraint allows children to learn words without having to work out what part of the object or which quality a particular word refers to. For example, when a child plays with a toy and is given the word *truck*, they will assume that this is a name for the whole object, not just the truck's tyres or the bonnet. By applying a new name to the object as a whole, word learning is focused on building categories that share features.

The Taxonomic Constraint suggests that children look for the common features of groups of objects and use words to label the groups. In doing so, the common features that children identify often differ from the features of adult categories. It has been argued that children's word meanings are either more general or narrower compared to adult meanings, thereby leading to extension errors (see the section on over- and underextensions). For example, a child might name a crayon *candle* (Kay & Anglin, 1982, p. 90). It is possible that the child's meaning of the word *candle* is wider than the adult's, such that crayons are included in the meaning. On the other hand, Kay & Anglin (1982) found that a number of extension errors were due to

---

Box 5.2: Constraints on word learning

Whole Object Constraint

According to this constraint, children will assign a given label only to the object as a whole, rather than any of the parts. If they learn the name of an animal, such as 'cat', the whole object constraint ensures that the label applies to the animal as such, rather than parts such as its paws or the tail.

Taxonomic Constraint

This constraint specifies that words refer to a group of objects that share common features. This constraint ensures that children build up conceptual representations of words, rather than just labelling specific objects in their environment.

Mutual Exclusivity Constraint

This constraint refers to children's tendency not to accept more than one label for a specific object.

---

the visual similarity between the target object (crayon) and the named object (candle). This is called the **shape bias**.

The Mutual Exclusivity Constraint refers to the tendency observed in children not to accept another label for the same object if they already have one word for it. An example is given in Aitchison (2012, p. 218) where a conversation is outlined between a father and a little boy, Brian, who does not believe that a horse can also be referred to as an *animal*. The child held up a plastic horse and asked 'What's this?' but did not accept the answer 'It's an animal'. Brian did not accept that a horse could be called *animal* because this would have been another name for the same object, thereby violating the Mutual Exclusivity Constraint.

Under- and Overextensions. The three components of word learning outlined earlier together with the suggested constraints on word learning ensure that children can build up word meanings and develop word concepts, mental representations of the group of referents that can be assigned the same label.

Children build up their word store gradually. As they initially comprehend more words than they are able to produce (Benedict, 1979), children have already developed some concepts before they can produce the corresponding words. However, their concepts are not necessarily exactly the same as those of adults. Children often produce words in contexts that show that their concepts are too wide or too narrow.

For example, a child might use the label *ball* when touching a *bauble* (overextension). Both share common characteristics, as they are both round, however, they differ in material and in their function. Overextensions of this kind are common in early child language. On the other hand, the opposite pattern also occurs, where a child applies a word only in a specific context (underextension). For example, a child might produce the word *banana* only in relation to the real fruit, and does not provide this label when seeing pictures of a banana.

Hoek, Ingram & Gibson (1986) investigate possible reasons for children's use of overextensions. One possible cause is a limited vocabulary. If the child has learnt the word *apple* but not yet the word *orange* or *peach*, then the associated meaning with *apple* is such that it incorporates other *round fruit*, at least until other words are learnt and the concepts for each are refined. Another possible reason is the phonetic form of the target word which might be difficult for the child to produce.

Another reason for overextensions is due to incomplete features that children have assigned to word concepts. For example, Bowerman (1980) describes a child's use of the word *moon* between the ages of 16 months and 2 years. Although the child was able to recognise the moon in all its different phases, the word was also used to describe a slice of lemon, a dial on a dishwasher, kidney-shaped paper, cow horns and others. The common feature to all the objects that were described as *moon* was their crescent shape.

Noun Bias. Children's early language has been found to contain a lot of object labels, rather than other word classes, such as verbs. When comparing nouns and verbs in early language, it becomes clear that there is a bias towards nouns over verbs (Noun Bias) (Gentner, 1982). This suggests that perhaps nouns are more transparent and therefore easier to learn than labels for actions.

This is what Gentner suggested. She argued that nouns are easier to learn because they refer to 'perceptual entities', objects that can be perceived with the senses, whereas verbs refer to events that pass fairly quickly.

The noun bias is confirmed for a number of different languages where nouns have been found to be more frequent than verbs (including English, French, German and Spanish). Gentner thought that the noun bias was universal, yet there are a number of languages where this is not the case. Tardif (1996) showed that children learning languages like Mandarin and Korean do not show the noun bias to the same extent as in the European languages.

Issues in the early lexical development of bilingual children

As was said before, bilingual lexical development is not essentially different from that of monolingual children. Therefore, what was said in the previous section about children's lexical development also applies to bilingual children. Two issues are discussed here: the acquisition of cross-language translation equivalents on the one hand and the acquisition of words that are similar in form and meaning (cognates) on the other.

Translation equivalents. It was thought that the occurrence of cross-language synonyms would result in a conflict for bilingual children, given the Mutual Exclusivity Constraint. This assumption has been used to explain why children tend to reject second labels for the same object at an early age. Applied to bilingual children, this constraint potentially leads to a problem as children should reject the label in the other language. However, we have seen from the example in Box 5.1 that this is clearly not the case.

Box 5.3:   The Principle of Contrast

The Principle of Contrast was put forward as a general principle that speakers of a language observe, including young children. It is different from the Taxonomic Constraints as these apply specifically to word learning. Clark states that:

> 'Words contrast in meaning so there are no true synonyms' (Clark, 1987a, p. 3).

What Clark is concerned with is that the meaning of two lexical items can overlap but differ in the contexts that they apply.

Example: **Charge – Payment**

The two words *charge* and *payment* for example can be synonyms in the context of a purchase. However, *charge* can occur in a variety of other contexts (care, electricity, accusation) where *payment* would not be appropriate. For this reason, they cannot be generally regarded as synonyms.

The Principle of Contrast is outlined in Box 5.3. According to this principle, there are no true synonyms within a language. This means that two words can overlap in meaning but each of them applies in different contexts. If children come across such an overlap in meaning, mutual exclusivity should prevent the adaptation of the second word.

Clark does not discuss the case of cross-language equivalents as such but mentions dialectal differences such as *fall* versus *autumn* for example. Differences in the contexts where the word applies can also be the case for translation equivalents. For example, French and English distinguish between the terms *watch* and *clock*. While a watch is an instrument that can tell the time and is worn on a person's wrist, a clock is a similar device but is bigger and usually mounted on a wall or freestanding. In German, on the other hand, the translation equivalent, *Uhr*, covers both *watch* and *clock*, therefore the term is wider in its application.

Studies of bilingual children's early words show that cross-language synonyms confirm that these are used from quite early on in children's productive language. The case of Manuela was already discussed in Chapter 1 (Deuchar & Quay, 2001, p. 59) where nine pairs of equivalents occurred between 0;11 and 1;5. They are listed in Box 5.4.

Box 5.4 shows that while the first equivalent emerged at 0;10, the others occurred at the age of 1;4 and 1;5 in quick succession. This clearly shows that the child acquires different words for the same concept and that the Principle of Contrast does not apply across languages.

While most of the equivalents in Box 5.4 are represented by different phonological forms in the two languages, the word for 'mummy' is similar in

---

Box 5.4: Manuela's early translation equivalents

	Word	Equivalent	Age of emergence
1.	Bye	**tatai**	0;10.25
2.	Mummy	**mama**	1;4.8
3.	**más**	more	1;4.14
4.	**bajar**	down	1;4.18
5.	**zapato**	shoe	1;4.19
6.	duck	**pato**	1;4.22
7.	hand	**mano**	1;4.22
8.	apple	**manzana**	1;5.4
9.	**pappá**	daddy	1;5.6

*the words in bold indicate the language where the equivalent first occurred.

English and Spanish. We will consider the question whether similarity in form helps acquisition in the next section.

Cognates. Cognates are translation equivalents that are similar in word form and meaning. For example, the English word *star* is derived from the Old English word *steorra* and is of Germanic origin. The Dutch translation equivalent is *ster* and the German equivalent is *Stern*. The words are cognates in the three languages. Given the similarity of form across languages, there is the question whether bilingual children acquire cognates faster.

Schelletter (2002) outlined a case study of a German–English bilingual girl between the ages of 1;11 and 2;8. She analysed all the noun pairs that occurred with translation equivalents in the observation period and distinguished between equivalents that are form similar (cognates) and those that are dissimilar (non-cognates). An example of a form similar equivalent is *bed* (German form *Bett*), as the pair differs just in the final phoneme. An example of a form dissimilar equivalent is *cup* (German form *Tasse*) as there is no overlap of phonemes.

Overall, there were 32 noun equivalents in the observation period, of these, 15 were form similar and 17 were dissimilar. In a number of cases, the equivalents occurred in the appropriate language contexts, in other cases, only one of the language equivalents was initially used in both language contexts. Box 5.5 gives examples of the child's use of equivalents.

Box 5.5 gives an example of a form similar equivalent *book-Buch* and also a dissimilar equivalent *boy-Junge*. The equivalent pair *book-Buch* differs in terms of the last phoneme, whereas the dissimilar pair *boy-Junge* does not share any phonemes.

Let's take the equivalents in turn. The English equivalent *book* was first recorded in the German context at the age of 1;11. Two months later, at 2;1, when the German equivalent *Buch* emerged in the German context, both equivalents were used in their respective language-appropriate contexts.

Box 5.5: Use of translation equivalents

Form similar: book-Buch

German context 1;11   **English context, 2;1**

C *book[ENG].*   E   I just go and get the other book.
E *wo   is das Buch?*   C   Papa[GER] ana[GER] book.
   where is the book?   Daddy   other   book.

C *eine Buch. (2;1)*
   a   book

Form dissimilar: boy-Junge

German context 2;1   **English context 2;2**

C *Junge.*   E   d'you know what that is?
   boy.   C   a fish.

C *wo   is die   Junge? (2;2)*   C   xx Junge[GER] x fish.
   where is the (fem) boy?
                                        C   boy want to go in there. (2;7)

On the other hand, the form dissimilar German equivalent *Junge* (boy) was first used language appropriately in the German context at the age of 2;1 and again at 2;2. The German equivalent also occurred once in the English context at the age of 2;2. The English equivalent *boy* was not recorded until the age of 2;7.

The observation that equivalents from one language are, at times, used in the other language context, confirms that the child has made a connection between the equivalent in the other language and the context. The use of the other equivalent can be seen as a form of borrowing where there is a gap in the child's lexicon. Once the language-appropriate form is learnt, there is no longer any need for borrowing to occur, hence the borrowing disappears.

The two examples also show a difference in the time it took for the other language equivalent to occur. For the form similar pair, this was 2 months after first emergence, for the form dissimilar pair it was 6 months. The overall gap between both equivalents emerging in the data was generally found to be 9 months less for form similar pairs compared to form dissimilar pairs.

On the basis of the findings, Schelletter (2002) suggests that form similarity facilitates lexical acquisition in bilingual children. A similar trend was found by Bosch & Ramon-Casas (2014) for Catalan and Spanish. They compared 24 simultaneous Catalan–English-speaking children aged 18 months with the same number of monolingual children who were either Spanish or Catalan speakers. They used a parental questionnaire to identify words that children were able to produce in both languages and grouped words as being form identical, form similar and form dissimilar. For example, the noun *coche* (car) was identified as form identical in Spanish and Catalan, as there was only a slight difference in the way the final vowel sound is produced. Words like *cat* were form similar as the equivalents only differ in the final phoneme, *gato* in Spanish and *gat* in Catalan. For dissimilar words, the forms did not overlap in their form, for example the word *dog* differs between Spanish and Catalan: *perro* in Spanish and *gos* in Catalan.

They found that identical forms made up the largest category of words with translation equivalents among the bilingual children. There were more translation equivalents among form similar words than form dissimilar words. Their results support the idea that similarity in form facilitates acquisition in bilinguals.

Overall, the studies discussed here make clear that Clark's (1987) Principle of Contrast as well as the Mutual Exclusivity Constraint clearly do not hold across the two languages of a bilingual. Both still apply within the two languages though, such that children will not accept two labels for the same object in the same language.

Lexical mixing. Mixing and code-switching were discussed in Chapter 3. In the context of lexical acquisition, one reason for 'mixing' languages is that children have not yet learnt equivalents for particular words in the other language. This creates a 'lexical gap'. From the example in Box 5.4 it is clear that children fill this gap by 'borrowing' words from the other language, at least until they have learnt the appropriate translation equivalent.

Lexical acquisition in sequential learners

Much of what was said before about monolingual and bilingual children's lexical acquisition also applies to sequential learners. As sequential learners have already acquired a certain number of words when they start learning another language, it seems that mutual exclusivity is not a problem that would prevent the acquisition of translation equivalents. In any case, the constraints only hold for beginning learners, as all children learn the names for parts of an object as well as within language synonyms.

Mixing has been found to occur frequently in sequentially bilingual children, for example in Raivo, as discussed in Chapters 1 and 3. This can involve a number of function words as well as content words.

Finally, for simultaneously bilingual children, form similarity was found to have a facilitating effect on word learning. Does the same hold for sequentially bilingual children? This is of course also dependent on the language combination that children learn. Schelletter (2002) also included a picture-naming and translation task, including 16 German–English bilingual children aged 8–9. Half of the children were simultaneous bilinguals, the other half came from a monolingual German background and started being exposed to English when coming to live in the United Kingdom. All children were found to translate form similar nouns more quickly than form dissimilar nouns. In the picture-naming task, some children used semantically similar nouns that had a greater phonological overlap between the two languages to label objects. For example, some children named the picture of a horse as *Fohlen* (foal) rather than *Pferd* (horse). A foal is semantically related to a horse and the translation equivalents *foal-Fohlen* are phonologically similar. They were also found to name a picture of a cloud (*Wolke*) as *Wind*. The noun *wind* is semantically similar to *cloud* and the translation equivalents *wind-Wind* which are form identical between English and German.

Based on these results it seems that form similarity between lexical items in the two languages is important both for simultaneous as well as sequential learners.

STUDY ACTIVITY 5.1

1. Consider the types of words that occurred with translation equivalents in Box 5.4 in terms of word frequency and the noun bias.
2. Are cognates easier to learn? Discuss in relation to simultaneous and sequential bilingual learners.

Assessing vocabulary in monolingual, bilingual and sequential language learners

In this section you will learn about different ways in which children's lexical skills can be measured. Assessing children's vocabulary at different stages is important to either confirm that the child is developing normally or to find out whether there is a developmental delay, for example.

When a child with a background in more than one language is assessed, the exposure to different languages needs to be taken into account as bilingual children often differ from monolingual children of the same age in terms of the number of items they produce in a vocabulary test. We will outline different tests and then discuss studies that have used the tests for bilingual children. We will discuss the results in relation to what has been called the 'bilingual disadvantage'.

Normative tests

When children start to understand and produce words, it is desirable to be able to measure the number of words they know. In this way, we can get an idea of the number of words children at a particular age should know. This can then be used as a guide. Tests are often normed on a large sample of children. This means that normally developing children have been tested and averages derived for particular ages. Particular children can then be compared to the averages and age equivalents can be determined.

Such norms generally only include children from a monolingual background. This means if a bilingual child is compared to the monolingual norms, this might not give an accurate picture of the number of words that the child knows, as their word knowledge is divided across two languages. It has therefore been suggested that the experimenter should count the number of different concepts that the child uses, irrespective of the language that these are expressed in. This is feasible for children's early vocabulary when the number of concepts is small but becomes more difficult when the child has a larger vocabulary.

CDI. An early assessment of children's vocabulary can be made using the McArthur-Bates **Communicative Development Inventory** or CDI (Fenson et al., 1994). This is a checklist which parents complete and it has an option for parents to confirm that the word or phrase is understood or whether it is both understood as well as produced. The CDI is divided into two age groups (infant form from 0;8 to 1;4 and toddler form from 1;4 to 2;6).

The first part of the infant form starts by parents confirming that the child reacts to certain phrases, for example turning when the child's name is called or responding to a request by the parent, such as *give me a kiss*. It also asks whether children imitate sound sequences and how often they label objects. The checklist includes animal sounds and a number of early words that are ordered by different semantic categories. For example, it includes the categories animals, vehicles, household items, people and action words as well as words about time. The second part of the form includes gestures (such as pointing or nodding), games (such as peekaboo), pretending to be the parent (by feeding a teddy or doll) or imitating the adult (by putting a key in the door).

The toddler form for older children includes more semantic categories in the first part, as well as grammatical words such as pronouns, prepositions and question words. The second part of the form includes grammatical endings (such as plural and past tense marking) as well as overregularisations (such as *goed* or *mouses*). It also asks about the complexity of children's sentences by suggesting different possibilities, for example *where mommy go*.

The CDI has been adapted in a variety of languages and is now available for 61 languages. In addition, based on the CDI, an open online database of children's vocabulary development has been developed, (Jørgensen et al., 2010). It can be accessed at http://wordbank.stanford.edu/. The wordbank provides vocabulary norms and item trajectories for words in the CDI in 29 different languages.

Box 5.6 gives the proportion of American children comprehending and producing the word *cat* as derived by the wordbank norms. The proportions are based on a sample of 105 children on average for each month. It is clear that the bars representing comprehension are higher than the bars representing production. Over the period of 8–16 months, comprehension of the word increases from 28% at 8 months to 80% at 16 months. Producing the word, on the other hand, is slower. Only 3% of children produced the word at the age of 8 months, whereas at 16 months it was 39%.

While the CDI is a useful tool and has been used widely to assess the vocabulary skills of young children, it is not objective as it is based on parents making a judgement about their children's language knowledge. Parents might under- or overestimate their children's knowledge, hence the test might not be as reliable as a measure where the child was recorded to have understood or

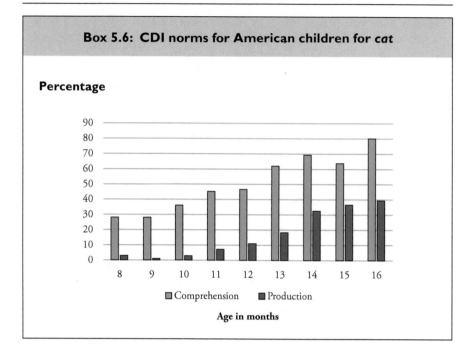

Box 5.6: CDI norms for American children for _cat_

produced the word. Nevertheless, the CDS gives a fairly accurate assessment of young children's early word comprehension and production.

Receptive vocabulary tasks. When children get older, assessment of their lexical skills is often carried out using normative tests of either comprehension and production, or both. One of the measures for receptive vocabulary skills for American English is the Peabody Picture Vocabulary Test (PPVT-4) (Dunn & Dunn, 2013). The test can be used from the age of 2;6 upwards. For the test, children are shown an array of four pictures and are asked to point to the picture that corresponds to the word read by the experimenter.

The tests consist of 204 items overall. They are divided into 17 sets of 12 items. The test starts with early acquired concrete words, such as _bus_ and actions such as _fly_, but items get progressively more difficult and more abstract. Depending on the child's age, the test can be started at the beginning or with a later set, as long as the child has no more than one error in the first set (basal set). The test concludes with a ceiling set, where the child has eight or more errors. The number of correct responses make up the child's raw score, which can be compared against the norms for the child's age.

A similar receptive vocabulary task is the British Picture Vocabulary Scale (BPVS III) (Dunn, Dunn & Styles, 2009). The BPVS is normed for children between 3 and 16. It consists of a total of 168 items which are divided into 14 sets of 12 items. Similar to the PPVT, the BPVS also requires a basal and a ceiling set. The BPVS norms are based on monolingual English children, but they also include a scale for children with English as an additional language.

Productive vocabulary tasks. Receptive vocabulary tasks measure how many words children can understand, however, comprehension is generally more developed than production. To assess children's production, the Expressive Vocabulary Test (EVT-2) (Williams, 2007) is a test to measure word retrieval in Standard American English. It can be used either on its own from 2;6 onwards or in conjunction with the PPVT-4 to assess both receptive and productive vocabulary skills. Children are shown a picture and are asked to produce a word relating to the picture. The EVT-2 consists of 190 items and includes nouns and verbs as well as attributes of nouns.

For British English, the Renfrew Language Scale (Renfrew & Mitchell, 2010) assesses children's word production between the ages of 3 and 8. As in the EVT-2, children are shown a set of picture cards and are asked to produce a word relating to the picture. The Renfrew vocabulary test consists of 50 pictures of objects that vary in the degree of difficulty. Initial pictures are *cup* and *window* and the final picture shows a *steeple*.

In addition to receptive and productive vocabulary, the Test of Word Knowledge (TOWK) (Wiig & Secord, 1992) does not only assess word comprehension and production, but it additionally includes tasks that measure children's ability to define words and to find words with a similar or the opposite meaning. There are two levels. The first level includes children aged 5–8 and includes all of the above, the second level ranges from 8–17 years and also includes figurative use of language, as in the use of idioms such as *barking up the wrong tree*.

We have outlined a number of tests that can be used to monitor the progress of monolingual English-speaking children. Similar tests are available for monolingual children of other languages, or some of the tests have been adapted for other languages. There are no specific tests or norms to assess the comprehension and production skills of children who have grown up with two languages. If bilingual children are assessed against monolingual norms, their language skills might be underestimated, as discussed in the next section.

Assessment of simultaneous bilingual learners

In this section, we will discuss results of studies that have used some of the tasks outlined in the last section to compare the lexical skills of monolingual and bilingual children. When comparing young bilinguals and monolinguals, there seems to be no particular disadvantage for bilingual learners, provided the children are matched on socio-economic background.

The CDI has been used to assess the comprehension and early production of monolingual and bilingual children. For example, de Houwer, Bornstein & Putnik (2014) compared the lexical skills of 31 bilingual Dutch–French and 30 Dutch monolingual children at 13 and 20 months using adult estimations of children's word knowledge based on the French and Dutch adaptations of the CDI. For both test ages, scores were calculated for both comprehension and production. It was found that all children were able to understand more words than they produced. When children were compared in just one language, Dutch, no significant differences were found between monolinguals and bilinguals at the age of 13 and 20 months. Children differed from each other though in the number of words they were judged to understand or produce.

When words were combined across both languages, bilingual children were found to understand more words than monolingual children at the age of 13 months but monolingual children knew more words in Dutch at 20 months. It therefore seems that at the start of lexical acquisition, bilingual children's vocabulary is similar to that of monolingual children in both languages, or they know more words than monolinguals if the words from both languages are combined.

The picture is different for older bilingual learners though. Quite a number of studies have reported lower lexical skills for bilingual children for at least one of their languages, or for both. Bialystok et al. (2010) compared the receptive vocabulary of 772 monolingual English children with a group of 966 bilingual children, using the PPVT-III. The children were between 3 and 10 years old. They found that the monolingual children's mean standard test score was significantly higher than that of the bilingual children for each age group. This result suggests that bilinguals generally know fewer words in one of their languages than children who have grown up as monolinguals in that language.

In a study of the vocabulary skills of 30 monolingual and 30 bilingual German–English pre-school children aged 3–5, Schelletter (2016) compared comprehension and production in English (BPVS and Renfrew) as well as word production in both languages. The results are outlined in more detail in Box 5.7. They show an effect of language dominance and community language as well as differences between comprehension and production of words.

The cause for the bilingual disadvantage is seen in the fact that bilingual children have less exposure to each of the languages, compared to monolinguals. As was discussed in Chapter 3, exposure to two languages per se does not necessarily mean the exposure in each language is reduced, however, as language is learnt in contexts, those differ across languages, therefore leading to differences in vocabulary knowledge.

The status of the languages in the community the child grows up in, as well as home languages, are also important aspects affecting the child's vocabulary knowledge. All the children in the study outlined in Box 5.7 were living in the United Kingdom, though both languages were spoken at the bilingual pre-school where the bilingual children were tested.

What if a child grows up with two languages that are spoken in the community? Wales is an example of such a community. Particularly in the north of Wales, both English and Welsh are common and all children are exposed to Welsh at school. Not all children grow up fully bilingual though. Children's home environment varies, depending on whether parents and children speak only Welsh, Welsh and English, or only English. It has to be said though that all Welsh speakers know both languages and frequently borrow words from English. Nevertheless, the different home language strategies provide a good

Box 5.7: Bilingual vocabulary

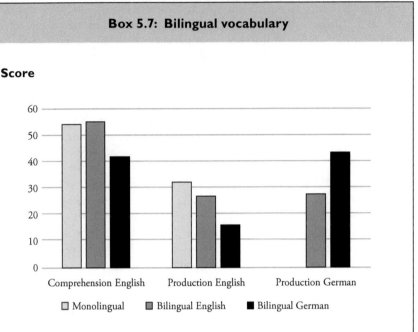

The bilingual group was further divided into two groups. There were 22 children where either the primary caretaker was German, or both parents were German, although all children were resident in the United Kingdom. They are described as Bilingual German. The remaining eight children have one parent who was a native speaker of English. They are described as Bilingual English. The children were tested in Comprehension in English as well as Production in both languages.

The results show that the Bilingual E group achieved a similar average score in the BPVS compared to the monolinguals. However, their production score was lower than that of the monolinguals. The Bilingual G group were lower than the monolinguals in both comprehension and production. Although their score in the productive German task was higher than that of the Bilingual E group, both groups scored below monolingual German norms.

basis for comparing simultaneous bilinguals with children who have grown up with mainly one of the languages.

A study comparing the different child groups in Wales was carried out by Gathercole, Thomas & Hughes (2008). They assessed the comprehension skills of bilingual Welsh–English children between 7 and 11 years in the Welsh language. Children were grouped according to home language: only Welsh, Welsh and English or only English. The home language provides an indication of the amount of exposure children have received in each of the languages. They developed a receptive vocabulary task for Welsh for this purpose.

Some of the criteria for designing such a task were similar to those of other tests, for example the requirement to cover a range of frequent and less frequent words, words with different degrees of complexity, as well as words that can be represented in picture form. Other criteria were specific to the language combination: the test did not include any cognates or borrowed words from English. The initial test consisted of a total of 240 items and each item was presented as an array of four pictures. Unlike the PPVT and the BPVS, the bilingual Welsh test can be administered in a group. Children are given a booklet with a questionnaire and the test items and see the array presented on a screen. When they hear a word, they are required to circle the picture that corresponds to the word.

In total, 611 children between 7 and 11 were tested with the bilingual Welsh vocabulary test. There was an almost equal number of children in each of the subgroups: only Welsh at home (214), only English at home (201) and both English and Welsh at home (196). There were a number of words in the task that were found not to discriminate between the children. These were eliminated, leaving a set of 111 significant words for the analysis. When children's scores were compared for the remaining words, there was a significant difference for age as well as home language background. Children's word knowledge increased with age but was also in line with the amount of input in Welsh they received. The children from a home background where only Welsh was spoken had higher scores compared to the children where the language background was both Welsh and English. The children who had input in both languages at home had higher scores in the task than the children with home English only.

Children's receptive English language skills were also compared, based on home language background (see Box 5.8).

Box 5.8: Receptive language skills in a dual language community

Gathercole, Thomas, Roberts, Hughes & Hughes (2013) compared children's English receptive vocabulary using the BPVS for different ages. They distinguished different home language groups (only English at home, only Welsh at home, English and Welsh at home) and also included a group of English monolingual children.

As for the Welsh test before, age and home language predicted vocabulary skills from the age of 2. Vocabulary skills increased with age but monolingual English children knew more words at each age level than children with both English and Welsh at home. The bilinguals in turn had higher scores than the children who only heard Welsh at home.

At the upper end of the age range, 13–15, differences were found to disappear. This suggests that the differences in vocabulary levels are not necessarily permanent and that in the course of development, bilinguals might be able to 'catch up' with their monolingual counterparts.

The results of assessments of bilinguals' lexical skills suggest that vocabulary acquisition is an area of language proficiency where the amount of exposure (e.g. in terms of home language) needs to be taken into account when assessing bilingual children. Furthermore, any difference between groups of children at a particular time can only be seen as a snapshot of a particular moment in time.

Assessment of sequential and early second language learners

When early sequential or early second language learners are exposed to another language (e.g. through immersion at a bilingual nursery school) they will need to learn about sound and sound sequences of the other language and then identify them as second language words.

These children are in the position where they have already learnt a certain number of words in their L1 at the point where an L2 is introduced. This means that their word knowledge of L1 and L2 differs in size, however, they already have a certain amount of word knowledge and have reached a particular stage in their cognitive development.

Children who learn a second language early seem to go through similar stages of language acquisition to their first language (McLaughlin, 1977), yet the acquisition is fairly rapid, such that children have been observed to be indistinguishable from native speakers of the same age after 9–12 months. At the same time, early second language learners have been found to translate from the non-native language, to borrow words from the native language (and pronounce them in the way that made them sound like the L2), to supply native endings on L2 words and to focus on cognates between the languages (ibid.: 449).

We have seen that the vocabulary skills of simultaneous bilingual children are dependent on the amount of input in each of their languages. This is similar for sequential bilinguals as well. The particular circumstances of when and how a second language is introduced, as well as the status of the second language in the community, has an influence on the children learning the second language.

In the study of children in Wales (Gathercole, Thomas & Hughes, 2008), the children growing up with English at home, of course, are sequential learners of Welsh, and they were found to have a smaller vocabulary in Welsh than the Welsh home language as well as the bilingual speakers. But given that Welsh is spoken in the community, the children could have had some exposure to Welsh prior to starting school.

Let us therefore consider a case of children who become immersed in another language when starting pre-school. Immersion is a term that was first used in relation to education programmes in Canada, where children from a different language background are able to attend schools in one of the official languages. So, for example, a child from a mainly English background can attend a French immersion school, where either a certain percentage or all of the classes are held in French.

Within the European Union, on the other hand, different countries have different official languages, but few countries have more than one official language. In 2003, the European Commission set up an action plan for 2004–2006 to advance early language learning and language diversity in the member states. Since then, there have been a number of initiatives in different member states to support early language learning by setting up immersion pre-schools and schools.

Within this context, the language learning of children attending different bilingual German–English pre-schools in Germany has been investigated as part of the Early Learning and Intercultural Acquisition Studies (ELIAS) project, a Comenius project funded by the European Commission (Kersten et al., 2010).

The project included 200 children aged 3–7 who were attending seven bilingual pre-schools in Germany, as well as one in Belgium and one in Sweden. They were compared to 20 monolingual English children attending a pre-school and school in the United Kingdom. The children were tested with the BPVS-II as well as a grammar comprehension task. Rohde (2010) compares children's BPVS results with those of English monolingual children at two points of observation, 6 months apart.

The children in the study were on average 4;8 years at the first time of testing and 5;4 at the second point of testing. The L2 learners had been exposed to English between 1 and 50 months at the time of the first testing. The chart in Box 5.9 shows the children's raw scores in the BPVS at both points, represented by 1 and 2. It is clear from the chart that both the monolingual children, as well as the L2 learners, increased their BPVS scores within 6 months. It is also clear though that the L2 learners understood significantly fewer words than the monolingual children of the same age.

We saw that home language was an important factor in the children growing up with Welsh and English in Wales. In the case of the children investigated here, the home language of most of the L2 learners was German. We can therefore not use home language to distinguish between the children. Instead, the children were grouped according to the length of time they had been exposed to English. This showed that the groups who had been exposed to English for the longest period of time, had higher scores than the other groups. They also increased their scores more than the groups with lower input intensity. The study confirms that length of exposure time affects the level of language.

The bilingual disadvantage

We have considered children's lexical development as well as the assessment of bilingual children's word knowledge in relation to monolingual children. While bilingual toddlers are comparable to monolingual children in their lexical skills, assessments of school-age bilingual children seem to show a

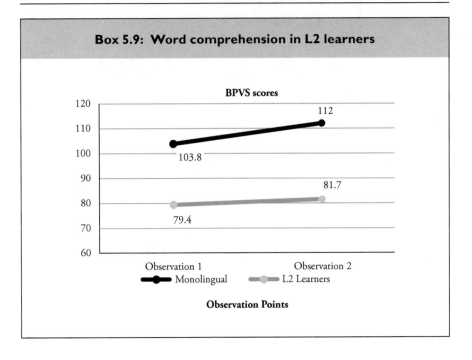

Box 5.9: Word comprehension in L2 learners

bilingual disadvantage, whereby bilingual children score below the monolingual norms in at least one of their languages.

But can we really say that bilingual children have a lexical disadvantage? They know many translation equivalents, even if they don't know all the concepts that monolingual children comprehend or produce. So, the problem is perhaps not so much the lexical knowledge of the bilingual child, but rather the method of assessing a bilingual against monolingual norms.

In designing a new vocabulary task, Gathercole, Thomas & Hughes (2008) aimed to develop new norms that can be applied to bilingual children. Given the process of selecting suitable words within different frequency ranges, the task is not that easily adapted to other languages, as frequencies can differ for different languages.

STUDY ACTIVITY 5.2

1. How have vocabulary skills in monolingual and bilingual children been compared? What factors need to be taken into account in such a comparison?
2. Do the differences in lexical development between monolingual and bilingual children really amount to a bilingual disadvantage?

Monolingual and bilingual word processing

A different way of looking at children's lexical skills is to consider the way words are processed and whether there are differences between monolingual and bilingual learners. We started out with words being linked to concepts which represent a group of objects. When we want to activate a word that we have stored in our mind, this process differs according to the task at hand. If we hear a particular sequence of sounds, we recognise the string as making up a particular word. If the task is to match the word with a particular picture, for example, we need to compare the meaning of the word with concepts that are represented in a set of pictures. If, on the other hand, we see a string of letters, we need to recognise the sequence of letters as a particular word and then convert the letters into sounds, if the task is to read the word aloud.

Processing a word therefore involves the levels that were identified at the beginning of the chapter as being associated with word learning, namely the sound or letter sequence associated with the word, as well as the concept. It is well known that the effort to access a particular word is dependent on different factors, including, for example, the frequency of the word and the word type as well as the word complexity. Frequent words are generally accessed faster than less frequent words. Concrete nouns (referring to objects that can be perceived through the senses) are accessed faster than abstract nouns.

Picture naming is often used to assess children's lexical skills in the normative tasks outlined earlier. This task has also been used to investigate factors affecting word retrieval, such as word frequency, age of acquisition and familiarity as well as word class.

The observation that children tend to acquire nouns earlier than verbs, which was discussed at the beginning of the chapter, gives rise to the question whether there is a difference in processing both word types and whether this differs for particular languages (given that the noun bias was found not to be universal). Bilingualism should not as such affect the processing of different word types, except perhaps where a child acquires two languages which differ in terms of the magnitude of the noun bias.

Noun and verb processing was investigated in monolingual children by Masterson, Druks & Gallienne (2008) who conducted a picture-naming study with 62 children aged 3 and 5 years. The children were shown 200 pictures with black and white line drawings on a computer screen, half of them showing objects, the other half showing actions. A picture resource is given in Box 5.10.

The noun and verb pictures were matched for complexity and age of acquisition. The children were tested individually in a quiet room at their school or nursery and were asked to name the object or action with a single word. The percentage of incorrect and correct responses were compared for the two age groups.

Not surprisingly, the error rate of the 5-year-olds was lower than that of the younger children for both nouns and verbs. The 5-year-olds had an error

---

Box 5.10: The International Picture-Naming Project (IPNP)

The IPNP is a project at the Centre for Research in Language of the University of California, San Diego. It provides a picture-naming database with downloadable object and action pictures, as well as picture-naming norms for seven different languages. There are black and white line drawings for 520 object and 275 action pictures. The languages include American English, German, Mexican–Spanish, Italian, Bulgarian, Hungarian and the Taiwan variant of Mandarin Chinese. The pictures and database can be accessed at http://crl.ucsd.edu/~aszekely/ipnp/.

---

rate of just under 20% for both word classes. The 3-year-olds, on the other hand, had an error rate of just under 40% for nouns and just under 45% for verbs. A more detailed analysis of the errors showed that the younger children had a higher rate of 'don't know' responses, but overall, among both groups, the most frequent error was semantic, that is, children responded to a picture with a name that was semantically similar to the target, but not the target name itself. For example, children might name a picture of a *cherry* as *apple* or *fruit*.

In a second experiment, 32 children at the age of 5 were tested with the same pictures and in addition to their accuracy rating, children's reaction times for each picture were also measured. The children had a similar error rate to the older children in the first experiment and they also had similar accuracy ratings for nouns and verbs. However, their reaction times for verbs were significantly higher than for nouns. This finding suggests that the retrieval of a verb requires a higher degree of mental effort than a noun. Masterson, Druks & Gallienne (2008) suggest that the results show different underlying semantic representations for nouns and verbs.

Why would this be the case? Nouns differ from verbs in that they refer to fixed concepts. An object will always have some of the particular qualities that are part of the concept, for example, a cat will have whiskers, four legs, a tail, etc. Verbs, on the other hand, refer to the relations between objects. The objects that are involved in the actions can be different. For example, the verb *buy* can refer to a relation between different people and objects: *Mary bought a coat, the child bought ice cream*, etc.

Given the differences in naming noun and verb pictures in monolingual children, let us now look at noun and verb naming in bilingual children. A study by Klassert, Gagarina & Kauschke (2014) investigated picture naming of nouns and verbs in a group of 60 Russian–German bilingual children aged 4–6 years, 60 monolingual Russian and 120 monolingual German children. The children were grouped by age (4, 5, 6). Their aim was to investigate the word processing skills of both groups and to determine whether there are differences between the two groups. The bilingual children were tested by native speakers in both languages. There were 36 noun and 36 verb pictures for the German test and 31 noun and verb pictures in the Russian version. The number of correctly named nouns and verbs was recorded and analysed.

For all children, the number of correctly named pictures increased with age from 4 to 6. The monolingual children showed a clear noun advantage, as there was a higher number of correct responses for noun pictures compared to verb pictures. For each age group, the monolingual children named more noun pictures correctly compared to the bilinguals. This is in line with the findings on most of the normative tests that were discussed earlier.

However, verb naming was similar across monolingual and bilingual groups, thereby showing a much reduced noun bias in the bilingual children. These results show that the bilingual children have no difficulties with the semantic complexities posed by verbs. The differences between monolingual and bilingual children are due to the lower lexical skills in the bilinguals but do not show any differences in the processing of nouns and verbs as such.

STUDY ACTIVITY 5.3

1. Bilinguals have often been found to take longer to access a word compared to monolinguals. Can you think of reasons why?
2. What have the picture-naming studies shown about noun and verb processing in monolingual and bilingual children?

SUMMARY

Overall, this chapter focused on the background of word learning and the lexical development of children who grow up with one or two languages. While the mechanisms of word learning are essentially the same for the different types of learners, children who grow up with more than one language have an early awareness that words for the same concept differ across languages, as shown by the early occurrence of translation equivalents. This means that one of the constraints on word learning, mutual exclusivity, only holds within a language, but not across languages.

While an assessment of vocabulary skills in children is common and desirable for different reasons, the outcomes of such assessments can be misleading in the case of learners with a background of other languages. The observation that the lexical skills of bilingual learners are below those of monolinguals, is often seen as the 'bilingual disadvantage'. However, factors, such as home language of the learner, as well as the length of exposure to the languages, need to be taken into account. Norms that take the background of the learner into account are desirable.

Children's word processing skills are often assessed by picture-naming tasks. When comparing noun and verb processing, monolingual children learning languages such as English, German and Russian, showed a noun bias. Their naming rate for nouns was higher than for verbs. In the English study, reaction times for nouns were lower than for verbs. The results of the monolingual-bilingual comparison show no differences in the processing of nouns and verbs.

FURTHER READING

For more details on children's very early lexical development see Conboy & Montanari (2016). The case study of Manuela is discussed in more detail in Deuchar & Quay (2001). The question of a cognate facilitation in early development is discussed in Bosch & Ramon-Casas (2014). Issues in the assessment of bilinguals as well as possible solutions are further discussed in Gathercole (2013a) and Gathercole (2013b). For more details on children's picture naming in different languages see Szekely et al. (2004). For a cross-linguistic lexical task (CLT) see Haman, Łuniewska & Pomiechowska (2015).

Bilingual Morpho-Syntactic Development

6

In this chapter we shall discuss monolingual and bilingual children's morpho-syntactic development. Morpho-syntactic development includes the acquisition of grammatical inflections as well as word order. A **morpheme** is defined as the smallest grammatical unit that has meaning. Morphemes can be smaller than a word or they can stand on their own. In English, inflections such as the *–s* plural and the past tense *–ed* are **bound morphemes** as they cannot occur on their own without the noun that they are attached to. However, when morphemes can occur on their own, they are **free**. This means that words are free morphemes (morphologically simple) when they cannot be further broken down, for example *apple* or *cook*. When they occur with **suffixes**, as in *apple-s* or *cook-ed*, words are morphologically complex.

Languages can differ in the area of morpho-syntax. There are different word order patterns, for example in the placement of the verb, but also in the grammatical marking that languages use to specify plural, case, gender, tense and aspect, which all differ. Take, for example, English and Turkish. Both languages differ in their word order, as in English the verb occurs after the subject and before the object. In Turkish, the verb is generally placed after the object. The noun endings also differ, and Turkish distinguishes different cases, grammatical markers that specify the function of the noun in the sentence, that is, whether it is the subject, the object, the indirect object etc.

Given the differences between languages, it is clear that a bilingual child needs to work out how the grammar in each of the languages works. In this chapter, we shall outline children's morpho-syntactic development in general, and then apply this to bilingual acquisition. We shall get back to the theories outlined in Chapter 2, as well as some of the issues discussed, such as the question as to whether a 'critical mass' is necessary for acquisition, as well as the question of transparency.

The chapter will also address the assessment of grammar development in monolingual and bilingual children, both at an early age, as well as when children are of school age. We shall also discuss the question whether inflectional endings that follow a particular pattern (regular morphology) are regulated by a different cognitive mechanism, as opposed to patterns that do not follow this pattern (irregular morphology).

Morpho-syntactic development in monolingual children

In this section we shall outline the morpho-syntactic development of mono-lingual children. We shall start with English as the language that has been studied in considerable detail. On the other hand, compared to other languages, English is quite sparse in terms of its grammatical morphology. By sparse we mean that the number of different morphemes in English is limited. The acquisition of grammatical morphology in English can therefore not be taken as a role model for the acquisition of the system in languages with richer morphologies.

Monolingual English development

Children's development of inflectional morphology involves the child starting to use adult inflectional endings added to stem forms of nouns and verbs. The investigation of the morphological development of English started with Brown (1973), who followed the development of three American children (Adam, Eve and Sarah). They were recorded on a regular basis from the time they were 2 years old. Brown was concerned with the acquisition of 14 particular morphemes and their order of acquisition. These include inflection in both nouns and verbs, as well as different function words.

In order to get an idea of children's grammatical development, Brown calculated the children's mean utterance length (**mean length of utterance – MLU**). MLU is determined by dividing the number of morphemes in an utterance by the number of utterances in a given transcript. For example, if a child produces the two utterances *teddy doing* and *this daddy's car*, the child has produced two utterances. The first utterance is three morphemes long, as the noun *teddy*, the verb *do* and the present progressive form *–ing* are all counted as separate morphemes, therefore the number of morphemes totals three. In the second utterance, the pronoun *this*, the noun *daddy*, the possessive *–s* and the noun *car* are all separate morphemes, totalling four. The child's MLU for the two utterances is the total number of morphemes, seven, divided by two utterances, resulting in an MLU of 3.5.

As children produce longer utterances as they get older, their MLU increases with age. MLU is therefore a valuable measure of English-speaking children's stage of grammatical development, at least between the ages of 2 and 4 (Miller & Chapman, 1981).

One issue in the investigation of children's acquisition of morphology is the question as to whether they use the endings productively, that is, whether they know the meaning of morphemes and can apply them to different lexical categories. For this reason, Brown used a particular criterion: children are required to produce a particular morpheme 90% correctly at least three times in so-called 'obligatory contexts'. These are contexts where an adult would have regarded the use of the morpheme to be necessary.

Let us take an example. Let's say a child produces the plural *–s* morpheme in English nine times with three different nouns. On one occasion, the child did not mark the plural, but the context clearly indicated that the noun was used in the plural. We can say that the child has acquired the plural, because it was used more than three times correctly in obligatory contexts and the proportion of correct use (nine times) out of all obligatory contexts (10 times) is 90%.

Brown also suggested a particular order in which the 14 morphemes occur in English, together with their assumed age of acquisition. This is given in Box 6.1. According to the list, the present progressive –*ing* is the first morpheme to occur in English child language. Children produce utterances such as *teddy doing* at an early age. The next two items that are listed are the prepositions *in* and *on*. These are free morphemes and also emerge early.

Notice that in Brown's order of acquisition, irregular past tense forms are acquired earlier than regular forms. This reflects the observation that children initially learn a number of irregular past tense forms before they acquire the rule for the regular past tense form. Irregular plural forms, on the other hand, are not represented in the list because they are not very frequent in English. Brown's list of morphemes also does not consider any case-marked pronouns, that is the distinction between *he* and *him*, whereby *he* occurs as the subject of a sentence, whereas the form *him* occurs in the object position after the verb.

Box 6.1: Morpheme acquisition in English

Morpheme	Example	Age of acquisition (months)
1. Present progressive	daddy driv-**ing.**	19–28
2. Preposition *in*	Ball **in** car.	27–30
3. Preposition *on*	Milk **on** table.	27–33
4. Regular plural	ball-**s.**	27–33
5. Irregular past tense	man **fell.**	25–46
6. Possessive	daddy**'s** chair.	26–40
7. Uncontractible copula	this **is** hot.	28–46
8. Articles	**a** cat. **The** cat.	28–46
9. Regular past tense	she walk-**ed.**	26–48
10. Third person regular	he work-**s.**	28–50
11. Third person irregular	she do**es.**	28–50
12. Uncontractible auxiliary	the horse **is** winning.	29–48
13. Contractible copula	he**'s** a clown.	29–49
14. Contractible auxiliary	she**'s** drinking.	30–50

The table gives the impression that English-speaking children have acquired the grammatical morphology of their native language by the time they are 4. However, Balason & Dollaghan (2002) investigated American children's use of the morphemes at the age of 4. They found considerable variation of use, based on 15-minute speech samples of 100 children. Monolingual 5-year-olds still use forms like *drawed*. These are **overregularisations**, irregular verb forms that children treat like regular verbs.

It is not clear what determines the order of acquisition of morphemes. One possible factor is the frequency of occurrence in the parents' speech. Brown (1973) stated that there is no evidence that parental frequency affects the order of acquisition in English, however, frequency of occurrence is now seen as an important predictor of lexical and morpho-syntactic development (see Chapter 3).

Cross-linguistic development

The morphological development of children acquiring languages other than English has been documented by Slobin (1985) for a number of different languages. While the morphological development of other languages is not fundamentally different from English, there are nevertheless differences reflecting the structure and degree of marking in the languages to be learnt, the frequency of inflections and phonological salience, as well as transparency of the particular inflection.

We shall discuss the acquisition of Italian morphology as an example of the acquisition of the morphological marking of a language other than English (Pizzuto & Caselli, 1992). Like many languages, Italian has a rich verb inflectional system consisting of a stem form with different endings depending on the particular person. The Italian inflectional system is outlined in Box 6.2.

Box 6.2: Italian verb morphology

Noun morphology: *cavallo* horse, *yogurt* yoghurt, *sedia* chair

	Singular		Plural	
Masculine	*un/ il cavall-o*	a/the horse	*i cavall-i*	the horses
	un/lo yogurt	a/the yoghurt	*gli yogurt*	the yoghurts
Feminine	*una/ la sedi-a*	a/the chair	*le sedi-e*	the chairs

Verb morphology: *parl-are* to speak, *arriv-ere* to arrive <u>Present</u>

Person	Singular		Plural	
1	*parl-o*	I speak	*parl-iamo*	we speak
2	*parl-i*	you speak	*parl-ate*	you speak
3	*parl-a*	he or she speaks	*parl-ano*	they speak

Present perfect

Person	Singular		Plural	
1	*ho parl-ato*	I have spoken	*abbiamo parl-ato*	we have spoken
	Sono arriv-ato	I have arrived	*siamo arriv-ato*	we have arrived
2	*hai parl-ato*	you have spoken	*avete parl-ato*	you have spoken
	Sei arriv-ato	you have arrived	*siete arriv-ato*	you have arrived
3	*ha parl-ato*	he/she has spoken	*hanno parl-ato*	they have spoken
	è arriv-ato	he/she has arrived	*sono arriv-ato*	they have arrived

Like a number of languages, Italian marks nouns according to gender (masculine and feminine) and the articles also differ. This means that instead of the distinction between the articles *a* and *the* in English, a child acquiring Italian needs to learn two different forms of the indefinite determiner (*un* and *una*) as well as at least six different forms of the definite determiner, depending on the gender of the noun. In terms of verb morphology, whereas an English child needs to learn the distinction between the stem and the third person singular *–s*, an Italian child needs to learn six different endings, depending on the subject.

Pizzuto & Caselli (1992) compare the acquisition of inflectional morphology of three Italian children aged 1;4 to 4 with the morpheme acquisition of the children observed by Brown (1973) according to the same MLU stage. Comparing MLU across languages is a problem if one of the languages has more morphological endings compared with the other. It would make the child learning the more inflected language look more advanced. For this reason, cross-language comparisons are based on MLU in words rather than morphemes.

As the children were matched to the children studied by Brown in terms of their MLU stage, it becomes possible to compare the acquisition of morphemes across languages to some degree. In the comparison between English and Italian children, there were some similarities in terms of the type of morphemes that reached the criterion for acquisition. For example, when the children had an MLU in words of about 2.25 to 2.74, verb endings emerged in both Italian and English. While the Italian children acquired singular person endings of the verb, English children acquired the present progressive form *–ing*. Within each category, the particular morpheme that reached criterion was found to be linked to factors such as frequency, but also how easily noticeable the morpheme was. The inflectional endings in Italian often end with a vowel and are more salient than in English. One difference between the acquisition of English and Italian, on the other hand, seems to be in terms of the acquisition of the third person singular main verb inflection, which was observed by Pizzuto & Caselli at a significantly earlier stage than in English.

You might have noticed in the outline of Italian inflections in Box 6.2 that the form *parlo* translates as *I speak*. This is because Italian is a language where the subject pronoun does not need to be present in a sentence (pro-drop), rather, the person is already incorporated into the verb ending (see Chapter 2). This means that the verb ending carries more information compared to non pro-drop languages like English. Also, there is more stress on the final syllable of the verb in Italian, such that the final syllable of an Italian verb is more phonologically salient than verb endings in English. And finally, the fact that verb endings change according to the subject (first, second, third person) means that there is more evidence that the ending of the verb is important.

We saw that the cross-linguistic comparison between English and Italian suggests that the third person singular ending of the verb in Italian is acquired earlier than in English. Do such cross-linguistic differences also affect bilingual acquisition? If there are differences in frequency as well as saliency, this could lead to a situation where a bilingual acquires a particular morphological form earlier in one language than in the other, hence the order of acquisition of morphemes can differ for the two languages.

On the other hand, while some morphological marking is acquired early in Italian, Pizzuto and Caselli (1992) found that other patterns take some time to be mastered. For example, Italian subject pronouns and the full acquisition of the Italian tense and aspect system were found to be delayed compared to English.

We have focused here on Italian, and compared the acquisition of inflections in both languages. What about other languages? A study by Xanthos et al. (2011) compared the acquisition of morphology of nine monolingual children between the ages of 1 and 3 who all spoke different languages (French, Dutch, German, Russian, Croatian, Greek, Turkish, Finnish and Yucatec Mayan).

The languages involved vary in the degree of morphological marking. Morphological richness was determined by the 'average number of distinct inflected word-forms per lemma' (Xanthos et al., 2011, p. 465). A lemma is a word form in the mental lexicon (see Chapter 7) which also includes inflectional markings. Morphological richness was determined for the languages involved by measuring the number of inflected forms in 1,000 tokens of the input language divided by the number of different lemmas. According to this measure, Turkish had the highest degree of morphological marking, followed by the language group including Croatian, Finnish, Russian and Yucatec Mayan. The group with the lowest marking included the languages Dutch, French, German and Greek.

When comparing the morphological richness of the different languages with children's speed of acquisition, it was found that there was a relationship between the two, such that the children acquiring languages with a high degree of morphological marking were faster at acquiring the inflections than children learning languages with a lower degree of morphological marking. This applied to both noun and verb inflections and raises interesting questions for bilingual acquisition. If children simultaneously acquire two languages with different degrees of morphological marking, these findings predict a 'lead-lag' pattern, whereby the inflections of the language with the richer system are acquired faster than the inflections of the less inflected language.

Theoretical accounts of morpheme acquisition

We discussed different theoretical accounts of acquisition in Chapter 2. We saw that verb inflections are included in the class of functional categories. The emergence of particular inflections therefore can signify whether or not the child has acquired the particular functional category. Their absence, on the other hand, can either be seen as a delay in the acquisition of tense, for example, or even as a diagnostic characteristic for the presence of a language disorder (Bishop, 2014).

How does the finding that a language with a richer morphological system can lead to faster acquisition relate to the Universal Grammar (UG) account? It certainly seems to show that exposure as well as maturation affect children's acquisition. Pizzuto & Caselli (1992) found that the acquisition of morphology in Italian and English children emerged at similar MLU stages, and this shows that a certain amount of language development is necessary before inflections are used. But the finding that a higher degree of morphological marking, and thereby a higher rate of exposure, affects the acquisition of inflections, is more in line with the Usage-based theory.

In the outline of the Usage-based theory, it is emphasised that acquisition is driven by intention reading and pattern finding, and that it proceeds in a piecemeal fashion. According to this view, the frequency of occurrence of forms in the input has an impact on the acquisition process, such that the most frequently occurring forms are acquired first. From the cross-linguistic evidence considered in the last section, it seems that this is supported, as some inflections in languages other than English (such as the third person singular in Italian) emerge early, while others emerge later. We shall discuss the impact of these findings on bilingual development in more detail in the next section.

The Constructivist account, which was also considered in Chapter 2, overlaps with the Usage-based theory in some of the principles that are outlined. Both assume 'piecemeal' acquisition of inflections, and also emphasise that exposure has an effect on the timing of acquisition. However, the Constructivist account also identifies the structure to be learnt as having an impact on the timing of acquisition. In the context of inflectional marking, it is clear that some structures are 'easier' than others and are learnt earlier. For example, we pointed out earlier that Brown's (1973) list of morphemes does not include irregular plurals. As irregular plurals are infrequent in English, the child will not have a lot of exposure to them. In addition, irregular forms differ for different nouns. The plural of *child* is *children*, the plural of *mouse* is *mice*. The low frequency, together with the forms which have to be learnt for each item, are likely to delay their acquisition.

When considering children's use of inflectional morphemes, a distinction is made between regular and irregular inflections. Regular inflections are assumed to follow a rule-based pattern (see Box 6.3), whereas irregular inflections need to be learnt for each item. Not all languages follow such a clear pattern though. We shall see in Chapter 9, for example, that Welsh has eight different regular plural forms (there are additional forms but they are not productive).

Box 6.3: The Wug test

In the well-known Wug test, children are given novel nouns, such as *wug*, and asked to form the plural of the words.

This is a wug   **Now there is another one.**
                           There are two of them. There are two ___

The assumption is that children have learnt a default rule that plurals are formed by adding an –s (pronounced either as /s/, /z/ or /iz/) to the end of a noun in order to form the plural. The Wug test shows that young children are able to apply the default form to words they have never heard before, therefore, they are assumed to have formed an implicit rule that can be extended to novel nouns.

Children who are between 2 and 4 have a tendency to apply the ending of a regular form to an irregular noun or verb, a process which is called over-regularisation. This has been seen as evidence that children have acquired a grammatical rule and that this is extended to forms where no irregular inflection has yet been learnt. Experiments like the Wug test (see Box 6.3) show that children apply the default rule to nouns that they have never heard before (Berko-Gleason, 1958).

STUDY ACTIVITY 6.1

1. Consider the different endings for verbs in Italian. Which person endings were acquired early? What factors might lead to an earlier acquisition of person endings compared to English?
2. What is 'piecemeal' acquisition in relation to the acquisition of morphological endings? Is the order of acquisition only affected by frequency?

Bilingual morpho-syntactic development

How do bilinguals acquire the inflections of both their languages? Given the importance of morphological richness of a language in the speed of acquisition, what does this mean for bilinguals? We have already discussed bilingual acquisition in relation to the 'critical mass' hypothesis (see Chapter 3), the idea that exposure to a form has to reach a particular critical mass in order for acquisition to occur.

Compared to monolinguals, there is an expectation that bilingual children's acquisition of inflections is delayed, due to the assumption that the input frequency of each of the languages of the bilingual is reduced. In Chapter 5 we found that the vocabulary skills of bilingual children are lower than those of monolinguals at school age. This has been described as the 'bilingual disadvantage'. Does this disadvantage also apply to the acquisition of inflectional morphology?

The situation regarding inflectional marking seems to be more complex. If a bilingual acquires two languages with a high degree of morphological marking, then the morphological richness should counterbalance the reduced amount of input, such that the bilingual child's morpho-syntactic development is similar to that of a monolingual child acquiring a language that is less rich in morphology.

In what follows, we shall consider different factors that influence the acquisition of morpho-syntax in both monolingual and bilingual children.

Issues for simultaneous bilingual children

Language-specific development. Following the single system versus separate development debate, it has become important to show that bilinguals produce language-appropriate forms most of the time, even where these differ.

Let us go back to the study by de Houwer (1990), where she investigated the morphological development of a child acquiring Dutch and English – Kate. The two languages differ in relation to word order. English is a language where sentence elements are ordered as SVO (subject, verb, object), as in the sentence *I have seen the film*, where the verb is *have seen*, consisting of a finite verb, *have*, and a non-tensed part, the participle *seen*. In Dutch, on the other hand, the two parts do not occur together. The non-tensed part of the verb occurs at the end of the sentence and the finite verb occurs after the subject in this case. The same sentence is therefore expressed in Dutch as *ik heb de film bekeken* (I have the film seen), where the finite verb *heb* and the participle *bekeken* occur in different parts of the sentence. This means that Dutch and English differ in terms of the placement of the non-tensed verb.

Box 6.4 shows examples from Kate speaking Dutch and English. Her placement of the non-tensed verb in Dutch is adult-appropriate and at the same time, her English utterances follow the English word order pattern. de Houwer found that inflectional endings for both noun and verb phrase developed in accordance with language-specific forms for both languages. There was no

---

Box 6.4: Verb placement in English and Dutch

Dutch 2;9	English 2;10
*CHI: *de tijger **gaat** ook **slape(n)**.* the tiger goes also to sleep. 'the tiger also goes to sleep'.	*CHI: I **would like** lollipop!
*CHI: *ik **heb** hij **gevange(n)**.* I have him caught. 'I have caught him'.	*CHI: mommy I **want to be** good.

mixing of morphemes, that is the use of morphemes from one language on lexical items of the other language. de Houwer calls this the 'principle of language stability' (de Houwer, 1990, p. 149). According to this principle, bound morphemes are acquired for each language separately and do not travel across to the other language. However, we have discussed examples where this principle is violated in Chapter 2.

Transparency. Transparency refers to the relationship between a particular grammatical form and the functions it can have. In English, the determiners *a* and *the* have one form, but different functions. For example, the indefinite determiner *a* is used to introduce a particular referent, as in *I saw a cat*, as the speaker has a particular cat in mind. On the other hand, it can mean *any one*, as in the sentence *have you got a pen?* In this case, the speaker does not mean a particular pen but asks for any pen that the listener can find.

Similarly, the definite determiner also has different functions. For example, it can either refer back to an already introduced referent, as in *the cat jumped into the car*, where *the cat* refers back to the referent that was introduced in the previous sentence. The definite determiner can also be used if a referent can be retrieved from the context. In the second use of the definite determiner, *the car*, it can be assumed that it was the speaker's car that the cat jumped into. Therefore, it is not necessary to introduce the car as a new referent. So we have seen that the English determiners have different functions.

If there is a one-to-one correspondence between a grammatical form and the function it has, then the grammatical form is transparent. An example of a transparent morphological system is Turkish. Turkish is a so-called **agglutinative** language where morphological endings map onto a specific meaning and are added consecutively to a word. For example, the English verb *come* translates into Turkish as *gel-mek*, where *gel* is the verb stem and the suffix *–mek* signals the infinitive form. In order to form the first person singular present, *I am coming*, the suffix *–iyorum* is added, resulting in the form *gel-iyorum*. In order to negate the verb, the suffix *–ma* or *–me* is added to the stem. However, the vowel is dropped if the addition of the suffix results in one vowel being followed by another. The sentence *I am not coming* therefore translates into Turkish as *gel-m(e)-iyorum*.

We can see that the way that endings are added to Turkish verbs makes grammatical marking transparent, which is one of the reasons why Turkish inflections are acquired at an early age, as we saw in the Xanthos et al. (2011) study.

We can therefore say that the structure of the languages that are learnt by a bilingual has an effect on the acquisition process. If the systems are both transparent, children will acquire both systems at similar times. If there are differences in the degree of transparency, this can lead to the situation where particular inflections in one of the languages are acquired earlier than in the other language. This is what has been called a **lead-lag pattern**. See Box 6.5 for more details.

Frequency of Occurrence. Both the Usage-based theory and the Constructivist account emphasise frequency of occurrence as a very important factor in the acquisition process. The Constructivist account assumes that a

---

Box 6.5: Lead-lag pattern

A lead-lag pattern can occur if the child's languages differ in the degree of morphological marking and/or the transparency of the morphological systems. The lead language will be the language that is more marked or transparent (or both), whereas the lag language will be the morphologically less marked (or transparent) language.

Serratrice (2001) investigated the simultaneous acquisition of English and Italian in a bilingual child. She found that the child's verb inflections in English were minimal at the age of 3, whereas in Italian, a number of different person and tense forms were produced at the same age.

This finding is compatible with the view of language-specific development and confirms a lead-lag pattern. However, Serratrice also points to similarities in the development of the child's two languages. In both cases, the forms are initially used with a small number of verbs, thereby pointing to slow and verb-specific acquisition of inflected forms (piecemeal acquisition), in line with the Usage-based theory of language acquisition.

'critical mass' of data is needed before a form is acquired. This leads to the possible assumption that bilinguals should be delayed in their acquisition of morphological forms, as they have had less exposure to the form compared with monolingual children.

Paradis (2010) investigated the acquisition of verb morphology in 43 school-age French–English bilingual children aged 6 in Edmonton, Canada. While English is the majority language in Edmonton and French speakers are a minority, the children all attended French immersion schools.

We saw in Chapter 5 that children's home language had a significant effect on their vocabulary levels. For this reason, the children in the study were also grouped according to their home language: mainly French, French and English, or mainly English. The children were tested in English with a standardised verb task, the Test of Early Grammatical Impairment (TEGI) – see the section on assessment of grammar for more details about the test. The children were given both the third person singular task and the past tense task as well as the grammaticality judgement task. In this task, the children had to judge the sentences of two toy robots who were supposedly learning English. The structures that children had to judge included tense errors, agreement errors and dropped *ing* forms. For example, in the sentence *he running away*, the auxiliary verb *is* is missing, which carries the tense in the sentence. An agreement error is given in the sentence *he am hurt*, where the form of the verb *am* does not match with the third person pronoun. A sentence with dropped *ing* is given in *he is smile*.

The results of the first two tasks of the TEGI showed that the children who mainly spoke French at home had the lowest proportions of correct verb endings for both the third person singular as well as past tense. This was expected, as they had the lowest input in English. Their proportion of correct verb endings was below that of the monolingual as well as the bilingual norm. On the other hand, the children who spoke French and English equally at home, and the children who mainly spoke English at home, performed at similar levels on both structures. Their scores were lower compared to the monolingual norm.

For the grammaticality judgement task, the results were similar. Again, the children who mainly spoke French at home had lower scores than the other two groups. The scores of the other two groups differed according to the structure. Performance on the dropping of –*ing* was similar, but there was a difference for tense errors, where the group who mainly spoke English at home, had a higher proportion of correct responses compared with the bilingual group.

The differences between the group who spoke mainly French at home and the other two groups, are seen as confirmation of the effect of frequency on the acquisition of inflectional marking. However, the finding that the target structure also had an effect on the proportion of children's correct responses, shows an interaction between both frequency and complexity of the structure, as predicted in the Constructivist account.

While we have seen effects of input frequency on vocabulary and the acquisition of morphology, Unsworth (2014) investigated whether input frequency also affects different domains of language. She compared children's judgements on gender marking in Dutch with their acquisition of restrictions on word order to express different meanings (scrambling). This is explained in examples 6.1 and 6.2.

Example 6.1

De jongen	heft		geen	(niet + een)	vis	gevangen
The boy	has.3ʳᵈ SG	no	(not	one)	fish	caught.PARTICIPLE

'the boy has caught no fish'

Example 6.2

De jongen	heft		(een vis)	niet	gevangen
The boy	has.3ʳᵈ SG	(a	fish)	not	caught.PARTICIPLE

'The boy has not caught a fish'

The examples make use of different types of negative elements, *geen* versus *niet*. In example 6.1, the negation *geen* (not one) relates to the noun and emphasises that no fish has been caught. On the other hand, the negation *niet* in example 6.2 relates to the verb and suggests that there is a (particular) fish that the boy has not caught.

Unsworth (2014) included 109 bilingual English–Dutch children aged 5–17 in the study. Of these, there were 29 children aged 5–6 that were compared with 19 monolinguals of the same age. The bilinguals showed effects of input frequency in terms of their judgements of gender marking but there were no significant differences between the monolingual and bilingual children. Scrambling, on the other hand, was found to be acquired in line with monolingual acquisition and did not depend on input frequency. These results suggest that frequency effects do not affect language acquisition in the same way for all areas.

Cross-linguistic influences. In Chapter 2, we discussed the effect of contact between language, which can lead to cross-linguistic influences, particularly at the interface of two modules of grammar, pragmatics and syntax. We discussed an example of an Italian–German child who seems to drop subjects in both Italian and German.

Do cross-linguistic influences delay the acquisition of inflectional morphology? As we said in Chapter 2, cross-linguistic structures occur only when certain conditions are fulfilled and depend on the particular combination of languages. In as much as they are a way of using the other language as a way to solve a particular problem or a bridge to fill a particular structural gap, the use of cross-linguistic structures is not as such delaying the child's development.

From the factors and evidence considered in Chapter 2, it does not seem that morpho-syntactic development in bilingual acquisition is delayed by cross-linguistic influences as such. Rather, the speed of acquisition of morpho-syntax in bilinguals seems to depend on a combination of factors, including the structure to be acquired, the degree of transparency and the salience of the inflections, as well as the frequency of occurrence. Most of these factors feature in the Constructivist account.

Issues for sequentially bilingual children

In the previous section, several factors were considered that affect the acquisition of inflectional marking in simultaneously bilingual children. For sequentially bilingual children, exposure starts later, and the frequency of exposure might be lower than for monolinguals. From the results of the Paradis (2010) study, it seems that sequentially bilingual children's acquisition of inflectional morphology is lower than that of simultaneous bilingual children, due to the fact that these learners have a lower exposure to the other language.

A longitudinal study conducted by Jia & Fuse (2007) is interesting in this context, as they investigated the acquisition of six morphemes over a period of 5 years. These were third person –s, regular and irregular past tense, the auxiliary *do* (DO), the auxiliary be (BE) and the progressive –*ing* form. Their subjects were 10 Mandarin Chinese L1 speakers who arrived in New York between the ages of 5 and 12. Two of the oldest subjects had some instruction in English before they arrived. They all attended English-speaking schools in the area of New York, where 70% of the students at the schools were English native speakers.

The subjects were tested from the time they had attended immersion schools for a period of about 3 months and continued for a period of 5 years. Subjects were recorded during free conversations, and their use of morphology in obligatory contexts was analysed. Mastery in this context was defined as correct use in 80% of obligatory contexts. Box 6.6 gives the average time from start of immersion until each of the morphemes was used in obligatory contexts.

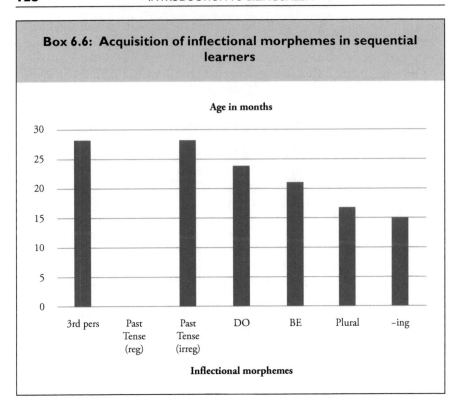

Box 6.6: Acquisition of inflectional morphemes in sequential learners

The chart in Box 6.6 shows that the –*ing* form was the morpheme that took the least amount of time to acquire and occurred in the free conversation of all of the participants after an average of 15 months. This is in line with the morpheme emerging first in monolingual children's acquisition of English.

Plurals were the second morpheme that emerged in the language of the participants after an average of almost 17 months. This is similar to monolingual L1 acquisition in terms of the order of acquisition. On the other hand, past tense and the third person were the slowest to emerge. Irregular past tense forms and the third person form were used by only a few participants. The regular past tense was the hardest to acquire and none of the learners reached the 80% criterion after 5 years. This is different from the acquisition of the regular past tense in first language learners, where this form is acquired between 26 and 48 months according to Brown (1973). The acquisition of the remaining morphemes varied across learners.

When grouping learners by age group (5–9 and 12–16), Jia & Fuse (2007) found that with time, younger learners showed a higher percentage of correct morpheme use for the most difficult morphemes, regular and irregular past tense. However, there was no difference between learners in terms of error type. All errors were errors of omission where the verbs were not inflected. This is again in contrast with the occurrence of overregularisations in first language learners.

STUDY ACTIVITY 6.2

1.   What is a lead-lag pattern in simultaneous bilingual acquisition? How can this pattern arise?
2.   How does the acquisition of tense morphemes differ between simultaneous and sequential language learners?

Assessment of grammar in different learners

This section gives an overview of different tests for measuring children's grammar skills. Similar to what we said for vocabulary measures, testing children's grammatical knowledge is important to ensure that a child is developing normally, but also to exclude the possibility of a disorder in the area of grammar.

Normative tests

When children have progressed to the multiword stage, and have started to use inflectional morphemes, it is desirable to assess their language development both in terms of comprehension and production. One tool to assess English-speaking children's language is the New Reynell Developmental Language Scales (NRDLS) (Edwards, Letts & Sinka, 2011).

The NRDLS consists of a comprehension and a production scale and is standardised on 1,266 children aged between 3 and 7. Picture books and toys support the activities designed to assess children's production and comprehension of a variety of different structures, including noun and verb morphology, comprehension of sentences including complex structures, and sentence imitation as well as sentence inferencing and a grammaticality judgement task.

The test also provides a multilingual toolkit with guidelines as to how to adapt the test to other languages and other cultures, though the test does not supply norms for children with different first languages.

Receptive Grammar tasks. The Test of Reception of Grammar (TROG 2) (Bishop, 2003) measures comprehension of 20 different structures (including negatives, passives, singular and plural inflection, as well as relative clauses, both subject as well as object relatives) and they are tested in blocks of four items. The child hears a sentence and has to point to the correct picture out of an array of four pictures. There are 80 test items in total. A child passes a block only if all four items are answered correctly. The test is discontinued when the child fails five blocks in a row. The test can be used from the age of 4 upwards and has been used with children as well as adults.

The TROG is now available as an electronic version and has been adapted for some other languages, for example German (TROG-D), but there is no bilingual version of the test available.

Box 6.7 outlines the Early Language and Intercultural Acquisition Studies (ELIAS) grammar task, which was developed for use in the ELIAS project, which was outlined in Chapter 5. The test consists of 36 items and has an A

Box 6.7: ELIAS grammar task

The ELIAS grammar task is a receptive test where the child has to choose one out of three options when hearing a particular structure.

Target Structure: *The dog who looked at the cat had an apple.*

The child has to select the picture that represents the structure among three pictures, all showing the referents *dog, cat* and *apple*. In picture (1) the dog is looking at the cat and the cat has the apple, in (2) the dog is not looking at the cat and the cat has an apple, in (3) the dog has the apple and is looking at the cat, hence this is the target.

An earlier version of the task has been tested with 30 English monolingual children, 30 German–English bilingual children and 148 early German L2 learners learning English in an immersion setting.

Exposure to English was found to affect the scores in the grammar task: the monolingual English children achieved the highest scores, followed by the bilinguals, and L2 learners were lowest. A comparison between monolinguals and bilinguals shows differences, particularly in relation to comprehension of pronouns and SVO word order. The L2 learners were lowest on comprehension of agreement and recognised plurals and possessives better than third person singular marking.

---

and B version, where the same structures are tested. The items in the later version include plural, negation, pronouns and passives as well as relatives.

The results show that while exposure to a language affects the comprehension of grammar, bilingual and sequential learners do not necessarily follow the same pattern in grammar comprehension as monolingual children.

Productive Grammar tasks. The South Tyneside Assessment of Syntactic Structures (STASS) (Armstrong & Ainley, 2007) is based on the grammatical development profiles put forward by Crystal, Fletcher & Garman (1989) and aimed at children aged 3–5. The grammatical profiles provide information about the children's language including the clause, phrase and word levels of different developmental stages. The pictures in the STASS aim for the child to produce the structures that are characteristic of each stage. The STASS has been used with bilingual children as well as children who speak non-standard English, though there are no specific norms for these populations.

Test of Early Grammatical Impairment (TEGI). One of the tasks that is used in studies of morphological development in different child populations is the TEGI (Rice & Wexler, 2001). The TEGI is a tool for clinical assessment and focuses on verb morphology, as this is an area of difficulty for children who have been diagnosed with Specific Language Impairment (SLI).

The tests consist of five different subtests, which are called probes. There is a phonological probe, a third person singular probe, a past tense probe, a BE/DO probe and a grammaticality judgement probe. The phonological probe is

---

Box 6.8: TEGI past tense probe

The past tense probe consists of 18 items. Each item has two pictures, one where a person is shown carrying out an action, the other where the person has completed the action.

Structure: *The boy is painting.* - *The boy painted.*

In the first picture, a boy is painting a fence yellow. The experimenter points out 'Here the boy is painting'. This is followed by the second picture where the fence is all yellow and the paintbrush is back in the paint pot. The experimenter says 'Now he is done. Tell me what he did'.

As the activity is completed in the second picture, the child is expected to use a past tense verb. Overall, the past tense probe includes 10 regular and eight irregular verbs.

---

included to ensure that the child can produce phonemes that are relevant for the production of tense marking, such as the phonemes /s/, /z/, /t/ and /d/ in final position in a word. The probe consists of 20 pictures representing objects and actions which the child is asked to name.

The third person singular probe consists of 10 pictures of people who are engaged in a number of actions. The child looks at the picture and is asked to say what the person does. For example, the practice item shows a teacher at a board. The child is expected to use a verb with a third person ending, such as *she teaches*.

The past tense probe is outlined in Box 6.8. The BE/DO probe is designed to test children's ability to produce the *be* verb as a copula or auxiliary and to produce *do* as an auxiliary verb. The procedure involves a puppet task where the child has to ask the puppet questions and make statements, using the two verbs. There are 36 items in this probe.

Finally, in the grammaticality judgement probe, the child has to judge the sentences of two robots who are presented as learners of English. There are 35 sentences including tense errors, agreement errors and dropping of *ing*, as outlined earlier in the study by Paradis (2010).

The TEGI was standardised on 393 English-speaking children between 3 and 7, as well as 444 children between 3 and 9 who were diagnosed as having a language disorder.

Bilingual grammatical assessment

Adapted TEGI. Assessing bilingual children's grammatical skills is particularly important in the context of what is normal and what constitutes a language impairment. Errors that are characteristic of language impairment (such as omitting grammatical morphemes) can also occur in simultaneous, and particularly in sequential, bilingual development, thus leading to a possible overidentification of bilingual children as being language impaired (Bedore & Peña, 2008). This means it is desirable to test children in both their languages

---

Box 6.9: Past tense in English and French

In this study, past tense acquisition in bilinguals was compared to monolinguals in English and French. Both languages have comparable structures. The TEGI was adapted for French by choosing and depicting suitable verbs in a similar way.

English	French
Regular past tense	
*the girl **picked** some flowers.*	*la fille **a** **mangé** une pomme.* the girl has eaten an apple.
Irregular past tense	
*the man **rode** a horse.*	*le garçon **a** **suivi** la fille.* the boy has followed the girl.

---

to establish whether the grammar of both languages is developed in line with the children's age and exposure. An example is outlined in Box 6.9.

In the adaptation of the TEGI for French (Paradis et al. 2011), comparable regular and irregular verbs were chosen and pictured. However, a general difference between the past tense in the two languages is that English past tense is formed either by adding the suffix *–ed* to the verb, or by using the irregular past tense form of the verb. In French, past tense is expressed in the form of the *passé composé*, which consists of the auxiliary verb *avoir* (have), or *être* (be), together with the participle form of the verb. Examples are given in examples 6.3 and 6.4.

Example 6.3

J'ai	parlé	avec lui
I have.1st SG	spoken.PARTICIPLE	with him

'I have spoken with him'

Example 6.4

Il	a	vendu	la maison
He	has.3rd SG	sold.PARTICIPLE	the house

'He sold the house'

Example 6.3 shows the regular participle form of the verb *parler* (speak) ending in the vowel *–é*, whereas example 6.4 includes the participle form of the irregular verb *vendre* (sell) which is *vendu*.

In the study, 23 bilingual children aged 4 were compared to their French monolingual counterparts in the acquisition of past marking in French and to the TEGI norms for English. The language background of the children was determined in more detail with the use of a parental questionnaire, and children were subdivided into a group who had more English and a second group with more French.

A comparison of the correct scores for children's English past tense forms with the TEGI norms shows that the bilingual children had lower mean scores on both, regular and irregular past tense forms. A comparison between the bilinguals and the French monolingual children also shows a similar discrepancy. When the bilinguals were compared according to subgroups, the children who heard more French at home achieved higher correct scores in both regular and irregular French past tense forms than the group who heard more English. On the other hand, the group who heard more English at home had a higher score in the regular past tense forms of the TEGI, but not the irregular ones.

Overall, these results confirm the relationship between language input that was discussed earlier. In the case of this study, an existing test was adapted for the other language of the bilinguals. However, this method is not always possible and requires new tests for different languages.

Bilingual Narratives. A different form of bilingual assessment was developed by Gagarina et al. (2015). The assessment is called Language Impairment Testing in Multilingual Setting: Multilingual Assessment Instrument for Narratives (LITMUS-MAIN) and assesses understanding and production of narratives in bilingual children between 3 and 9.

By using story retell as a form of assessment, both children's comprehension and productive language can be monitored, and it is possible to determine children's grammar levels at particular ages. The stories have been trialled with monolingual children in a number of languages, as well as bilingual children with different language combinations.

There are four stories that are comparable in terms of complexity and suitability for children from different cultural, linguistic and socio-economic backgrounds. An example of a story is given in Box 6.10.

Stories are comparable in terms of the number of referents as well as the internal structure. The story in Box 6.10 has three referents, a dog, a mouse and a boy. The words in italics refer to the internal states of the referents. The story also includes goals that the referents are trying to achieve, as well as attempts and outcomes. For example, the dog wants to catch a mouse, as well as grab a sausage a bit later on. In his attempt to catch the mouse, the dog leaps forward, yet the outcome is that the mouse runs away quickly.

So far, data has been collected from 267 monolingual and 302 bilingual children aged 3 to 9 with 14 different language pairs. Overall, they found that children's scores for story structure components increased with age. The bilinguals achieved similar scores in both languages compared with the monolingual children. These results suggest that the narrative instrument is a useful tool in the assessment of bilingual children and shows less bias than the normative tests outlined in the current chapter, as well as Chapter 5.

Box 6.10: Bilingual narrative example

Pictures 1/2:

One day there was a *playful* dog who saw a grey mouse sitting near a tree. He leaped forward because he wanted to catch it. Meanwhile, a *cheerful* boy was coming back from shopping with a bag and a balloon in his hands. He looked at the dog chasing the mouse.

Pictures 3/4:

The mouse ran away quickly and the dog bumped into the tree. He hurt himself and was very angry. The boy was so *startled* that the balloon slipped out of his hand. When he *saw* his balloon flying into the tree he cried: 'Oh no, no, there goes my balloon'. He was *sad* and wanted to get his balloon back. Meanwhile, the dog *noticed* the boy's bag and *thought* 'I want to grab a sausage'.

Pictures 5/6:

At the same time, the boy began pulling his balloon out of the tree. He did not *notice* that the dog had grabbed a sausage. In the end, the dog was very *pleased*.

STUDY ACTIVITY 6.3

1.   What particular instruments have been used to assess monolingual and bilingual children's grammatical skills?
2.   What difficulties arise in the assessment of bilinguals in both their languages?

The mental representation of regular and irregular morphology

Morphological marking is often described in terms of regular and irregular paradigms, as we have seen in the assessment in the previous section. Regular marking can be described in terms of a particular rule which can be applied to the stem form of a particular word. Irregular items, on the other hand, do not adhere to this rule, and form exceptions which need to be learnt on an item by item basis. This had led to the suggestion that there are two different cognitive mechanisms underlying the processes of regular and irregular inflections.

The Words and Rules Theory

The Words and Rules Theory was outlined in Pinker & Ullman (2002) and suggests that the human language faculty has two distinct mechanisms that are activated when we retrieve a regular or irregular morpheme. The mechanism for retrieving irregular inflections is lexically based and involves the retrieval of a form that is stored together with the base form. This means that in order to retrieve an irregular plural such as *mice*, the item is retrieved from the lexicon via the singular form *mouse*. Similarly, an irregular past tense form, such as *sang*, is retrieved from the lexicon via the present form *sing*. In order to account for the similar pattern found in several irregular verbs, such as *sing-sang*, *ring-rang*, similar-sounding words are linked via their phonemes, so that the patterns can be associated.

In order to retrieve a regular form, a rule-based mechanism is activated, such that a particular ending like *–s* for plural or *–ed* for past tense can be added to the word form if the lexically based mechanism has not been able to retrieve an irregular word form.

Proponents of the Words and Rules Theory have argued that most morphological systems have a default rule-based as well as a lexically based mechanism. Clahsen (2006) showed that lexically based forms have a 'frequency advantage', whereby high frequency word forms were more accurate, and were produced faster than low frequency forms, a pattern that was not found for regular forms.

Evidence for the existence of two distinct cognitive mechanisms comes from the overregularisations of children, as in *draw-ed* and *mouse-s*. Overregularisations always involve the overapplication of the rule-based mechanism to irregular forms, not the other way round.

Additionally, in adults with impairments that affect language, there is evidence that one of the mechanisms is more affected than the other. If this is the case, we can say that one of the mechanisms is selectively impaired. For example, dementia affects lexical knowledge, hence patients show a deficit in the lexical mechanism which in turn affects the retrieval of irregular forms. On the other hand, patients with Broca's aphasia are more affected in their retrieval of regular morphology.

The Words and Rules Theory works quite well for English, where the majority of noun and verb types are regular (98% and 83%), as outlined by Marcus, Brinkmann, Clahsen & Wiese (1995). The situation becomes more complex though when other languages are considered. Marcus et al., (1995) claim that the German *–s* plural is still the default form, even though the type frequency is very low (between 1% and 9%).

The Bybee model

Bybee (1995, 2006) takes a different approach to the way morphology is conceptualised. Her model is a Usage-based theory and recognises the importance of type and token frequency in the processing and storage of morphological strings. Frequently occurring forms get entrenched and are therefore more resistant to the application of productive patterns such as the regular past tense form.

Bybee's model does not postulate two different cognitive mechanisms. It assumes that the token frequency of a word results in different degrees of lexical strength. In English, words with a high token frequency are usually irregular, whereas words with a low token frequency follow a specific productive pattern, the regular past tense.

In line with models of semantic memory, Bybee also assumes that words have connections with other words, both in terms of phonological as well as semantic features (see Chapter 7). Again, the connections can vary in strength as well as in terms of the number of features that are shared. Words with high token frequency can be characterised as relatively autonomous and have weaker connections with other words, whereas lower frequency words have stronger connections. Bybee suggests that on this basis, high frequency words are better learnt on their own, whereas lower frequency words are better learnt in conjunction with related words.

Unlike models that claim that one single mechanism is sufficient for the derivation of both regular and irregular morphology (Rumelhart & McClelland, 1986), Bybee (1995) suggests two different processes, schemas, that can account for inflected forms. The first schema is *source-oriented*, which allows for a derivation of a form from a source via particular rules. The second schema is *product-oriented* and corresponds to generalisations over a group of derived forms, such as the group of verbs that follow a similar pattern (sing, ring, swing).

The product-oriented schema is different from the lexical mechanism proposed in the Words and Rules Theory because it is based on the phonological connections between members of this group of verbs. The regular English past tense is described as a source-oriented schema, yet it can also be product-oriented in that it includes verbs that do not change in the past tense form (put, cut, quit).

One source of evidence in support of the Words and Rules Theory has been the fact that children tend to overregularise the rule-based mechanism. Bybee's model, on the other hand, suggests that overgeneralisations are based on lexical patterns as well as type and token frequency. In cases where the two go together, as in the English regular past tense where the rule-based mechanism has a high type frequency (Marcus et al. 1995), though a much lower token frequency, the product-oriented schema is the default form. However, not all morphological patterns work in this way.

Take, for example, the German plural system. According to Marcus et al. (1995), there are five different plural forms (not counting vowel changes as separate forms). One form (the –s plural) is assumed to be the default form despite the fact that type frequency is less than 10%. The –s plural is used mainly for nouns that end in a vowel, common nouns or borrowings. Marcus et al. (1995) cite studies that have found a higher proportion of overgeneralisations of the –s plural compared to other plural forms. This would suggest that token frequency does not affect the use of the rule-based pattern.

However, when looking more closely at the use of the different plural forms in German, a different picture emerges. The particular affix used in German to mark plural on a noun depends on the gender of that noun. Contrary to Marcus et al. (1995), Bybee (1995) cites evidence to suggest that children overgeneralise the –en plural most often, the form that is commonly used for feminine nouns.

While Bybee does not deny that the German –s plural has the status of a default form that applies to common nouns, acronyms and borrowings, the fact that it has a low token frequency reduces its productivity. Contrary to Marcus et al. (1995), Bybee suggests that the assignment of the −*s* plural is not rule-based because it applies predominantly to nouns with a particular phonological shape.

Hence according to Bybee's Usage-based theory, morphological marking does not always have to follow a distinction between a rule-based and a lexically based mechanism. Rather, different patterns with different type frequencies and different degrees of productivity are possible.

Studies of regular and irregular morphology in bilinguals

The study of bilingual acquisition in relation to regular and irregular morphology can give an indication as to whether there is further evidence for the cognitive mechanisms involved in the Words and Rules Theory, or whether the acquisition pattern follows the type and token frequency encountered in the input. As bilingual children are assumed to receive less input in each of their languages compared to monolingual children, the token frequency of regular and irregular verb forms should also be lower. While the Words and Rules Theory assumes that token frequency only affects irregular verb forms, as they are lexically based and generally have a high token frequency, bilinguals should show a slower rate of acquisition only for irregular verb forms. On the other hand, according to the Bybee model, both regular and irregular verb forms are frequency dependent, hence bilingual children should show a slower acquisition rate for both regular and irregular forms.

We have already discussed the Paradis et al. (2011) study earlier. The study compared monolingual French–speaking children with French–English bilinguals in terms of their acquisition of regular and irregular past tense forms. In addition to the monolingual-bilingual comparison, accuracy ratings for regular and irregular past tense forms were also compared. It was found that all children were more accurate with regular past tense than irregular forms.

The bilingual children were divided into subgroups and compared on their scores for regular and irregular verbs. While the subgroup with more input in French had higher scores for the French task than the English subgroup on both regular and irregular forms, the group who spoke more English at home did not have higher scores on English irregular past tense forms. This is not in line with the Words and Rules Theory, as irregular forms are assumed to be affected by token frequency. This effect can possibly be explained by the high type and token frequency of French regular verbs. Overall, the results are interpreted as a confirmation that input frequency has an effect on acquisition, as suggested by the Bybee (2006) model.

In a different study, Rispens & De Brie (2015) investigated the production of regular and irregular past tense in 11 Dutch–Hebrew bilingual children of the age of 7, and compared the findings with age-matched and vocabulary-matched younger children. They used tasks similar to the TEGI for existing regular and irregular verb forms, but their tasks also included a number of novel verb forms.

Similar to the findings by Paradis et al. (2011), all groups showed higher scores for regular verb endings compared to irregular ones. However, there was no difference between monolingual age-matched children and bilinguals in the provision of the regular allomorphs for regular and novel verbs. The bilinguals were less accurate than age-matched monolinguals on irregular verbs and were at a similar level to the vocabulary-matched younger monolingual group. In terms of errors, the vocabulary-matched children tended to use the present tense form of the verb, whereas bilinguals were more likely to use the wrong allomorph. This is seen as a possible transfer from the other language, Hebrew.

STUDY ACTIVITY 6.4

1. Children go through a phase where they overregularise irregular past tense verb forms. How are these forms explained in the Words and Rules Theory and the Bybee model?
2. What do the findings on bilingual children's acquisition of morphology show about the influence of token frequency on acquisition?

SUMMARY

This chapter has considered the morpho-syntactic development of bilingual children. English can be described as a relatively sparsely inflected language, essentially consisting of the 14 morphemes listed by Brown (1973). Cross-linguistically, there are a number of languages that have a richer morphological system, yet acquisition of morpho-syntax is not slower than English. Children's acquisition of morphology is important in terms of proposed theoretical accounts as well as in order to understand possible factors that facilitate or hinder the acquisition process. While frequency of occurrence is one of the factors involved, there is evidence that other factors, such as the structure to be learnt, as well as the transparency of the structure, are important in determining monolingual as well as bilingual children's acquisition.

Similar to the issues in the assessment of vocabulary, tests for grammar are language-specific and normed on samples of monolingual children. Bilingual children often score below monolingual norms. An example of a bilingual assessment instrument is the narrative tool that was outlined, as there is a possibility of less bilingual bias.

In this chapter, we have also reviewed models like the Words and Rules Theory that assume two different cognitive mechanisms in relation to regular and irregular morphological forms and contrasted this with the Bybee model that emphasises type and token frequency as an important factor in processing and storing morphological strings. While the acquisition of regular and irregular verb forms discussed as evidence is more in line with the latter model, the pattern is not as clear-cut as expected.

FURTHER READING

For further details of the morpho-syntactic development in English and in particular, the Brown stages, see Brown (1973). Children's cross-linguistic development in different languages is outlined in Slobin (1985). The ELIAS project is outlined in detail in Kersten et al. (2010). Further details for the narrative task are available from http://www.zas.gwz-berlin.de/zaspil56.html. For an outline of regular and irregular items, and the Words and Rules Theory, see Pinker (2015). The Bybee model is outlined in Bybee (2006).

Bilingual Language Processing

7

This chapter gives more background to the psycholinguistics of bilingualism. First, we look at the mental lexicon in more detail in relation to both simultaneous and sequential bilinguals. Next, we'll investigate the question as to how words are connected in the mind of bilinguals and what happens when language is understood or produced.

While some of the assessment methods discussed in Chapters 5 and 6 are able to give some idea of the developing language system for both languages, they can only capture a specific aspect of the child's system at a given time. In general, they cannot give information about the way the stimuli are processed.

The term **language processing** refers to the mental processes that are involved in understanding and speaking language. Bilingual processing refers to the mental processes in speakers of more than one language when understanding and speaking those languages. The mental processes involved include the access of particular words (mental lexicon), as well as retrieving grammatical information (including inflectional morphemes such as plural *–s*, present progressive *–ing*, past tense *–ed*, etc. and derivational morphemes, such as the prefix *un–* which is added to a verb to express a reversal of the action, the suffix *–er* which changes a verb to a noun describing the person carrying out the action, etc.).

The processes involved in bilinguals are not fundamentally different from those of monolingual speakers, however, there are a number of questions relating to the way the different language systems are stored in the mind and activated during language tasks.

Psycholinguistic methods

In order to gain an insight into the mental processes of speakers, it is not possible to rely on language output. A spoken sentence is the result of the mental processes, and therefore can only confirm that a speaker is able to process language, but not how mental processes have enabled the sentence to be produced.

Most of the tasks that were outlined in Chapters 5 and 6 are so-called **offline** tasks. Offline tasks measure behaviour that occurs as a result of a particular stimulus. For example, when a child points to a picture or gives a verbal response, what is measured is the result of the child processing the particular stimuli. An incorrect response to a picture suggests that the child has not yet acquired the particular object name or the structure associated with the picture. A correct response could be accidental (if the child points to a picture out of an array of several pictures) but if given systematically, a correct response shows that the child has indeed acquired the word or structure that is tested.

The development of new technologies has meant that the focus of investigations into bilingual processing, as well as bilingual acquisition, has changed. Rather than investigating how many words the subjects can understand or produce, researchers are interested in the underlying mechanisms that enable participants to comprehend and produce words and sentences.

The experimental methods that enable us to get information about the mental processes involved in processing language are outlined in the next section. They are so-called **online** tasks. They are online, because the measurements give us an indication of the mental effort involved, or the eye movements or brain activity during a particular task, which give us an insight into the processing taking place. We will outline each of these methods and discuss them in relation to children.

Reaction time measurements

Measuring reaction times is a method that has been used for some time in adult language processing. By measuring the reaction time of different types of stimuli, it is possible to get an idea of the complexity of processing the stimuli. Psycholinguistic experimental software, such as Superlab and E-prime, display trials and also measure the time it takes for subjects to complete the task (reaction times, measured in milliseconds). The basic idea is that stimuli that have a higher degree of complexity will result in the subject spending more time on processing the items, therefore the mean reaction time of these items will be higher.

A classic reaction time experiment that has been used in adult language processing is the lexical decision task (Meyer & Schvaneveldt, 1971). The task is outlined in Box 7.1. Subjects have to make a decision as to whether they recognise both words in word pairs that are presented on a computer screen. There were four different types of items with varying complexity. The first word pair consists of two words that are related in meaning (semantically similar). In the example, the words *cat* and *dog* are semantically related, not only because both describe animals, but also because both animals share a number of features: both have fur, four legs, a tail, etc.

The second word pair are words that are not related in meaning. For example, the words *tree* and *cable* have very little in common. A tree belongs to the larger category of *plant* and occurs naturally, whereas a cable is a man-made object. They differ in size, colour, etc. The third word pair consists of a word

---

Box 7.1: Lexical decision task

In the lexical decision task, subjects see words or word pairs on the computer screen and have to respond with 'yes' if the word or both words are recognised as words, or with 'no' if one of the words is not a recognisable word. In the task by Meyer and Schvaneveldt (1971), there are four different word pairs:

Word pair	Example
Real pairs related in meaning	*cat* and *dog*
Real pairs not related in meaning	*tree* and *cable*
Pairs where one of the words is not a real word	*table* and *skell* (2nd word is not real) *tolag* and *mouse* (1st word not real)
Non-word pairs	*rond* and *blimp*

The results show that semantically related word pairs were responded to fastest: average reaction times were 855ms for related word pairs compared to 940ms for unrelated word pairs. For pairs where one string was a non-word, the position of the non-word made a difference: if the non-word occurred as the bottom string, the average reaction time was 1,087ms to reject the pair, compared to 904ms if the non-word occurred as the top string. Word pairs where both strings were non-words were rejected in 884ms on average.

---

and a string that is not a word. In the example *table* and *skell*, the second string is not a word in the English language. The participants need to realise that they have to reject the word pair for this reason. In the fourth word pair, both strings are not real words. The strings *rond* and *blimp* do not exist as words in English and do not have a meaning assigned to them.

The findings show that the subjects were fastest at responding correctly to the semantically related words. This is because of the meaning relationship between them. As we shall see a bit later, the mental lexicon is organised in such a way that related words are stored close together. This means that when we hear a word, such as *apple*, this word is activated in our mind, together with related words, in this case other types of fruit. We can also say that the first word **primes** the second word.

Priming is a process where a stimulus has an effect on the processing of a second stimulus. For example, if you see a picture of an apple and then a picture of a pear, the second picture is named faster. In the context of the lexical decision task, the first word acts as a prime and makes it easier for subjects to access the second, related word. This is why subjects are fastest to react to the related word pairs. For word pairs where there is no semantic relationship, there is no priming, therefore the average reaction times are generally slower than for related words.

In word pairs where only one of the strings is a real word, it matters which string is read first. Meyer and Schvaneveldt (1971) found that word pairs where the non-word occurred first were faster than word pairs where the non-word occurred second. This is because the non-word signals that the pair can be rejected. When the order of the strings is reversed, and the real word is read first, the decision whether or not to reject the pair depends on the second word. Finally, making a decision on strings of letters where both are not real words is again more straightforward, as the recognition of only one of the words as a non-word is sufficient to reject the pair.

In the context of children, we have seen in Chapter 5 that reaction times have been measured for monolingual children aged 5 in a picture-naming task which included objects and actions. In Chapter 8, we shall see more examples of experiments involving monolingual and bilingual children where this methodology has been used. This shows it is possible to gain insights into children's language processing by applying this methodology.

Eye fixations

One of the new technologies that measures online processing is eye tracking. Eye tracking enables us to measure where subjects are looking when they see a visual display and hear a word or a sentence that directs them to locate a particular item.

The visual display typically consists of line drawings of objects or semi-realistic scenes. This design is known as a **Visual World Paradigm** (Huettig, Rommers & Meyer, 2011). While the subject is engaged in the task, the eye tracker records their eye fixations and movements. The eye-tracking software combines the eye fixations and the visual display such that the eye fixations during the task can be measured and analysed. The mechanics of eye tracking are outlined in Box 7.2.

Similar to reaction time measurements, eye fixations are taken as evidence of the mental processes involved in a particular task. As subjects identify the target, eye fixations to the location of the target increase over time. If there is a competition between related targets, the eye fixations to the target and the competitor give an indication of the degree of the competition.

Box 7.2: Eye tracking

In eye-tracking equipment, eye fixations are measured via a device that is either fixed to the bottom of a computer screen or mounted onto a glasses frame in case of a mobile eye tracker (eye-tracking glasses).

Non-ionising infrared light is used as a light source that is directed towards the eye of the participant. In this way, the movement of the pupil can be captured by a camera while the participant is looking at a display on the computer screen or mapped onto a video recording taken from a recorder in the glasses.

Let us look at an example. Marian, Blumenfeld & Boukrina (2008) used a Visual World Paradigm consisting of four pictures which were displayed in the four corners of a computer screen. One of the pictures corresponded to a particular word that the subjects heard. Another picture sounded similar to the target word. For example, the words *hat* and *hut* only differ by one phoneme. When subjects hear the word *hut*, their eye fixations increasingly focus on the corresponding picture of a hut. However, the presence of a picture of a *hat* means that this picture is a possible competitor. If subjects are affected by words that sound similar to the target, it is expected that they will fixate on the competitor picture more than the other non-target pictures until they have identified the target picture and fixate on the target.

The study measured the proportion of subjects' eye fixations to the different pictures to gain insight into the way a spoken word was processed. A possible pattern of fixations for the task is given in Box 7.3, where each line represents a different picture, an **area of interest** (AOI). The graph gives the proportion of fixations for each AOI over a period of time, measured in milliseconds.

In the Marian, Blumenfeld and Boukrina (2008) study, the competitor was a word that was similar in sound to the target word. Similar to the graph in Box 7.3, the result showed that phonological similarity between the target and a competitor did result in a higher proportion of fixations to the competitor. This means that subjects were affected by the similar sounding word when processing the target word.

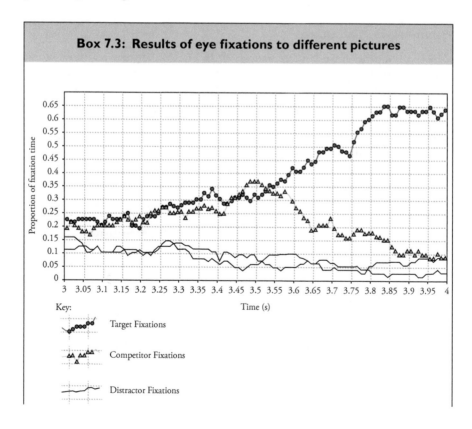

Box 7.3: Results of eye fixations to different pictures

Proportion of fixation time (y-axis)

Time (s) (x-axis)

Key:
Target Fixations
Competitor Fixations
Distractor Fixations

The chart displays the proportion of fixations to different areas of interest from a particular point in the display, usually from the point where the target word was heard. The different areas of interest are the target, the competitor and two distractors. It is clear from the chart that eye fixations to the target increase up until a certain point where participants react to the target stimulus, for example by clicking with the mouse on a particular picture.

The chart also shows quite a high proportion of competitor fixations up to a certain point, where the competitor fixations drop off. It can be assumed that the competitor fixations decrease because subjects have recognised the target and are increasingly focusing on it.

Fixations to the distractor are low throughout. This suggests that the subjects did not look much at the distractors while engaged in the task.

Children's eye gaze has been used in different methodologies. For example, in tasks involving preferential looking, children are presented with two displays and a stimulus. Their eye gaze to one of the displays reveals something about their understanding and processing of the stimulus. Eye-tracking studies have been carried out with children as well, though the process might not be suitable for young children, as they might not be able to focus on the screen long enough in order for the eye fixations to be measured accurately.

Event-related potentials

The method of event-related potentials (ERP) is another new technology that was developed to gain insight into the activity of the brain during particular tasks. Brain activity is measured while subjects carry out a particular task so that any changes in brain activity at any particular point can be observed.

In particular, the ERP technology measures the electrical activity at the scalp of a person via electrodes that are attached to the subject's head, and in turn, this indicates brain activity. The measurements are 'event related' because they are linked to a particular point of interest, such as the occurrence of a particular stimulus (Podesva & Sharma, 2013). This method measures the neurological response of subjects while processing a particular task, rather than their behavioural response, as in eye fixations. It is another online task.

The ERP methodology has been used to investigate different aspects of language processing, including speech perception, phonology, syntax and semantics. The brain responses to certain stimuli are represented in terms of waves that can be either positive (neuronal discharging) or negative (neuronal charging). Depending on when these responses reach their peak, the particular point in time is labelled. For example, an N100 response suggests that there is a negative wave which occurs about 100ms after the beginning of a particular stimulus. On the other hand, a P600 response refers to a positive wave that occurs about 600ms after the onset of a stimulus.

The processing of particular linguistic information is associated with particular neurological responses. For example, in grammaticality judgement tasks, where subjects have to decide whether a given sentence is grammatical or not, subjects tend to have a P600 response. In contrast, semantic violations have been found to trigger an N400, a negative wave after 400ms.

In addition to these labels, the brain activity that results from a particular stimulus can also be described in terms of its location, namely in terms of the hemisphere of the brain where it was observed, and in terms of the particular brain region. A negative wave that occurs in the frontal part of the left hemisphere is identified as left anterior negativity (LAN), and if this occurs early on, it is described as ELAN.

When processing sentences with morphological errors, subjects have been found to have a neural response consisting of a LAN around 400ms. On the other hand, an ELAN response was triggered when subjects were given an ungrammatical sentence such as *the food was in the eaten.*

In Chapter 6 we discussed regular and irregular morphology and suggestions that there are different cognitive mechanisms underlying both. In a study using ERPs, Newman et al. (2007) presented subjects with marked and unmarked regular and irregular past tense forms in a set of sentences. They found that violations of regular past tense forms first triggered a LAN, followed by a P600. On the other hand, violations of irregular past tense forms only triggered a P600. These results suggest partially different neurological responses for regular and irregular morphology.

The ERP technology has been used with children for the purpose of gaining further insights into the process of language acquisition, as well as the way children develop their ability to process language. As the methodology directly measures brain responses, it is independent of any particular behavioural stimuli from the child.

STUDY ACTIVITY 7.1

1. What is the difference between online and offline tasks? Give examples of each type of task.
2. Give examples of studies that have used lexical decisions, eye tracking and event-related potentials in studying language. What insights can be gained from using these methodologies?

The monolingual mental lexicon

In this section, we shall look more specifically at how words are stored in the mind. In order to express sentences, we need to be able to insert different words into different places in the sentence. The words are selected from our **mental lexicon**. While neuroscientists are concerned with questions such as where in the brain the words are stored, psychologists and psycholinguists focus on the organisation of the word store, and the factors that facilitate or hinder the access of a particular word.

In a study by Huth et al. (2016), areas of neuronal activity during a task where subjects listened to narratives were mapped onto regions of the brain. They found that there is no specific place in the brain where all words are stored. Words are distributed all over the brain and over both hemispheres. When looking closer at a particular region where a word was stored, it is clear that semantically similar words are stored in the same area.

For example, they found that words describing people are stored in the front of the brain. These include *women, father* and *mom*. On the other hand, terms like *child, innocent* and *children* are stored in the temporal lobe of the brain. The atlas also shows that the same words can occur in different places in the brain as well. Overall, the map of the brain in terms of word storage confirms that words that are related in meaning are stored in a similar area of the brain.

Semantic relationships between words

The really interesting question is, of course, how the different language words in a person who speaks more than one language are organised. But before looking at the bilingual mental lexicon, let us first discuss the monolingual mental lexicon in more detail. Aitchison (2012) describes the mental word store as a web of words, a network of connected words that overlap in meaning. Evidence for the mental lexicon as a semantic network comes not only from early studies, such as the lexical decision task outlined in Box 7.1, but also from **word association** studies (Aitchison, 2012, pp. 101–102). A word association task is a simple experiment where subjects are given a particular word, such as *child*, and they have to respond with the first word that comes to their mind. The word that subjects respond with allows some insight into the immediate neighbourhood of a word in the word store.

It has been found that during word association tasks, people come up with words that are related to the initial word in terms of meaning (Aitchison, 2012). For example, a frequent answer to *salt* is the word *pepper* and in answer to *dog* people often associate *cat*. The pairs *salt and pepper* as well as *dog and cat* often occur together in spoken language (collocation). In addition, they are both members of the same larger category. In the first example, both are *condiments* (substances used to flavour food) and in the second example, both are members of the category *animal*. The organisation of the mental word store is such that concepts that are similar in meaning are stored close to each other and can be accessed more quickly.

Semantically related words can have different types of relationships. One such relationship is that of **hyponymy**. This relationship is illustrated in Box 7.4. The words in such a relationship are related in meaning but differ in how specific the set is that they refer to. The words *apple* and *fruit* have this relationship, as the term *apple* refers to fruit that have specific characteristics (grows on trees, has an oval shape, the outer peel is green, yellow or red, the inside is softer and sweet, it has several small seeds inside), whereas the word *fruit* includes different edible objects, such as pears, oranges, bananas, etc. and also includes apples.

The word *fruit* is the **superordinate** term that includes the word *apple*, as an apple is a type of fruit. Terms that are at a similar level in terms of the set they describe, are **co-hyponyms**. *Apples* and *pears* are co-hyponyms as they are both contained within the category *fruit*.

As Box 7.4 also shows, the term *apple* can be both a hyponym of the larger category *fruit*, but at the same time be a superordinate category in relation to more specific categories that are specific types of apples, such as Cox, Golden Delicious and Braeburn.

In addition, specific features that apply to a certain concept are stored together with the concept. For example, the category *fruit* can be said to have the feature *is edible*, as well as *is sweet*, as fruit generally has these two characteristics. The items lower down the hierarchy all have the features of the category at the top. In addition, the hyponyms of fruit that are listed in Box 7.4 have specific characteristics relating to their shape or colour.

Hyponymy is not the only relationship between words. For example, in response to the word *butterfly*, the word *wing* was found to be a common response. While butterflies have wings, a wing is not a type of butterfly, instead, a wing is a part of a butterfly. This type of relationship is called a **meronymy** (part-whole relationship).

Box 7.5 illustrates this relationship for the category *bird*. Both *wing* and *bill* are parts of the bird, and the category *wing* in turn has parts, such as *feathers*.

We have outlined two types of relationships that hold between nouns, however, there are more relationships and they involve other word classes. One of them is **antonymy**, where words relate in the sense that they are opposite in meaning. For example, the adjectives *hot* and *cold* are antonyms because they are on opposite sides of the temperature scale.

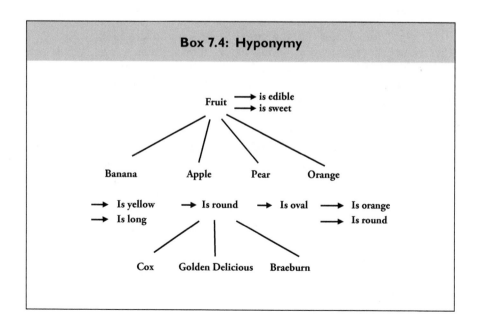

Box 7.4: Hyponymy

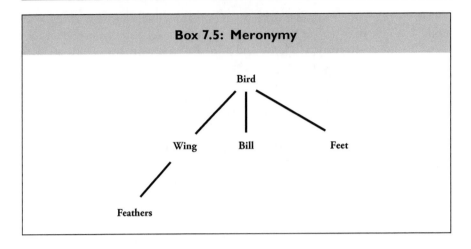

Box 7.5: Meronymy

A systematic way of illustrating different semantic relationships between different words is given in Word Net (Miller, 1995), an online lexical database that includes semantic relationships for different word classes, as well as different semantic relations between words. Verbs are an interesting category in this respect, as they mostly have a 'shallow' structure and do not fit into the kind of relationship that we have discussed for nouns. An exception is the verb *communicate*, as there are different ways in which communication can take place. For example, *talk*, *whisper* and *text* are all ways of communicating.

Word access

Accessing a word means that the stored concept in the mind is activated, such that the speaker is able to recognise the word or produce it (e.g. in a picture-naming task). When the word is activated, it is assumed that concepts that are close by also become activated to some extent. For example, when a word such as *bird* is activated, similar words such as *robin* (a type of bird), *fish* (an animal) and *animal* are also activated.

This can explain why we tend to choose semantically related words in word association tasks: a word and the related concept is activated and this in turn partially activates related concepts. The word that comes to mind is chosen from an already partially activated word concept. The types of words that are activated are not just from the same word class. Associations are often related to the given concept in different ways, for example parts of the associated concept or its characteristics are also in a semantic relationship to the stimulus word.

The related concepts that are partially activated can, for example, represent attributes of the stimulus word. When asked for a response to the word *fire*, subjects might think of the adjectives *hot* or *red* as this is what a fire looks like or feels like.

Models of semantic memory

An early model of semantic memory was suggested by Collins and Quillian (1969) which is based on the relationship of hyponymy that was discussed in the last section. It assumes that the mental representations of words are organised in a hierarchy where the most general categories are at the top and the most specific ones are at the bottom, as outlined in Box 7.4.

Word concepts are stored together with their semantic features. For example, a specific feature of birds is that they can fly, or that they have feathers. Therefore, the features *can fly* and *has feathers* are stored together with the concept *bird*. It is assumed that every time we mentally move to a higher or lower level of the hierarchy, or access one of the features, the mental effort takes time. On the other hand, this model cannot explain the semantic relationship between words like *child* and *innocent* which were found to be stored in a similar location in the brain.

As a result of the shortcomings of the early model, Collins and Loftus (1975) introduced the **spreading activation theory** of semantic processing. This theory assumes that concepts are organised within a network of semantically related nodes. They do not specify the type of semantic relationships between words but assume a network of interconnected nodes. An example of such a network is given in Box 7.6. You can see that a concept like *rose* can have connections to a variety of semantically related concepts. On the one hand, there is a connection to related concepts at the same level, for example, co-hyponyms such as *lily*. On the other hand, *rose* is also connected to the superordinate term *flower*. But the network also allows this concept to connect to colour words such as *red* and *white*, as well as the meronym *thorn*.

Nodes in the network have a particular resting activation. When a particular word, such as *rose*, is heard, it activates the concept associated with the word and this activation is then assumed to spread to connected nodes.

Spreading activation thereby can explain the concept of priming. Priming occurs when a stimulus presented after another stimulus affects the recognition process. As we saw earlier, in a lexical decision task, the word pair *bread butter* is reacted to faster compared to unrelated words such as *table cloud*. Spreading activation theory can explain this effect by assuming that the spreading activation temporarily lowers the activation threshold of a word that is related to the first stimulus, therefore reaction times will be faster.

Collins and Loftus (1975) assumed that the conceptual representations are also linked to a lexical network which is organised according to phonemic and orthographic similarity. This can explain phonological and orthographic priming. When presented with a word, for example *crab*, and then with a second stimulus that is similar to the first either in terms of sound or the spelling, for example *crib*, the reaction time of the second stimulus is lower. This shows that similarity at different levels has an effect on processing time.

One of the criticisms of the spreading activation theory is that it does not take into account whether the particular representation of a particular concept that subjects come across, is **prototypical** of the concept. A prototypical member of a particular category displays all the features and is easily recognisable as a representative of the concept. Take, for example, a picture of a sparrow to represent the concept of a *bird* in Box 7.5. The size and the features of a sparrow are more prototypical of the category *bird*, than, for example, an ostrich. An ostrich is much larger than a prototypical bird, and the feature *can fly* does not apply.

Box 7.6: Spreading activation theory

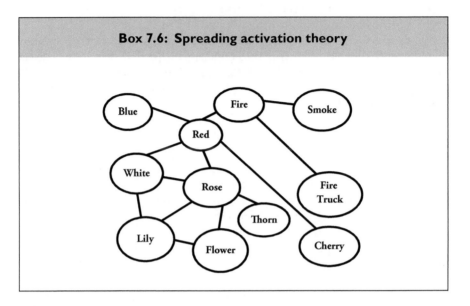

STUDY ACTIVITY 7.2

1. Give examples of different semantic relationships between words. Are there differences for different types of words?
2. Can spreading activation theory account for different relationships between words?

Models of the bilingual mental lexicon

Having considered models of the monolingual lexicon, we shall now discuss the organisation of the bilingual mental word store. While the way concepts are organised is not different from the monolingual word store, the question is how the two language systems are linked to the conceptual level, and in what way they interact with each other. As we discussed in Chapter 5, translation equivalents are acquired quite early, suggesting that children are aware of the link between words from different languages and can use equivalents in the different contexts.

Back in Chapter 1, we discussed Weinreich's (1953) classification into co-ordinate, compound and subordinate bilinguals. In co-ordinate bilingualism it is assumed that word forms and concepts of the bilingual are both separate, which suggests that the bilingual has two completely separate bilingual lexicons. In compound bilingualism, there is an assumed common meaning representation, but the word forms differ. This suggests that the bilingual mental lexicon has a shared conceptual level with links to word forms in either language. Finally, subordinate bilingualism assumes that words in the weaker language are connected through words in the first language. We shall consider different models of the bilingual lexicon and how they relate to Weinreich's classification.

Bilingual dual coding theory

An early model of the bilingual lexicon was suggested by Paivio & Desrochers (1980). In general, they suggested that information can be coded in two ways, either visually or verbally. This is known as the dual coding theory and is illustrated in Box 7.7. Dual coding brings together two different cognitive mechanisms, the processing of perceptual information (image system) on the one hand, and the verbal system on the other.

When processing an image, we have to recognise the objects or object that is represented, which in turn activates the relevant stored concepts. For example, when seeing a picture of a bird, the concept of the word is activated. On the other hand, when we hear a word, we recognise the sound sequence and in turn activate the same concept. The model suggests that objects are coded in two ways: in terms of image representations and as verbal representations. In other words, an object can be described verbally, using the label that is commonly assigned, but it also has a corresponding concept that includes the perceptual information relating to the object. In the case of *bird*, it is the word itself as well as perceptual information, such as the bird having wings, feathers, a beak, etc.

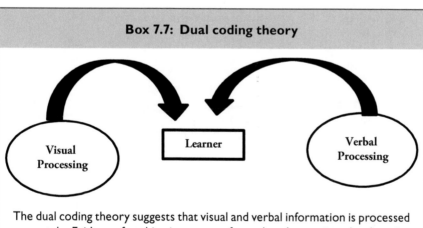

Box 7.7: Dual coding theory

Visual Processing — Learner — Verbal Processing

The dual coding theory suggests that visual and verbal information is processed separately. Evidence for this view comes from the observation that learning increases when the information is illustrated by pictures or video clips.

When someone knows more than one language, they will still code objects in the same way, except that there are different verbal representations for the two languages. The model assumes that the level of image representations is shared between the languages, at least for compound bilinguals. They access the same image system through either of their languages.

Co-ordinate bilinguals, on the other hand, are assumed to have a different conceptual as well as verbal system. This would mean that in terms of dual coding, they have different image representations. However, Paivio & Desrochers (1980) state that the distinction between compound and co-ordinate bilingualism is a matter of degree. This means that for both types, some concepts overlap between the two languages, while others differ.

Box 7.8 gives an example of overlapping concepts across languages, as well as an example where there is no overlap.

Finally, subordinate bilinguals access the verbal system of the second language (L2) through the first language (L1). Therefore, their verbal representations would link words in the two languages, but there is no difference at the level of image representations between monolingual and subordinate bilinguals.

Experimental tasks aimed at distinguishing different types of bilinguals did not show any reliable differences. This raises the question as to whether the distinction between different bilinguals is as clear-cut as suggested by Weinreich.

Box 7.8: Cross-language concepts

Conceptual overlap

Equivalent concepts across languages are not necessarily completely equivalent in the two languages as the boundaries or what is considered to be a prototypical member of a category may differ. For example, take the category *bread*. What is considered to be a 'typical' type of bread can differ across countries: in France, it is a white baguette, in Germany dark rye bread, in Ireland it is soda bread, etc.

No overlap

Not all concepts have equivalents in the other language, or at least they are not exactly the same. This often gives rise to 'borrowing' from the other language. For example, the concept associated with the German word *Schadenfreude* (joy at someone else's misfortune) has no translation equivalent in English, though the emotion itself is known to speakers of English.

The revised hierarchical model of lexical and conceptual representation

The revised hierarchical model (Kroll & Stewart, 1994) gives some more details of the different pathways between image representations, concepts and word forms in bilinguals, and is outlined in Box 7.9. This model also suggests that there are links between the shared conceptual level, and different word forms. However, the links between the conceptual level and each of the languages can differ in terms of how strong they are. Links to the L2 are weaker than to the L1.

Weaker connections mean that it is more difficult to retrieve a word, and also that it will take more time. For example, a beginning learner of an L2 will know a certain number of words in their L2 and what they mean in the L1. When they want to use a common word in their L2, they will be able to go directly from the conceptual level to the word level, but for most other words, they are likely to access the word in the L1 initially and then translate the word from their L1 into the L2.

As an L2 learner becomes more proficient and has acquired more words, the connections between the conceptual level and the L2 increase in strength. A very proficient speaker of an L2 will have links to both languages that are similar in strength. Similarly, a child who grows up with two languages simultaneously will develop connections to words in both languages, hence the links are similar for both languages.

The revised hierarchical model of lexical and conceptual representations also assumes that there are direct connections between L1 and L2 words. These

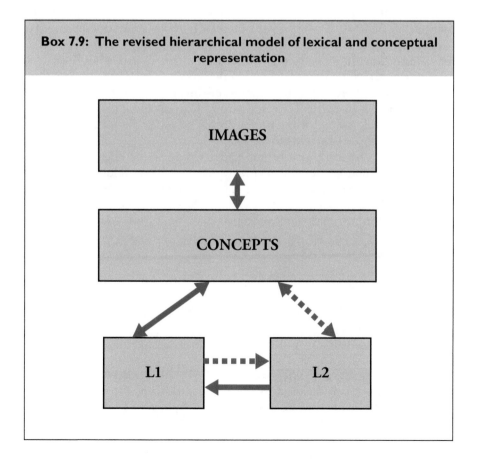

Box 7.9: The revised hierarchical model of lexical and conceptual representation

connections allow speakers to translate words directly from one language to the other without involving the conceptual level. The process of translation is mediated via the lexical links between L1 and L2 words, whereas tasks such as picture naming require activation of the semantic level and are therefore conceptually mediated.

Again, there are differences in the strength of the connections. The connections from L2 to L1 are stronger than the connections from L1 to L2. This is because L2 learners find it easier to translate words from the L2 into the L1, but more difficult the other way around.

We saw in Chapter 5 that children growing up with two languages develop translation equivalents quite early and can use the appropriate words in different language contexts. This means that they have developed connections between the words naturally, and without explicit instructions.

The revised hierarchical model has been tested using picture-naming and translation tasks. In picture-naming tasks, subjects are shown pictures of objects, and they have to respond with the word that corresponds to the picture. The mental processes involved in this task include the recognition of the object in the picture, access to the concept of the word, and then retrieving the word that corresponds to the concept.

For L2 learners, the model makes different predictions, namely that pictures are named faster in the L1 as opposed to the L2. A picture-naming task is outlined in Box 7.10. The model also predicts that the connections from L2 to L1 are stronger than the other way round, hence predicting that the translation of words is faster in this direction. A translation task is outlined in Box 7.11.

The results from picture-naming studies involving adult L2 learners show that there are differences in the amount of time it takes to name pictures in both languages. In particular, results from different bilingual reaction time studies confirm that L2 learners take longer to name pictures in their L2, compared with the L1 (Snodgrass, 1993).

The longer reaction times for non-native words can be interpreted as confirmation that non-native speakers first retrieve the L1 word forms for the pictures, and then access the translation equivalents. For example, an L2 learner

---

Box 7.10: Bilingual picture naming

Non-cognates		Cognates	
Mouse	Souris	Violin	Violon
	(French equivalent)		(French equivalent)

In a picture-naming task, subjects are shown different pictures and they have to respond either in their first or their second language. Subjects' reaction times are measured to see whether the target language has an effect on word retrieval and, also, whether there is a difference depending on the cognate status of the target word and its translation equivalent in the other language.

Box 7.11: Bilingual translation

Non-cognates

English–Spanish		Spanish–English	
desk	escritorio	*freno*	brake
money	dinero	*tienda*	shop

Cognates

English–Spanish		Spanish–English	
accident	accidente	*traffic*	tráfico
fruit	fruita	*minuto*	minute

In a translation task, subjects read stimulus words in a particular language on a computer screen and have to respond by giving the translation equivalents of the stimulus items. The translation direction varies. Subjects translate words from their LI into the L2 or the direction is from L2 into the LI. Reaction times are measured to see if one of the directions is faster than the other. The stimulus words are varied and include cognate as well as non-cognate words.

of French who is asked to retrieve the French word for mouse, *ratón*, would first retrieve the English word and then access its translation equivalent, rather than retrieve the French word directly from the common concept.

Alternatively, the difference in reaction time could be due to the different strengths in the links between concepts and the L1 and L2 words. Either way, the results are in line with the revised model of lexical and conceptual representations (Kroll & Stewart, 1994).

But do these results also hold for child bilingual learners who have learnt their languages in naturalistic settings? If they do, we would expect to see a possible difference between sequential and simultaneous learners in the time they take to name pictures in the L2. If connections between the conceptual level and words in each language are similar in strength, the reaction times should not differ across the languages of the simultaneous bilingual.

Children's picture naming in both languages was investigated by Schelletter (2002) using a group of simultaneous bilingual children (German and English) aged 8–9, a group of sequential bilingual speakers (with German as their first language) of the same age, and a group of adults. The simultaneous bilingual learners came mainly from a German–English home background, whereas the sequential learners had a German monolingual home background but were exposed to English due to living in the United Kingdom. The results did indeed show similar reaction times for the simultaneous bilinguals for both languages, as well as similar accuracy levels. The sequential learners of English, on the other hand, were slower and less accurate at naming pictures in English. The children named pictures more slowly than the adults. These results also support the revised model of lexical and conceptual representations and show that simultaneous bilinguals have equally strong connections to both their languages.

The results of studies involving picture-naming tasks also showed an influence of the similarity of the phonological form of the word across languages. We have already discussed the status of cognates in Chapter 5 in relation to bilingual acquisition. In a study by Costa & Caramazza (2000), pictures of cognate and non-cognate words were given to monolingual Spanish and bilingual Catalan–Spanish speakers. For example, non-cognates included the pair *taula-mesa*, the Catalan and Spanish words for *table*, whereas cognate pairs included the pair *gat-gato*, the Catalan and Spanish words for *cat*.

They found that the bilingual subjects were faster to name cognates than non-cognates. For the monolingual group, the cognate status of the word associated with the picture did not make any difference. This is what we would expect, as monolinguals do not have another language system.

The finding that the cognate status of a word made a difference in the picture-naming task is interesting, as the task required subjects only to activate one of their languages, namely Spanish. These results cannot be explained by the revised model of lexical and conceptual representations, as the model does not distinguish between words that are cognates across languages, and words that do not have this status.

Snodgrass (1993) suggested that both picture naming and translation activate the semantic memory system. However, the revised model of lexical and conceptual representations also includes lexical links between words and their translation equivalents. It is therefore possible that a translation task just activates the two lexical forms.

Translation studies with unbalanced bilinguals (Kroll & Stewart, 1994) suggest that translating from L1 to L2 is more difficult and takes more time than translating from L2 to L1. This means that it is easier to retrieve a native-language word when hearing a word in an L2 than to find the equivalent of a native word in the L2. Also, it makes a difference whether the equivalents are cognates, as these words were translated faster in both directions.

In order to find out whether translation involves just the lexical links between the words of both languages, the translation task was varied so that all the words to be translated came from the same category. For example, a 'categorised' list of words includes words from the same semantic category such as 'furniture' and includes *chair, table, sofa, armchair*, etc.

Categorisation makes translation harder if subjects activate the concept, rather than just the lexical links between a word and its translation equivalent. It was found that the reaction times of the translation direction from L1 to L2 were slower when the stimulus list was categorised, but this was not the case from L2 to L1. This suggests that subjects make use of the lexical links from L2 to L1 when translating in this direction (lexical mediation) but they activate the conceptual level when translating from L1 to L2 (conceptual mediation).

What do these results mean for simultaneous and sequential bilingual learners? This was examined by Schelletter (2002) as her study also included a translation task with all groups. The simultaneous bilingual children and the bilingual adults showed similar reaction times and accuracies when translating in both directions. This result confirms that high proficiency in both languages results in equally strong connections between words in both directions.

The adults were able to translate words a lot faster than the children though. It is possible that adults translated via lexical links in both directions, whereas the children activated the conceptual level. On the other hand, the adults were all L2 learners of English who had been resident in the United Kingdom for some time. All groups showed a cognate facilitation effect in both directions.

The cognate facilitation effect was found for both picture-naming and translation tasks, and included different speakers. The revised model of lexical and conceptual representations is not able to explain the effect as it does not distinguish between different word types.

In the next section, we shall therefore discuss a model that can account for the cognate facilitation effect.

The distributed lexical/conceptual feature model

An alternative model which can account for the cognate facilitation effect, is the distributed lexical/conceptual feature model (Kroll & de Groot, 2014). This model is outlined in Box 7.12.

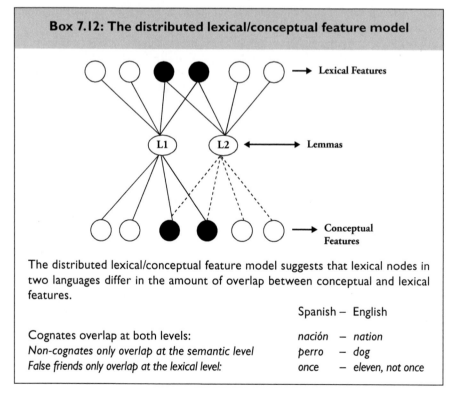

Box 7.12: The distributed lexical/conceptual feature model

The distributed lexical/conceptual feature model suggests that lexical nodes in two languages differ in the amount of overlap between conceptual and lexical features.

	Spanish – English
Cognates overlap at both levels:	nación – nation
Non-cognates only overlap at the semantic level	perro – dog
False friends only overlap at the lexical level:	once – eleven, not once

The model has three levels: conceptual features, lemmas and lexical features. In contrast to the revised hierarchical model of lexical and conceptual representations that was discussed earlier, this model represents the levels for individual word forms, rather than words as a whole.

The lexical level consists of phonemes that make up the spoken word. If words across languages sound similar, they share phonemes. For example, the English–Spanish word pair *minute-minuto* shares the phonemes /m/, /i/, /n/ and /t/.

The same principle is applied to the conceptual level. If the same concept is shared across languages, the features overlap. If the concepts partially overlap, only some of the features are shared.

The term **lemma** describes a language-specific word form in the mental lexicon that includes syntactic aspects of word knowledge. For example, a verb like *sink* can occur as *sinks* if the subject of the verb is a third person form. It can also occur in the past tense form *sank*. In the present context, lemmas are described as 'patterns of activation between form and meaning' (Kroll & de Groot, 2014, p. 191). If lemmas are activated within a particular context, then the activations also include syntactic features.

The model can explain the earlier findings that cognate words are translated faster than non-cognates by assuming that more overlap leads to faster processing. In the case of cognates, more features overlap at the lexical level. In a translation task, when a cognate word is given, some of the phonemes of the translation equivalent are already activated, therefore the translation equivalent can be accessed faster. In the case of a non-cognate word, there is much less overlap at the lexical level, which leads to slower translation of the word.

We can also imagine a situation where words overlap at the lexical level but do not share features at the semantic level. The similarity in this case is accidental. For example, the English–German word pair *tailor-Teller* (plate) differs in one phoneme, yet the meaning of the words is quite different. Words that share their orthographic or phonological form across languages, but have different meanings, are often called 'false friends' because the overlap at the lexical or orthographic level suggests to the L2 learner that the meaning should overlap too. An example is given in Box 7.12 where the word *once* in Spanish looks like the English word but differs in meaning. In the Spanish context the word means *eleven*.

The distributed lexical/conceptual feature model also suggests that the connections between the conceptual features and L2 words can initially be weaker than the connections to L1 words. In this way, the differences in the time taken to name pictures in the L1 and L2 as well as the differences in the translation directions can be explained.

The model can be applied to different experimental tasks, such as picture naming and translation, as outlined in Boxes 7.10 and 7.11. One difference between the tasks though is that picture naming first activates the conceptual level, then the lemma level, and then in turn activates the lexical level. In translation tasks, the stimulus is a written word, therefore the letters making up the word need to be processed first and then the lemma level activated.

The shared (distributional) asymmetric model

The last model that we are considering in this context is the shared (distributional) asymmetric model (Dong, Gui & MacWhinney, 2005) as this takes us back to the question of whether concepts are shared across languages, which was discussed earlier in this chapter. The distributed lexical/conceptual feature model in Box 7.12 suggests that concepts can be partially shared, as the overlap in features can vary.

However, it is not clear what information the conceptual features encode, or how specific they are assumed to be. When we looked at the semantic relationships between words, we looked at characteristics of objects, such as *is edible* to describe the concept *fruit*. If there are differences between concepts across languages, it is not clear whether they would be captured by these features.

Pavlenko (2009) outlines different possibilities for a conceptual overlap: **equivalence, partial equivalence** and **non-equivalence**. A translation pair is equivalent when all, or nearly all, of the items that native speakers of a language A call by a particular word, are labelled with the translation equivalent by native speakers of a language B. For example, the English word *cup* and the French word *tasse* were found to be equivalents. This means that the types of objects that English speakers labelled *cup* were more or less the same objects that French speakers labelled *tasse*.

For partial equivalence, the conceptual domain of a word in one language is contained either fully or partially in a larger category of the other language. Pavlenko (2009) calls this relationship **nesting**. An example of nesting is the English word *jar* as this is contained in the concept of the Spanish word *frasco*. This word describes containers that have both the shape of a bottle but also include the equivalent of *container*. The concept of *frasco* is therefore larger than that of the English word and it contains the English concept of *jar*.

Finally, non-equivalent concepts occur where a word in one language does not have a counterpart in the other, either because the particular object does not occur in the other culture, or there is simply a lack of translation equivalent. We have already discussed the example *Schadenfreude* in Box 7.8 where there is no translation equivalent in English.

The model in Box 7.13 suggests that the concepts of L1 and L2 words are either shared, or they are separate across the languages. Separate conceptual representations mean that the concepts are non-equivalent, whereas concepts that have common elements across languages can either be equivalent or partially equivalent.

The model was tested using two experimental tasks (Dong, Gui & MacWhinney, 2005). The first was a lexical decision task where the subjects had to make a decision as to whether or not the second word of a word pair was a real

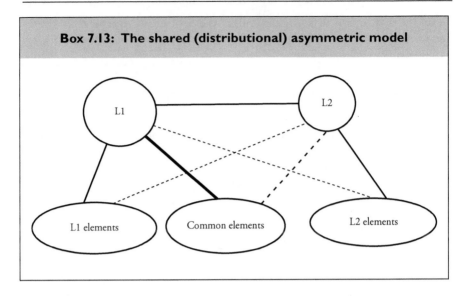

Box 7.13: The shared (distributional) asymmetric model

word. The words making up the word pairs were semantically related and represented different conceptual relations between verbs and other words. For example, the word pair *bark-dog* represents the relationship *Action-Agent*, where *dog* is the agent and *barking* the action that the agent is frequently engaged in. The word pair *take-give* are **antonyms**, because the verbs are opposite in meaning.

The word pairs included in the task were either words from the same language (English or Chinese) or from both languages. Subjects were 17 Chinese L2 learners of English aged 21–22 who had learnt English for 6 years at school.

It was found that subjects accepted semantically related word pairs faster than unrelated word pairs (priming). The priming effect occurred in both: within-language pairs, as well as across-language pairs. The fact that priming occurred within both languages suggests that the concepts are indeed related. The fact that priming also occurred across languages shows that the concepts are shared across both languages. They also found that targets in the L1 were responded to faster than L2 targets, thereby suggesting stronger connections between L1 and the shared conceptual representations than between L2 and the level of common elements.

A second task was designed to find out more about the organisation of words in the bilingual lexicon that do not share a conceptual basis. For this purpose, different groups of Chinese learners of English, as well as Chinese monolingual speakers, were asked to judge how close in meaning a group of eight words was to a particular head word (e.g. *fruit*). Their findings suggest that L2 speakers initially adopt separate conceptual representations for L1 and L2 words: they keep the L1 concepts for their native words and adopt the conceptual system of the L2 for L2 words. As they become more proficient in the L2, they integrate the conceptual differences of the two systems.

The experiments support the model which suggests both shared concepts for L1 and L2 words, as well as some representations which are separate. As the L2 learner becomes more proficient, conceptual knowledge across languages becomes more integrated.

STUDY ACTIVITY 7.3

1. What is 'cognate facilitation'? How can this effect in picture-naming and translation tasks be explained?
2. Find examples of translation equivalents with different conceptual overlap. How is conceptual overlap accounted for in the distributed lexical/conceptual feature model and the shared (distributional) asymmetric model?

The developing mental lexicon

How do children acquire their mental lexicon? And how do bilinguals acquire semantic representation for both languages? Children build up the mental word store gradually as they learn new words and their meanings. In general, children's first words represent concepts that are fairly specific, such as *cat* or *bird*. These are included in larger categories such as *animal*, yet children do not initially seem to understand this relationship.

According to Clark (1995), children learn only **base level** terms initially, terms where concepts are not too broad but not too specific either. She looked at a child's early animal repertoire and found that early acquisitions included words like *doggy*, *duck, mouse, bird* and *horse*. The inclusive term *animal* did not emerge until age 1;7 and more specific words such as *robin, sparrow* and *trout* occurred in the child's lexicon after the age of 2. Once some terms at different levels are established, it is possible to build a network. For example, the terms *animal-bird-robin* represent a network where each term is included in the larger category (see Box 7.14).

Box 7.14: Children's early categorisations

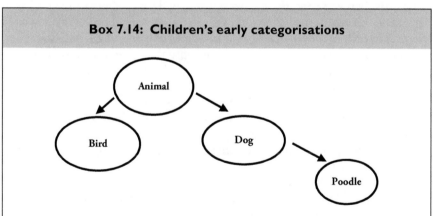

Early experiments to test children's categorisation have involved sorting tasks, where children were asked to sort objects according to different categories. It was found that 3-year-olds were more accurate when the categories were base level terms (dog, bird), rather than superordinate (animal) or subordinate categories (poodle).

This is in line with Clark (1995) who found that children's early words are base level terms and that superordinate and subordinate level terms are produced slightly later.

Children who grow up with two languages from birth or from some point in their life will develop the mental word store in a similar way to monolinguals. However, rather than one word being linked to a particular concept, the results from picture-naming and translation tasks suggest that there are connections between the concept and the words in both languages and direct connections between a word in one language and the translation equivalent in the other language. In this way, it is possible to retrieve the words of both languages directly after activating the concept.

Bilinguals have either built two different networks, or a network with integrated conceptual representations and links to the different word forms. There is also the question as to how bilinguals acquire differences in the application of the concepts across languages.

So how do monolinguals and bilinguals differ in relation to the development of their mental lexicon? One crucial difference, of course, is the fact that a bilingual develops more than one word form for a similar concept. We saw in Chapter 5 that bilingual children start to learn translation equivalents from early on, and that they increase when more words are learnt. Children learn words in contexts. In order to link words from both languages, presumably they will have come across both forms separately in similar contexts. It is possible that at an early age, a bilingual can link the different word forms before completing the aspect of network building. On the other hand, the concepts of later acquired translation equivalents might initially be separate and become integrated as the child realises that the word forms describe the same or similar referents.

A child learner who is regularly exposed to two languages will build up the network for both languages gradually, however, the connections between word forms, and between concepts and word forms, will have a similar strength. As we have seen, this means there is no difference in the amount of time it takes to name pictures in each of the languages or to translate from one language to the other.

In terms of the distributed lexical/conceptual feature model, we have seen that phonological similarity between the words in the two languages facilitates access, particularly in translation. Research on early bilingual lexical acquisition (Bosch & Ramon-Casas, 2014) has indeed shown that form similarity between the words in both languages facilitates the acquisition of these words.

One challenge for bilingual children as well as adult learners is the fact that the way concepts are applied is not always equivalent in the two languages. If the semantic category derived from a concept is wider in one language than the other, will bilingual children initially regard them as equivalent and gradually adjust the categories of both languages?

Gathercole et al. (2016) investigated the development of semantic knowledge in 36 monolingual adult English and Spanish subjects, as well as a group of 108 adult bilingual English–Spanish speakers. The bilinguals were grouped by home language, and included simultaneously bilingual English–Spanish speakers, sequential bilinguals living in the United States from birth who only spoke Spanish at home, and sequentially bilingual speakers who were born in a Spanish-speaking country but emigrated to the United States between the ages of 2 and 12.

The bilingual subjects were given words in both English and Spanish where the translation equivalent had a wider application in the other language. This is illustrated in Box 7.15. The subjects were given a set of six pictures as well as particular words in each of the languages. There were two targets, corresponding to the words in the narrower language, as well as related distractors. For example, the list of pictures for the target *tree* contained both types of trees, as well as related words, such as flower, leaf and coconut.

Box 7.15: Cross-language semantic categorisation

The application of the meaning of particular words can differ across languages. Some categories can be wider, but others can be narrower. As an example, consider the words *reloij* in Spanish and *tree* in English.

Wider in Spanish: *reloij*   Wider in English: *tree*

Clock   Watch   Deciduous tree: *arbol* Palm tree: *palmera*

The Spanish word 'reloij' includes both the English word 'clock' as well as the word 'watch', therefore it is wider than the English meaning. On the other hand, the English word 'tree' includes both the Spanish word 'árbol', which means 'deciduous tree', but also the word 'palmera' which means 'palm tree'.

The results showed that the bilingual subjects were closer in accuracy levels to the monolinguals in English, the dominant language of their country of residence, rather than Spanish. Their performance was related to vocabulary knowledge as well as home language. In general, for semantic categories that are close in terms of the underlying concept (classical categories), it was easier to adopt the semantic category of the other language when this was wider, but harder to separate a category into different subcategories, when the semantic category in the other language was narrower.

There were also some differences between the various bilingual groups. The simultaneous Spanish–English bilinguals and the speakers who were exposed to only Spanish at home, had earlier exposure to two languages than the sequential bilinguals who came from a Spanish-speaking country. In relation to the semantic categorisation in Spanish, it was found that the performance of the later sequential bilinguals was closer to that of the Spanish monolinguals. This suggests that the early exposure and competition between the semantic categories of two languages has an impact on conceptual development.

Differences between simultaneous and sequential bilingual learners

Earlier in this chapter we considered different models of the bilingual lexicon. These were developed to account for adult L2 learners who vary in the amount of language exposure to another language. Balanced simultaneous bilingual learners have similar language levels and hence connections with similar strengths to both systems. When we consider a sequential child learner on the other hand, we cannot assume that their mental lexicon resembles that of an L2 learner.

Depending on the timing of the onset of an L2 in the case of a sequential bilingual, the child will have acquired a certain number of words in the L1 and will have started building up the conceptual network based on this language. At the same time, they will not have completed the network building process, as they are still learning new words and building up concepts. The onset of a new language at some point during this process suggests that there will be an integration of the concepts already acquired, as well as new ones that are directly linked between languages.

In their study, Gathercole et al. (2016) found that the later sequential learners did not differ from the other groups as far as their semantic categorisation in English is concerned. This suggests that the age of onset did not affect their ability to acquire the semantic categories of the later language.

On the other hand, the finding that the later sequential bilinguals were closer to the monolingual Spanish speakers in the semantic categorisation of Spanish, suggests that early exposure to two languages can have an effect on children's semantic categorisations.

STUDY ACTIVITY 7.4

1. Children start building their network with base level terms such as 'dog' rather than broader or more specific categories. Can you think of possible reasons?
2. Semantic categories can differ across two languages. How do different types of bilingual learners learn these differences?

SUMMARY

In this chapter, we have considered different psycholinguistic methodologies as well as models of the mental lexicon for both monolingual and bilingual speakers. Models of the monolingual lexicon focus on the semantic relationship between different words, as experimental evidence suggests that words that are related are stored close together.

Models of the bilingual lexicon focus on the links between the two languages, and the observation that increasing proficiency in the later learnt language can affect the way the language is conceptualised. The models show development from an initial system where L2 words are accessed, through the conceptual level of the L1, to a system where connections between concept and language forms in both languages are equally strong. The observation that cognate words facilitate tasks such as translation has led to the distributed lexical/conceptual feature model, where words and their concepts are represented in terms of features that can have varying degrees of overlap.

Children build up the conceptual representations of both languages slowly, and they first acquire base level terms before adding more general and more specific categories. Bilingual children link translation equivalents in their languages early when they are exposed to similar situations in both language contexts. Children who start exposure later will initially have more concepts linked to only L1 words but develop a more even system as exposure to the L2 continues.

Concepts can be shared, overlap or differ across languages. The semantic categories associated with different concepts can have a different scope in different languages. Children's acquisition of these categories can be affected by exposure to another language.

FURTHER READING

At the beginning of the chapter, we outlined different online methods to investigate language processing. For further details on using these methods with children, see Sekerina, Fernández & Clahsen (2008) as well as Blom & Unsworth (2010). For more details on the software packages see https://cedrus.com/and https://pstnet.com/products/e-prime/.

Different semantic relationships between different types of words and the online database Word Net are illustrated in Miller (1995). Relationships between verbs, in particular, are discussed by Fellbaum (2005). For a more detailed outline of bilingual lexical access and different models see Kroll & De Groot (2005) and Pavlenko (2009). For more details of children's conceptual development see Bowerman & Levinson (2001).

Bilingual Metalinguistic Awareness

8

In this chapter we return to the question as to whether bilingualism has advantages, and the reasons why bilingualism delays the onset of dementia. We have already seen in Chapter 1 that bilingual children were found to be better at accepting different names for objects in the 'sun moon' task, and that they were better at a grammaticality judgement task where they had to refrain from responding to grammatical but not meaningful sentences. So, we can say that bilingual children have an enhanced metalinguistic awareness.

Metalinguistic awareness refers to abstract knowledge about language that children develop. Part of this awareness is the ability to control attention. It is in this aspect of metalinguistic awareness that bilingual children show better performance. On the other hand, metalinguistic awareness also includes abstract knowledge of language, an aspect that develops with age, and where bilingual children do not seem to show enhanced skills. We saw that the younger children in the word knowledge task (see Chapter 1) responded only with content words as the last word they heard, whereas the older children showed more flexibility.

In this chapter we begin with the question as to how children develop skills that enable them to carry out mental tasks; that is, we outline what is commonly known about children's cognitive development in the early years. With the bilingual advantage in mind, we explore some non-verbal cognitive skills that are known as executive functions (EF). We then investigate which cognitive skills are enhanced by bilingualism, and what aspects of language are affected by increased metalinguistic awareness skills.

We also look at the question: how much exposure to another language is needed in order for the cognitive advantages to be effective? Does the onset of another language need to take place by a particular age? Does it make a difference if the two languages of a bilingual are balanced, or if one of the languages is more dominant than the other? By looking at these questions, it will become clear what the bilingual advantage is, and what conditions must be met in order for it to be effective.

Children's cognitive development

In the course of this book, we have at times made reference to children's cognitive skills. Cognitive skills relate to the way the mind works. The mind is able to receive, store, transform, retrieve and transmit information (Karmiloff-Smith, 1999). Cognitive development refers to children's increasing ability to perform these functions as they get older.

We saw in Chapter 4 that infants at birth have sound perception skills that enable them to distinguish between their own versus other languages. This was shown by measuring the sucking rate of newborn infants when listening to the language spoken by the parents, and then changing the stimulus to another language. This finding shows that infants are able not only to receive information (such as the sound of a language), but they react to a new stimulus by increasing their sucking rate.

Other cognitive skills that children make use of in order to learn language are intention reading and pattern finding. We saw in Chapter 2 that these social cognitive skills play an important role in the Usage-based theory as a way for children to understand the intentions underlying particular actions carried out by adults for the purpose of achieving a particular goal.

In Chapter 5, we saw that word learning involves not just a string of sounds in relation to a particular object, but the ability to develop a particular concept linked to a particular word that applies to a group of objects that have similar characteristics. The ability to form concepts is assumed to be one underlying reason for the vocabulary spurt that children go through between 18 and 24 months when word learning accelerates.

Even in relation to the acquisition of morphology, we saw in Chapter 6 that the Words and Rules Theory suggests that regular and irregular morphemes are linked to two different cognitive mechanisms. The mechanism related to regular morphemes is a rule-based one, which children apply to regular words, and overapply to irregular words.

We can therefore see that language development relies on a number of cognitive skills which are independent of any specific innate linguistic knowledge. We outline some influential work on cognitive development and relate this to bilingual children's cognitive skills.

Piaget's account of cognitive development

Piaget (1936) was concerned with children's understanding of the physical world around them, not specifically their development of language. He suggested the notion of a 'schema', a building block of knowledge and intelligence. A schema refers to the mental representation of an aspect of the physical world. These can include objects and actions, as well as more abstract representations. Piaget believed that schemas were not static but that they could change through different processes. The schemas of young children are quite simple, but as they change, they become more complex. An example of a schema could be bath time, a routine that is familiar to children before bedtime and involves water in the bathtub, particular toys that swim in the water, such as rubber ducks, and getting dried at the end.

Changes to schemas occur as a result of two processes: **assimilation** and **accommodation**. Assimilation is the process whereby a new object or situation is adapted into the existing schema. For example, if a new toy, such as a fish, is added to the bath time routine, this object becomes part of the existing schema. On the other hand, accommodation occurs if the new object or situation does not fit into the existing schema and has to be revised.

Box 8.1 gives an example of both assimilation and accommodation. The child in the example has a schema of a clown which includes a male with a bald head and frizzy hair doing funny things. When encountering a bald man with frizzy hair on the sides, the child assimilates the man into his schema of a clown. When the father explains that the man might have some similarity with a clown but that he does not do funny things, the child is able to accommodate his schema such that it is closer to that of the adult schema.

Box 8.1:   Assimilation and accommodation

Assimilation

A 2-year-old child sees a man who is bald on top of his head and has long frizzy hair on the sides. To his father's horror, the toddler shouts 'Clown, clown'.

Accommodation

In the 'clown' incident, the boy's father explained to his son that the man was not a clown and that even though his hair was like a clown's, he wasn't wearing a funny costume and wasn't doing silly things to make people laugh. With this new knowledge, the boy was able to change his schema of 'clown' and make this idea fit better to a standard concept of *clown*.

When a child's schema fits in with the physical world encountered, or new objects or situations can be assimilated, there is balance. When a new situation is encountered, there is a drive towards restoring the balance, which is called **equilibration**.

Piaget suggested four developmental stages which are outlined in Box 8.2.

Object permanence is a gradual process where the child initially does not look for an object when this is hidden (4–8 months). At a later stage (8–12 months) the child will look in the place where the object disappeared, but not in other places when the object has been moved. It is not until 18–24 months that the child has mastered full object permanence and will look in various possible locations for the hidden object. The child is also able to comment verbally that the object is *gone*.

Egocentricity is expressed in children's language, for example, when they talk about people they know, but do not specify their relation to the people for someone who has not got the same knowledge. For example, in the utterance *she bought me a pen*, the child has not specified who the pronoun *she* refers to.

Box 8.2: Piaget's stages of cognitive development

Sensorimotor period (0–2)

In this period the child comes to know the world in terms of physical action. The child also achieves **object permanence**, the insight that an object exists, even if it is hidden from view.

Period of pre-operational thought (2–7)

In this stage, children acquire representational skills and learn that a word or an object can stand for something else. Children are still 'egocentric', which means that they view the world from their own perspective and do not take someone else's perspective into account.

Period of concrete operations (7–11)

This period marks the beginning of logical thought, where children are able to understand transformations of objects and the reversibility of operations. The child is now able to take other perspectives into account.

Period of formal operations (11–adult)

When children have reached the stage of formal operations, they are thought to be able to think logically and abstractly. This is considered to be the ultimate stage of cognitive development.

To test children's cognitive development, Piaget developed a number of different tasks. We have already discussed the 'sun moon' problem back in Chapter 1. An example of number conservation is given in Box 8.4.

Bilingual children have been found to show more advanced cognitive development on different Piagetian tasks (Ben-Zeev, 1977). These early findings have prompted more investigations into the nature of the bilingual advantage.

Piaget's theory has been criticised on a number of counts. First of all, he underestimated the abilities of young children. Regarding language, Piaget (1997) divided the function of speech of children at the age of 6 into 'egocentric' and 'socialised'. As we explore in the next section, children are not as egocentric as Piaget assumed them to be.

Theory of Mind (ToM)

Theory of Mind (Baren-Cohen, Leslie & Frith, 1985, p. 39) refers to the ability 'to make inferences about what other people believe in a given situation', and to understand that other people do not necessarily share your own knowledge or mental state. This means that it is possible to draw conclusions about what someone believes in a particular context. On what basis can we draw those conclusions? On the one hand, we can imagine ourselves in the situation and draw conclusions about how we would feel ourselves. On the other hand, we can assess what the other person in a situation believes, based on what we know about the person or their circumstances.

Theory of Mind is related to intention reading and contrasts with Piaget's notion of egocentricity. A common way of testing children's Theory of Mind is the Sally-Ann task which involves two dolls, a marble, a basket and a box, and is outlined in Box 8.3.

In order to pass the task, children have to realise that they cannot answer the question based on what they know to be true (the marble is in Ann's box) but have to consider what Sally believes to be true (the marble is still in her basket). In general, children pass the task at the age of 4–5 and around 4 if simpler versions of the task are used (Doherty, 2009). For example, children might get confused by the fact that both dolls are female and forget which doll is Sally and which one is Ann. This can be rectified by choosing a male and a female doll in the task. In general, children's performance changes quite rapidly from 3 to 4. At the age of 3, the majority of children give the wrong answer, based on what they believe to be true. As they approach 4, their performance is mixed and over 4 they are more likely to give the correct answer.

How does Theory of Mind develop? Baren-Cohen (2001) sees children's pretend play at the age of 18–24 months as a first sign of ToM emerging. At the age of 4, a ratio of 85% of normally developing children will pass the Sally-Ann task, yet only 25% of autistic children do. Autism is a developmental disorder which affects a child's communication abilities and is characterised by impaired abilities to make inferences about other people's intentions. The disorder also affects language use and the understanding of non-literal meanings, as in the use of metaphors and idioms. As we saw in Chapter 2, the language abilities at the interface between grammar and pragmatics are vulnerable if one of the areas is not developed.

Are bilingual children more advanced than monolinguals in the development of Theory of Mind? Not all studies have found such an advantage. We will look further into children's cognitive skills connected with Theory of Mind.

Box 8.3: Theory of Mind

The Sally-Ann task

In the Sally-Ann task, a child sees two figures, Sally and Ann. Sally has a marble which she puts in her basket. Then Sally goes away.
While Sally is away, Ann takes the marble out of the basket and puts it in her own box.
(The child witnesses the action but Sally would not know about the change as she has gone away.)
Then Sally returns. The question is 'Where will Sally look for her marble?'

Representational re-description

We have seen that Piaget's model of cognitive development lacks detail and underestimates children's abilities, both in terms of their early abilities to interpret the world around them, and in particular the language that they hear, but also in terms of their ability to infer the mental states of others. New methodologies have enabled us to gain more insight into young children's abilities to interpret the stimuli around them.

Karmiloff-Smith (1999) looked at the way mental representations develop in children. She follows suggestions that the mind is organised in different domains that are concerned with different aspects of knowledge. These aspects include the physical world, language, the concept of number, Theory of Mind and literacy.

One domain is knowledge about the physical world. As children interact with the outside world, they become aware of the properties of objects and their relation to each other. We have already seen that children develop object permanence at an early stage. Another domain is, of course, language. As children get older, their comprehension of words increases, and they learn to produce words and the way words combine to express meaning.

Box 8.4: Conservation of number

Children are shown two rows of objects that line up. Then one of the lines is spaced out more so the objects no longer line up.

● ● ● ● ● ● ●   ●   ●   ●   ●   ●   ●   ●

● ● ● ● ● ● ●   ● ● ● ● ● ● ●

Are there the same number in each row?   **Now, are there the same number in each row, or does one have more?**

Regarding the concept of number, this was thought to develop significantly when children enter Piaget's period of concrete operations around the age of 7, the time they realise that the quantity of a number of objects does not change (see Box 8.4), even if the layout of an array is different (period of concrete operations). However, it has been found that children under the age of 5 can complete the number conservation task if no more than three or four objects are used.

Regarding Theory of Mind, processes like intention reading at an early stage and pretend play are precursors of the fully developed skill to draw conclusions about the mental state of others. Finally, while literacy skills are taught when children start school, young children develop relevant skills earlier, for example they make a distinction between 'drawing' and 'writing' by lifting the pen more often when they 'write', and they also develop an awareness of rhyming and syllables in a word before starting school.

The observation that children's skills in these areas develop more gradually has led to the suggestion of the model of representational re-description, or the R-R model (Karmiloff-Smith, 1999). The model suggests that children's knowledge in each area is re-described as their experience with the environment as well as social interaction becomes more refined. Children are said to go through four stages of development where their knowledge changes from an implicit level to different levels of explicitness (E1–E3). While implicit knowledge is characterised by a response to an external stimulus, it is tied to a particular context and not available to conscious control.

Let us look at an example. Pine & Messer (2003) examined children's knowledge of the task of balancing a beam in relation to the stages of the R-R model. Of course, we know that in order to balance a long object, such as a beam upon a fulcrum, the balancing point is in the middle of the beam. Within the model, children at the implicit level (I) are able to balance different beams at the age of 4–5 but do not have an explicit understanding that they are determining the middle point of the object.

Children who have moved to the first stage of explicitness (E1) have generalised their knowledge about balancing, assuming that all things balance in the middle. This knowledge representation would lead them to balance a beam in the middle, even if a weight is placed on one end of the beam, so that the balance point is no longer in the centre.

As children's knowledge representations become more explicit (E2), they gain conscious access to the knowledge representations. This means they are able to make predictions about the balancing point but are not yet able to give reasons for their predictions. When prompted, they reply with 'don't know' or 'I just did it' (Pine, Messer & St. John, 2002, p.1256). It is not until they have reached the final stage (E3) that children are able to consciously access the knowledge representations and give reasons for any predictions. For example, they can express that 'this side's got more weight on so I make this side longer so it has the same weight' (ibid., p. 1256).

The stages of knowledge representation outlined in the R-R model can also be applied to language, for example the acquisition of the past tense forms in English (see Chapter 6). Monolingual children have been observed to initially use some correct regular and irregular past tense forms. After this, they go through a period where they tend to use the regular past tense form, –ed, for both regular and irregular verbs, resulting in forms such as draw-ed. After learning more irregular verbs, overregularisations become less and the child is able to use both past tense forms correctly.

In terms of the R-R model, children are initially at the implicit level where they can use inflected forms but have no conscious access to the knowledge representations underlying the forms. When prompted, children would not be able to say why they have chosen a particular verb ending, similar to the responses in the beam-balancing task.

At the E1 level, children apply the regular inflected form to both regular and irregular verbs (overregularisation), but cannot yet verbalise the rule that past tense is formed by adding –ed to the end of verbs. At the E2 level, they are able to self-correct, for example from drawed to drew, but are not able to give reasons for the correction. At the E3 level, children have conscious access to the knowledge representations and can verbally express the rule, namely that the ending is used for the past.

Similar to the Piaget stages of cognitive development, Karmiloff-Smith's R-R model does not give any details about the mechanisms that are responsible for the child moving from one stage on to the next, other than age and increasing maturity.

STUDY ACTIVITY 8.1

1. How does cognitive development relate to language development? Discuss in terms of object permanence as well as 'egocentricity'.
2. Can you think of the different stages of the R-R model in relation to the development of Theory of Mind?

Metalinguistic awareness and attentional control

Let us now look more closely at the cognitive advantage in bilingual children. While cognitive development per se is not essentially different for monolingual and bilingual children, any cognitive advantage is due to the exposure to two languages.

When considering the 'sun moon' task in Chapter 1, the difference between monolinguals and bilinguals seemed to be based on the fact that bilingual children are more aware that names for objects are arbitrary. Bialystok (2001) suggested that bilingual children are better at attentional control, which is one of the processing components she suggests in the Analysis Control framework.

The Analysis Control framework

What is the Analysis Control (A/C) framework? It was suggested by Bialystok (2001) to explain the development of children's metalinguistic awareness. In the framework, she distinguishes two processing components, **analysis** and **control**. The analysis component is similar to the stages that were outlined earlier for the R-R model (Karmiloff-Smith, 1999), where the child is able to mentally represent more and more explicit and abstract structures. In this process, knowledge that has been implicit initially becomes gradually more accessible.

The word knowledge task that was discussed in Chapter 1 is an example of children's developing representations. In the task, a story was read to children and the story was stopped at certain points. Children were then asked to repeat the last word, which could be either a content or a function word. Younger children were found to repeat only the last content word, even if this was followed by a function word. For example, when the child heard the string *missed the* and was asked what the last word was, they said *missed* but left out the article *the*.

Older children, on the other hand, were able to repeat both content and function words as the last word. They would correctly say that the last word was *the*. We can therefore say that older children's knowledge representation of a word is different from that of younger children. Whereas younger children's representation of a word only includes content words, older children's representation includes both content and function words.

The way the task was conducted did not include asking children for reasons for their word choice. If children had been prompted to give reasons, a similar pattern to the one discussed earlier for the stages of the R-R model should emerge. Initially, children choose the last content word but are not able to give reasons for their choice, in line with the implicit level of knowledge representations. As their knowledge representations become more explicit, children should be able to give explanations, showing an understanding that both content and function words are valid words.

The second processing component is control of attention. This component enables the child to attend to a particular aspect of a representation or a stimulus. Bialystok outlines that when a child is faced with a particular problem where there is a conflict or some ambiguity, the child is able to construct two mental representations initially, and then attend to one of the representations in order to arrive at a solution. An example of the process of control of attention is the 'sun moon' task (see Chapter 1) where children were asked to exchange the names of the planets and then engage in a task where they had to remember that the names had been exchanged.

The A/C framework has been applied to different areas of language, including phonological awareness, word awareness and vocabulary as well as syntactic awareness. We can look at different tasks in relation to the different processing components that are suggested in the A/C framework. Some tasks require the representation of more abstract structures (analysis), whereas others involve attentional control. Bialystok (2001) suggests that the bilingual advantage only affects attentional control but not the analysis component. This means that differences between monolingual and bilingual children should only be found in tasks involving a higher degree of attentional control.

Phonological awareness

Phonological awareness refers to children's ability to identify and manipulate sounds and syllables and has been identified as an important skill in learning to read. While some phoneme awareness develops from the age of 2 years, children's awareness of rhymes, syllables and phonemes has been found to improve between the ages of 4 and 6. Syllable awareness develops before phoneme awareness. Syllable awareness tasks often require children to clap as they say each syllable of a given word. In phoneme awareness tasks, children need to identify each separate sound of a word.

Campbell & Sais (1995) carried out a study where they compared two groups of 5-year-old children, one group was monolingual English, the other Italian–English bilinguals with different degrees of proficiency in Italian. There were 15 children in each group who were able to complete the task. Children were matched, where possible, by socio-economic status as well as ethnicity and teaching regime.

The children were given sets of four pictures where three of the objects started with the same phoneme and three pictures showed objects that were semantically related. The items for the task are given in Box 8.5.

For example, in the first test array – 'cow, cat, *cup*, dog' – there are three words referring to animals (cow, cat, dog) and there are three words beginning with the same phoneme (cow, cat, cup). The item *cup* is the odd one out semantically as it does not fit in with the semantic category of the other three words, whereas the word *dog* is the odd one out in terms of the initial phoneme, as the other three words start with the phoneme /k/.

They found that the bilingual children were significantly better at both the semantic sorting task as well as the phoneme identification task, showing that bilingual children seem to have some advantage relating to the perception of sounds in spoken language.

On the other hand, Bialystok, Majumder & Martin (2003) conducted a range of different phonological awareness tasks with children aged 5–7 and included two different bilingual groups: Chinese–English as well as Spanish–English bilinguals. They found no differences between bilingual and monolingual children in their performance of a phoneme substitution task. In the

---

Box 8.5: Phonological awareness task

In the phonological awareness task children were shown pictures and asked to select the 'odd one out'. They were expected to select the picture that was not semantically related to the other pictures. This picture was then hidden and the children were asked to find the picture that starts with a different sound.

				Semantic category	Odd phoneme
1.	**Training set:**	a)	cake <u>bread</u> carrot *clock*	food	/b/
		b)	*key* comb <u>brush</u> clip	hair accessories	/b/
		c)	foot *fish* <u>leg</u> face	body parts	/l/
		d)	bird *banana* bee <u>fly</u>	insects	/f/
2.	**Test set:**	a)	cow cat *cup* <u>dog</u>	animals	/d/
		b)	pink <u>blue</u> purple *pencil*	colours	/b/
		c)	<u>spade</u> *biscuit* bricks ball	toys	/s/
		d)	<u>car</u> bike bus *bed*	vehicles	/k/
		e)	<u>moon</u> sun *saw* star	planets	/m/
		f)	pear <u>grapes</u> peach *pullover*	fruit	/g/
		g)	<u>shoe</u> *sun* socks skirt	clothes	/ʃ/
		h)	dog duck *door* <u>pig</u>	animals	/p/

The item that is not part of the semantic category is given in italics, the word with the initial phoneme that is the odd one out is underlined.

task, children were asked to take away the first sound of a particular word, that is the /k/ sound in a word such as *cat* and replace it with the first sound of another word, such as the /m/ sound of the word *mop*, and expected them to produce the word *mat*.

A further set of phonological awareness tasks were given to the children to see whether there were differences between monolinguals and bilinguals. In one of the tasks, children were asked to count out the phonemes in a list of words (Phoneme Segmentation task). For example, the phonemes of the word *fish* are /f/, /ɪ/ and /ʃ/. This task was the only one that distinguished between the groups. The Spanish–English bilingual children were significantly better than the monolinguals, who in turn performed better than the Chinese–English bilinguals.

Do bilingual children have an enhanced phonological awareness? If there is an advantage, different studies looking at different language combinations should be consistent and show the same advantage. This was not the case. The study by Bialystok, Majumder & Martin (2003) included bilinguals with different languages but found an advantage only for one group of bilinguals, the Spanish–English group.

This suggests that there is no general advantage in phonological awareness for bilingual children. The language combinations considered in both studies, Italian–English, Spanish–English and Chinese–English, differ with regard to the similarity of the languages. The first two are more closely related than Chinese–English. Any advantage in phonological awareness is dependent on the language combination being closely related.

Word awareness

Regarding word awareness, we have already seen that bilingual children were better than monolinguals in the 'sun moon' task. Ricciardelli (1993) designed a number of metalinguistic awareness tasks, which she tested on a group of 83 monolingual children aged between 5 and 7 who lived in Australia. This included a word renaming task, similar to the 'sun moon' task, as well as a symbol substitution task where the child had to substitute one word for another in a sentence. Overall there were eight different tasks. Details of two tasks are given in Box 8.6.

The first task, the word renaming task, is similar to the 'sun moon' task because children were asked to imagine that the names for categories are swapped around. They were then asked questions about the particular category. For example, when swapping the names for *cat* and *dog*, the child would be expected to name the picture of a cat *dog*. When asked what noise it would make, the child would need to remember that the animal still has the same characteristics, that is it meows.

In the symbol substitution task outlined in Box 8.6, the child has to swap the word occurring as the subject of the sentence and replace it with a given word as well as modify the verb of the sentence to agree with the new subject. While the first task requires the first processing component of the A/C framework, control of attention, for the second task the children also need to use the analysis component, because they need to apply their knowledge of grammar.

Box 8.6: Word renaming and symbol substitution task

1. **Word renaming task (Control)**
   Imagine that the names of cats and dogs were changed around. Let's call cats 'dogs' and dogs 'cats'. What would you call this animal (cat)? What noise would it make?

   Items: a) sun/moon, b) cat/dog, c) people/fish, d) trucks/tables, e) books/pillows

2. **Symbol substitution task (Analysis)**
   This time when we ask you to swap words, I also want you to change things so that it does not sound wrong. So we say 'mum is home' but 'they are home'.

Items:

Exchange	Sentence	Substitution
1. they/water	They are cold.	Water is cold.
2. she/I	She is running.	I am running.
3. he/we	He likes walking.	We like walking.
4. winter/they	Winter is cold.	They are cold.
5. dog/sheep	The dog is resting.	The sheep are resting.
6. she/mice	She likes eating cheese.	Mice like eating cheese.
7. they/he	They are having lunch.	He is having lunch.
8. Anne/they	Anne is waiting outside.	They are waiting outside.
9. children/she	Children are playing with water.	She is playing with water.
10. she/we	She is driving to work.	We are driving to work.
11. pond/boats	The pond is full of tiny fish.	Boats are full of tiny fish.
12. they/Paul	They go camping on fine weekends.	Paul goes camping on fine weekends.

All tasks were grouped according to the processing component that children were required to use, and the results for each of the processing components were compared. It was found that there was a relationship between the tasks that apply the same processing component (either control or analysis), such that children who scored highly on one of the tasks that involve control of attention for example, also did well on other tasks that involve the same component. The results confirm that the tasks involve two different components, as suggested in the A/C framework.

Ricciardelli (1992) compared 55 monolingual English with 57 Italian–English bilingual first grade children who lived in Australia. The children were 5–6 years old. She tested proficiency in each language with the Peabody Picture Vocabulary Test (PPVT). The test was translated into Italian in order to assess children's language level in this language. She also tested the children on a number of metalinguistic awareness tasks, including three tasks on word awareness. The bilingual children were divided into further groups to distinguish high and low proficiency for each of their languages.

She found that the bilingual children achieved higher scores than the monolingual children. However, when looking at children's performance in relation to language proficiency, she found that the cognitive advantage only applied to bilinguals who have a high degree of proficiency in both of their languages. This supports the Threshold theory which predicts that bilingual children need to have a high level of proficiency in both languages in order to benefit from enhanced cognitive development. Bilingual children who have a high proficiency level in only one of their languages will not have a higher level of cognitive development compared to monolingual children.

Regarding word awareness, the studies confirm a bilingual advantage for control of attention but suggest that the advantage only exists for individuals with a high degree of proficiency in both languages.

Syntactic awareness

Syntactic awareness is often tested by giving subjects a grammaticality judgement task, where they are given a sentence and have to decide whether or not the sentence sounds correct. For example, Ricciardelli (1993) used a word order task where children heard sentences like *I chocolate like* and were asked to say the sentence correctly. Grammaticality judgements are tasks that require control of attention, whereas the instruction to modify the sentence so that it is grammatical requires the analysis component.

In a study by Foursha-Stevenson & Nicoladis (2011), they compared a group of 39 French–English Canadian children aged 4 with a group of 51 monolingual English children of the same age. They tested children on sentences with word order differences between English and French. The structures included adjective-noun structures, subject-object placement and structures that differed between languages in terms of whether or not a determiner was needed.

For example, while adjectives always occur before the noun in English, in French they are often placed after the noun, as outlined in example 8.1.

Example 8.1

La	voiture	<u>noire</u> est	rapide
The car		<u>black</u> is.3rd SG	fast

'The black car is fast'

Regarding word order, English SVO sentences always place the object after the verb, regardless of whether the object is a pronoun, as in *Paul called her*. In French, on the other hand, pronouns are placed before the verb, as outlined in Example 8.2.

Example 8.2

Elle <u>la</u>   lave

She <u>her</u> washes.3rd SG

'She washes her'.

Example 8.3

Mon ami   est   médicin

My   friend   is.3rd SG   doctor

'My friend is a doctor'.

Finally, English and French differ in the presence or absence of a determiner. For example, in example 8.3 no article is needed in French before *médicin* (doctor), whereas the English sentence requires an indefinite determiner: *my friend is <u>a</u> doctor*.

In the study, the bilingual children were tested in both languages and were asked to judge sentences that were ungrammatical in one language but correct in the other. Both groups were also compared in relation to their vocabulary in English. They found that the monolingual children had higher vocabulary scores than the bilinguals.

For the grammaticality judgements, children had to say whether the sentences were right or wrong and their answers were noted. They found that the bilingual children had a higher proportion of correct responses for all three structures, particularly for structures that differed between languages, thereby showing a higher degree of control of attention for the bilingual children. This is in line with the A/C model.

A bilingual advantage in the analysis component

So far, we have seen that a bilingual advantage has been found for tasks that involve control of attention and, in particular, for tasks that test word awareness and grammaticality judgements. From discussing children's development of knowledge representation earlier (the R-R model) we saw that Karmiloff-Smith (1999) showed that representations become more and more explicit as children become more mature.

So could it be possible that the bilingual advantage in the control of attention leads children to also develop more explicit knowledge representations? If this is the case, then it should be possible to show that bilingual children are at a later stage of representational knowledge than monolingual children.

Murphy & Pine (2003) investigated this question in relation to children's overregularisation of irregular past tense forms. We have already seen earlier that children go through different stages in the acquisition of this form. In terms of the R-R model, overregularisations would suggest that the children have formed a rule about past tense forms and apply this rule in a general fashion. This is considered to be the first stage of explicitness (E1).

If bilingual children's exposure to two languages has resulted in a greater degree of awareness of the regularities in each of the languages, they might have stronger mental representations, leading them to produce more overregularised past tense forms compared to monolingual children. The past tense task applied is outlined in Box 8.7.

For the task, 24 novel verbs, words that do not exist in English, were presented to the children on cards with a cartoon character who was seen carrying out an ambiguous action. For half of the items, children were asked to produce the past tense form of the novel verb (production version).

As outlined in Box 8.7, for the novel verb *spling* children were expected to produce either the form *splinged* or the form *splung*. As the form *spling* sounds similar to existing irregular verbs like *sing* and *ring*, the irregular form *splung* would be in line with the existing verbs. On the other hand, a child who forms the past tense in line with the rule to add the form *-ed* to the end of the verb, would be expected to produce the form *splinged*. For the other half of the verbs, the children were given the forced choice version, where they had to make a decision between *splinged* and *splung*.

Murphy & Pine (2003) tested 52 children aged 5–9 who were attending a school in Hertfordshire in the United Kingdom. They were split into three age groups, 5, 7 and 9. The study also included 18 bilingual children aged 6–7 who were attending the European school in Oxfordshire in the United Kingdom.

The study found that in the production task, bilingual children produced more overregularised past tense forms than the 5 and 7-year-olds, but fewer than the 9-year-old monolinguals. In the forced choice version of the task, the bilingual children did not differ from the older monolingual children in their choice of past tense form.

The results are taken as evidence that all children are at the first level of explicitness of representational re-description, E1, as they all produced overregularised forms. The fact that the bilingual group produced more regular

---

Box 8.7: Past tense task

1) Production version	2) Forced choice version
This is Michael. Michael knows how to *spling*. He is *splinging*. Yesterday he _____	This is Michael. Michael knows how to *spling*. He is *splinging*. Yesterday he *splinged*. OR Yesterday he *splung*.

forms is seen as evidence that their representations are more robust, compared to the monolinguals, showing that their exposure to more than one language did have an effect on their knowledge representations.

While Bialystok (2001) suggested that the bilingual advantage is restricted to the component of attentional control, the study by Murphy & Pine (2003) raises the possibility that the bilingual advantage also affects children's representations of knowledge.

STUDY ACTIVITY 8.2

1. Control of attention involves the ability to attend to a particular aspect of a stimulus. How is control of attention manipulated in tasks testing different aspects of metalinguistic awareness?
2. Do bilinguals show enhanced metalinguistic awareness in all tasks? Does the exposure to two languages affect children's representations of knowledge?

Children's development of executive functions

So far, we have discussed the bilingual advantage in terms of attentional control and considered different aspects of language. As bilinguals are exposed to more than one language, they are more flexible in terms of their control of attention. But it seems that this is not the only area where bilinguals have an advantage.

We saw in Chapter 7 that the two languages of the bilingual are active simultaneously in particular language tasks. More recent research (see Chapter 9) shows that this is also the case if the tasks only involve one of the two languages. For example, when the child is shown a picture of a swing and is asked to provide the name of the object, the word forms of both languages are activated, even though the language context specifies only one of the languages.

This means that in order to complete the task, the cognitive system needs to make sure that attention is directed to the language that is required at a particular time. The system that is responsible for directing attention to the target language is the EF system.

Executive functions are a set of mental processes that are involved in behaviour to achieve a particular goal. EF include inhibitory control, the ability to stop yourself from acting in a particular way, working memory, the ability to hold information in your mind in order to complete a particular task; and shifting, the ability to shift between mental states (Miyake et al., 2000). These functions are further explained.

EF and their development have been of interest, particularly in relation to bilingual development. We shall consider the development of these EF in children, and then discuss the question whether the regular access to two languages trains EF such that bilingual children are more developed compared to monolinguals.

Inhibitory control

Children develop some inhibitory control at a fairly early age, for example when they are able to delay eating a sweet that they have been given. This cognitive ability develops fairly quickly during early childhood. An example of a task testing inhibitory control is the bear/dragon task which is outlined in Box 8.8.

Box 8.8: Bear/dragon task

Nice bear	Mean dragon
'Put your hands on your head'	'Touch your toes'

In the bear/dragon task, the child sees two puppets, a bear and a dragon. The bear is the 'nice' puppet and the dragon is the 'mean' puppet. Similar to the game 'Simon Says', both puppets are giving instructions for the child to carry out an action. In this case, the puppets give conflicting instructions, for example, 'nice bear' tells the child to put its hands on its head, whereas 'mean dragon' wants the child to touch their toes. The child is instructed to listen only to the instructions of one puppet, 'nice bear', and to ignore the instructions of 'mean dragon'.

The bear/dragon task was carried out with 103 children aged 3–6 together with other tasks testing inhibitory control. For example, children heard a gift being wrapped for a minute and were instructed not to unwrap the gift until they were told that they could do so. In addition, parents were asked to fill in a questionnaire where they were asked to give information about the child's behaviour and temperament. Children were also tested in terms of their ability to sustain attention, the ability to focus continuously on specific stimuli.

The results found that inhibitory control develops with age, such that the older children get better at ignoring the stimulus that they were told not to follow. At the same time, children who were better at sustained attention showed a greater degree of inhibitory control.

Working memory

As children get older, they are able to hold increasing amounts of information in their memory. The term 'working memory' refers to a model of memory that was proposed by Baddeley (2007). It is a temporary storage system that is under the control of our attention, as we can decide what to keep in memory at a particular time. Working memory is also the basis of more complex thinking, as this often relies on information being temporarily stored.

The working memory model has different components and is outlined in Box 8.9.

Box 8.9: Working memory

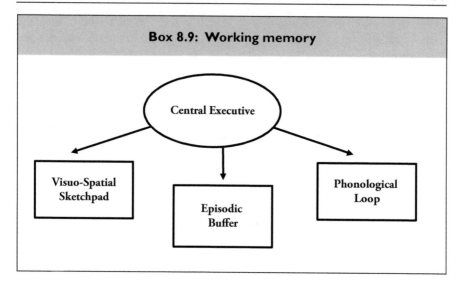

The main component is the **Central Executive**. This system is responsible for the control of attention. Henry (2011, pp. 34–35) gives the example of a driver who uses a particular route on a daily basis. For a skilled driver, taking a familiar route is quite an automated process that does not require the central executive. However, if the familiar route is blocked by an accident or a burst water pipe, the central executive needs to inhibit the automatic process in order for the individual to plan a different route.

The central executive has different subsystems: the **phonological loop**, the **episodic buffer** and the **visuo-spatial sketchpad**. The phonological loop is a particular system for temporarily storing information that is heard; in particular, speech. It is responsible for phonological short-term memory, the ability to temporarily remember information that one has heard.

For example, if you witness a car hitting a pedestrian and the car does not stop, you are aware that it is important to give a description of the car as well as the number plate. In order to remember the number plate, you are likely to repeat the letters and numbers on the plate to yourself a few times. Repetition results in longer-term storage, so that you are able to give the number plate when you are asked for a witness statement.

The visuo-spatial sketchpad is responsible for the temporary storage of visual, spatial and kinaesthetic information. It is a different system from the phonological loop and is assumed to be stored in the right hemisphere, whereas the storage component of the phonological loop is assumed to be in the left hemisphere of the brain. In the example of the car accident, while the memory of letters and numbers of a number plate are rehearsed via the phonological loop, the temporary memory of the colour and shape of the car involves the visuo-spatial sketchpad.

The third subsystem of the central executive is the episodic buffer. This system was not part of the original model of working memory. It is said to bring together different types of information. This includes information from the other two systems, namely auditory, visual, spatial or kinaesthetic information, but it also interlinks with long-term memory and integrates information from different sources.

An example of the way the episodic buffer integrates information comes from story retell in Box 8.10.

Box 8.10: Information integration: The Very Hungry Caterpillar

One Sunday morning the warm sun came up and – pop! out of the egg came a tiny and very hungry caterpillar.

> He started to look for some food.
> On Monday ...
> On Tuesday ...
> ...
> The next day was Sunday again
> ...

He built a small house, called a cocoon, around himself. He stayed inside for more than two weeks. Then he nibbled a hole in the cocoon, pushed his way out and ... He was a beautiful butterfly.

In the case of a story retell, such as *The Very Hungry Caterpillar* story, there are different levels of information coming together. Remembering the story involves the phonological loop and as well as long-term memory. First there is the story structure, in this case the caterpillar eating various kinds of food, becoming a cocoon and turning into a butterfly in the end. As part of the structure, the story goes through the days of the week and the kinds of food that are eaten every day. At the level of language, there is the vocabulary that is used, the grammatical structure and the meaning. The story repeats the word *ate* and the phrase *but he was still hungry.*

One of the ways of testing working memory, and particularly the phonological loop, is by testing children's memory span, the amount of information that children can keep in short-term memory. This is tested by getting children to repeat either a number of words or numbers in a particular order. In general, at the age of 5, children can repeat three words or numbers in the right order. At the age of 9, children can repeat four words and at 11 they can repeat five words (Henry, 2011, p. 82). The increase is thought to be due to an increase in capacity, that is, children can remember more information, as well as the speed of processing, which results in a faster rate of articulation.

Shifting

The last aspect of executive functioning that we are considering here is shifting. This is the ability to shift mentally between tasks. For example,

Miyake et al. (2000) outline different shifting tasks which they tested alongside other EF. One of them is the local-global task which is outlined in Box 8.11.

In the local-global task the shapes are presented on a computer screen. Depending on the colour, participants were asked to give the number of lines either of the global or the local shape. In this case, the global shape (the triangle) has three lines, the local shape (a square) has four lines. When the colours of the stimuli change, participants have to switch between naming the lines of either the local or the global shape.

Shifting is different from inhibitory control, which was considered earlier. In inhibitory control, a particular stimulus needs to be suppressed, as for example the instruction from the 'mean dragon' outlined in Box 8.8. Shifting, on the other hand, involves a switch between two different tasks.

Shifting has been found to improve with age in children (Best & Miller, 2010). At the age of 3–4, children were found to be able to switch between simple tasks that were set in a story context, yet accelerated development was found to occur between the ages of 5 and 6.

To summarise, in this section we have considered children's development of EF, in particular inhibitory control, working memory and shifting. All three functions were found to develop with age in children.

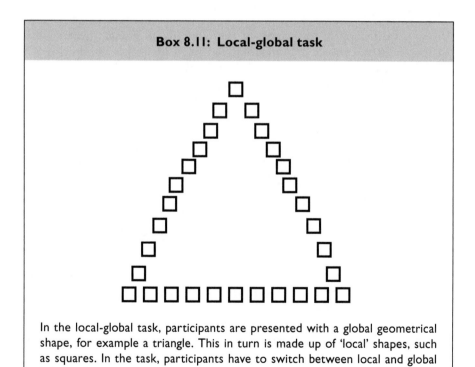

Box 8.11: Local-global task

In the local-global task, participants are presented with a global geometrical shape, for example a triangle. This in turn is made up of 'local' shapes, such as squares. In the task, participants have to switch between local and global information.

The bilingual advantage in executive functions

We described the bilingual advantage earlier in terms of the A/C framework (Bialystok, 2001). According to this model, the bilingual advantage exists for control of attention, but does not result in more advanced metalinguistic representations.

If both languages of the bilingual are activated as a default, this means that there is a greater demand for the EF that were outlined in the previous section, namely inhibitory control, working memory and inhibition. In this section we are going to outline results of studies comparing monolingual and bilingual children on tasks using EF. We shall also come back to the question whether only children who grow up with two languages simultaneously will benefit from any cognitive advantage.

Conflict resolution

In order to investigate the nature of the bilingual advantage involving EF, Bialystok (2010) compared 25 monolingual and 26 bilingual children aged 6 who attended English-speaking schools in North America. While the mono-lingual children only spoke English, the bilingual children had different other languages that were spoken at home, including French, Cantonese, Russian, Spanish, Hindi, etc.

The children were given several tasks, including verbal and non-verbal measures: a vocabulary and digit span task, as well as a global-local task, simi-lar to the task outlined in Box 8.11. In the letter version of the task, children saw big letters that were made up of little letters. They either had to respond to the global or the local shape. For some letters, the global and the local shape were identical, that is a big 'H' made up of little letters 'h'. This was the **congruent** condition. In the **incongruent** condition, the big and little letters were different. The shape version of the task also included congruent and incongru-ent items.

The tasks also included a trail-finding task, where children had to draw lines with a pen to connect points from 1 to 25 that were scattered randomly on a page. In a different version of the task, the children had to alternate between a number and a letter when connecting points. For example, they had to start at the number 1, then connect this point to the letter A and then go on to number 2, and so on.

It was found that all the children achieved similar results in the vocabulary as well as the digit span task. This confirms that the children were at similar levels of vocabulary development as well as memory development. There was a bilingual advantage for the global-local task and the trail-finding task. In the global-local task, the bilinguals were found to respond more quickly for both the congruent and incongruent conditions, compared to the monolinguals. In the trail-finding task, the bilinguals were faster for both, the number trails and the alternating number and letter trails.

While the results were expected for the conditions that involve a conflict (as in the incongruent condition for the global-local task and the number-letter version of the trail-finding task), the faster response time for the congruent condition and the number version of the trail-finding task cannot be explained in the same way. Bialystok (2010) concludes that the simple conditions of both tasks involve more processing effort by the children. Overall, the results confirm the bilingual advantage in relation to tasks involving switching as well as conflict resolution.

The bilingual children in the study spoke different languages at home. Also, according to a parental questionnaire, they were found to be fluent in both languages and were using both languages on a daily basis. No information was given as to whether the children acquired both languages simultaneously.

Non-verbal working memory

As was outlined in the last section, working memory is often tested by asking people to memorise a list of words or numbers (digit span). When monolingual and bilingual children were compared with regard to their ability to recall word lists or digits, children recalled a similar number of items, so there was no bilingual advantage. We have seen in Chapter 5 that bilingual children generally achieve lower scores on vocabulary measures in one language. Tasks that involve recalling a list of words might therefore 'disguise' a possible advantage.

A bilingual advantage was, however, found for tasks that involve non-verbal working memory. An example of such a task is the Simon task which is outlined in Box 8.12. Morales, Calvo & Bialystok (2013) carried out a variant of the Simon task with 29 monolingual and 27 bilingual children aged 5 who spoke different languages at home from birth and were using both languages on a daily basis.

In the task, the children saw different shapes occur either in the middle of the computer screen or on the left or the right side of the computer screen. They had to press different buttons indicating either the different shapes or the position of the shape on the computer screen.

The bilingual children were consistently found to be faster in all of the conditions. When either two or four shapes were presented in the middle of the screen, the children had to remember which button to press for which shape, but there was no conflict. The result is interpreted in a similar way to the global-local task, namely that even the non-conflict conditions require additional attention.

When two or four shapes were presented on the left- or right-hand side of the computer screen, this resulted in a congruent and non-congruent

---

Box 8.12: Simon task

LEFT   +   + LEFT

Congruent condition   **Non-congruent condition**

In the Simon task, a stimulus appears either on the left or the right side of a computer screen and the participant has to respond by pressing a corresponding button either on the left or the right side of the keyboard or a button box. The screen on the left is congruent as the word 'LEFT' appears on the left-hand side and triggers a left button press. The screen on the right is non-congruent as the word 'LEFT' appears on the right-hand side but still triggers a left button press.

---

condition, similar to the outline in Box 8.11. All children were slower to press the button in the non-congruent task, yet the bilingual children maintained their advantage over the monolinguals.

Taken together, the results show that the bilingual advantage holds for non-verbal working memory tasks, particularly where other processes in addition to working memory are needed to solve the task.

Inhibition

We talked about inhibitory control as one of the EF that children start to develop quite early. One of the tasks testing inhibitory control is the Flanker task, which is outlined in Box 8.13. As the stimulus that participants attend to is in the middle of a row of similar stimuli, the participant has to focus on the middle item and ignore the surrounding items, particularly in the non-congruent condition.

Children have been tested with an adapted version of the Flanker task where the arrows have been replaced by fish swimming in a particular direction. When comparing monolingual and bilingual children, a bilingual advantage has been found for non-congruent trials (Barac et al., 2014). Similar to the results in the Simon task, bilingual children were found to be faster and more accurate in the non-congruent trials.

But how can we be sure that the differences are due to the fact that children have more than one language, rather than different factors, such as socio-economic background or different cultural experiences? We have seen in Chapter 3 that children's socio-economic background can make quite a difference to children's language development. However, different studies have confirmed the bilingual advantage for different language combinations and different cultural backgrounds. This confirms that it is indeed the regular exposure and use of more than one language that affects EF.

Box 8.13: Flanker task

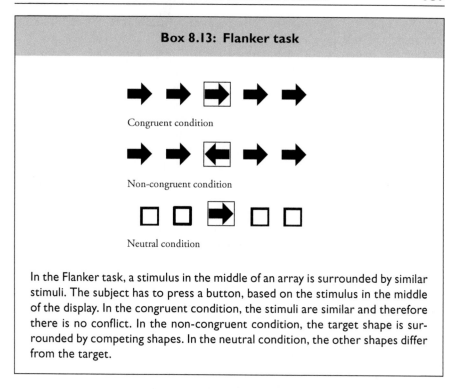

Congruent condition

Non-congruent condition

Neutral condition

In the Flanker task, a stimulus in the middle of an array is surrounded by similar stimuli. The subject has to press a button, based on the stimulus in the middle of the display. In the congruent condition, the stimuli are similar and therefore there is no conflict. In the non-congruent condition, the target shape is surrounded by competing shapes. In the neutral condition, the other shapes differ from the target.

Does the bilingual advantage extend to later learners?

Having confirmed that exposure to more than one language leads to an advantage in EF, the question is whether this advantage applies to both simultaneous and sequential bilinguals. We said earlier that the Threshold theory predicts a cognitive advantage only if the individual has a high level of proficiency in both languages. For a sequentially bilingual child, there is initially a lag in the language skills of the later acquired language.

This question was investigated by Bialystok & Barac (2012) in a study of metalinguistic awareness and executive control in school-age children at grades 2, 3 and 5. The children all had a monolingual background in either English, a variety of languages or Hebrew, but attended a school where they were immersed in Hebrew (study 1) or a school where French was spoken in class (study 2). All children except for the Hebrew native speakers therefore started learning another language when entering the immersion school. They were able to enter the school at any time and received intensive language instruction when they joined.

In the study, the children were given different tasks testing both their metalinguistic awareness and EF, as well as their level of vocabulary in both languages. Metalinguistic awareness was tested in English and based on either a Wug task (see Chapter 6) that contained a sentence with a nonsense word (study 1) and assessed the application of different morphological rules (such as past tense); or a grammaticality judgement task (study 2) where children had to decide whether a sentence was correct or not.

Incorrect sentences either contained a grammatical error, as in the sentence *Where does a horse like to runs;* or were semantically odd, as in *Where does a horse like to sail.* The sentences were presented on a computer screen and children had to make a decision as to whether the sentences were right or wrong.

The EF tasks were non-verbal and included the Flanker task, outlined in Box 8.13, as well as a switching task where children had to match stimuli either by colour or by shape. The children's language background was determined via a parental questionnaire which asked about home language as well as the length of time children had been attending the immersion programme.

For the metalinguistic awareness tasks children's performance was related to their level of English, the language they were tested in. The higher their level of English, the better children performed in the task. The length of time they were exposed to another language, on the other hand, did not affect their performance. This result is surprising compared to earlier findings that bilingual children had better metalinguistic awareness skills than monolinguals. The results are seen as evidence that it is not bilingualism as such, but language experience in general that enhances metalinguistic awareness. Exposure to more than one language can give a 'boost' in metalinguistic awareness, but this is also dependent on the language combinations and the level of proficiency in both languages, as expressed by the Threshold theory.

The results for the EF tasks, on the other hand, showed that there was a relationship between the length of time the children spent in the immersion school, and their performance in the EF tasks. Children who had been in the programme longer did better in the tasks than children who had joined more recently. This shows that the development of a bilingual advantage develops as a result of regular exposure to another language, and that it develops gradually. The fact that older children in immersion programmes also showed a bilingual advantage makes clear that this does not depend on both languages being learnt from birth.

It shows that learning another language at different ages leads to particular cognitive benefits that have been found to delay the onset of the symptoms of Alzheimer's disease, a condition that causes increasing loss of memory and reasoning. It has been found that in adults who are fluent in more than one language, the onset of the symptoms of Alzheimer's occur up to 5 years later than in adults who only speak one language.

STUDY ACTIVITY 8.4

1. How do monolingual and bilingual children compare with regard to their executive functions?
2. Are there differences in the development of executive functions in simultaneous and sequential bilinguals?

SUMMARY

In this chapter we have outlined children's cognitive development in terms of the Piagetian stages, as well as Karmiloff-Smith's model of representational re-description. This model assumes that cognitive functions develop from implicit to explicit representations. While bilingual children do not develop faster per se, there is the possibility that exposure to two languages could lead to children developing more explicit representations earlier.

The focus of the bilingual advantage has been on the development of enhanced metalinguistic awareness, in particular control of attention, as well as the development of enhanced EF which include inhibitory control, working memory and shifting. These functions are used regularly by bilinguals in order to make a language choice, or when switching from one language to another.

Metalinguistic awareness was tested for different areas of language, including phoneme awareness, word awareness and syntactic awareness, and with a variety of different verbal tasks. The bilingual advantage was found to be dependent on the language proficiency of the individuals as well as the closeness of the two languages.

The other aspect of the bilingual advantage, executive functions, is non-verbal and has been tested with a variety of non-verbal tasks, including the Simon task and the Flanker task. The bilingual advantage in these tasks has been found to hold for different language combinations and different speakers, including later learners. This means that the advantage in executive functions delays the onset of Alzheimer's in bilingual speakers.

FURTHER READING

We have outlined children's cognitive development according to Piaget's stages as well as their development of a Theory of Mind. For further details on the bilingual advantage in Theory of Mind see Nguyen & Astington (2014) as well as Barac et al. (2014). For more details on the development of working memory and executive functions in monolingual and bilingual children, see Henry (2011), Morales, Calvo & Bialystok (2013) and Best & Miller (2010). For more details on the bilingual advantage in sequential learners see Bialystok, Peets & Moreno (2014). Finally, to read more about the effect of bilingualism on delaying the onset of Alzheimer's disease see Craik, Bialystok & Freedman (2010).

Further Directions in Studying Bilingual Learners

9

This chapter summarises the outline that we have given of bilingual learners and sketches further developments in the area of bilingual acquisition. One of the aims of this book has been to bring together different ways of studying bilingual acquisition, including linguistic approaches, insights from studying cognition and cognitive development, as well as language processing in a second language. When the first case studies of bilingual language acquisition were documented more than 100 years ago, the study of bilingual acquisition was in its infancy. Particularly over the last 25 to 30 years, studies of different aspects of bilingualism have increased significantly. Different directions and methods of study have complemented each other, such that a more complete picture is emerging.

What has become clear is that bilingual acquisition has certain costs and clear advantages. The costs are associated with more limited input in at least one of the languages, leading to a narrower vocabulary range compared to monolingual children. This in turn can lead to possible delays in the acquisition of morphological marking. On the other hand, bilingual development does not end at a particular age. Depending on the community and different choices, the weaker system can further develop to narrow the gap.

In bringing together the study of language and the study of the processes that underlie language, the study of bilingual acquisition can make use of new technologies that enable us to observe those processes, as well as extending studies that have been carried out with adult bilinguals or second language learners, to the study of monolingual and bilingual children.

The bilingual advantage occurs in the area of cognitive development, particularly in the development of executive functions. These advantages have been found to have a long-term effect, such as delaying the onset of Alzheimer's. By observing sequential language learners, we can get a clearer idea of how enhanced metalinguistic knowledge develops.

Another aspect of bilingual development that we have not covered so far is bilingual literacy, the acquisition of written language in both languages. As different languages have different ways of representing sounds, learning to read can be a challenge or it could be that literacy in one language can facilitate literacy in the other language.

Bilingual language development

Can the bilingual disadvantage be overcome? Chapters 5 and 6 were concerned with lexical and morphological development in monolingual and bilingual children. While the acquisition process per se is not different, the comparison with monolingual norms has resulted in the finding that bilingual children can be at a disadvantage, particularly in their vocabulary knowledge in each of the languages, and also in the acquisition of morphology and some structures.

We have already discussed in Chapter 5 that one issue is the monolingual norms themselves. Developing specific bilingual norms would be a more suitable way to assess bilingual children's language skills. Given that children's language skills are a snapshot at a particular point in time, there is the question as to whether bilingual language can develop further over time, raising the possibility of a 'catch-up' at a later point.

Another way of finding out more about the acquisition process is to apply different methods in order to gain a more complete picture of the way children acquire language.

Bilingual catch-up

Can bilinguals catch up with monolingual children? As discussed in Chapter 3, language learning depends on the amount of input, that is, the length of time children hear each of their languages and, as they get older, the amount of time they actively engage in the languages by talking, watching television or videos, reading, etc. The language or languages spoken at school, and the topics children are required to engage with, all have an influence on further language learning.

The status of the language in the community is an important determining factor in long-term language acquisition. If the child grows up with a heritage language, a language that is not spoken in the community, it is unlikely that the child's language skills will be at the same level as the community language. Usually, the community language will become the child's dominant language in the course of time (see Chapter 3). A condition for the possibility of a catch-up is therefore that the two languages are part of the community already.

We discussed the status of the two languages in Wales back in Chapter 5. As both English and Welsh are spoken in the community, and there are a number of Welsh-medium schools, there is the possibility that bilingual Welsh–English speakers are comparable to their monolingual Welsh peers at some point. We saw that Gathercole et al. (2013) did not find any differences in children's vocabulary skills in children aged 13–15. This suggests a possible pattern in bilingual communities, such that the regular exposure to two languages leads to similar language skills in the longer term.

If this is the case, it could include both lexical and morpho-syntactic development as well. As we discussed in Chapter 3, the 'critical mass' hypothesis assumes that a certain amount of exposure is required in order for children to learn a particular structure. It seems that this period is longer in the case of bilinguals, but it is possible that they will have caught up with monolinguals at a certain point.

In Chapter 2 we discussed evidence from Spanish–English bilinguals which supports the Constructivist account (Gathercole, 2007). The same study also investigated different Welsh structures in children aged 5, 7 and 9, including their acquisition of gender. Children were grouped by the language that was spoken at home: only Welsh, English and Welsh, only English.

She found that the children who had the most exposure to Welsh performed better in the gender task than the bilingual and English-speaking children at home groups. Given that the catch-up in vocabulary occurred at the age of 13–15, can we expect that the other groups will have caught up on structures such as gender and plural at this age as well?

The question of whether there is a bilingual catch-up was investigated by Binks (2017) for vocabulary as well as gender and plurals in Welsh. We shall first give a brief outline of the way gender and plurals are formed in Welsh and then discuss the findings.

Welsh gender. Gender in other languages is often marked by the determiner, for example *le* and *la* in French mark masculine and feminine nouns respectively. While Welsh also has the two genders masculine and feminine, these are marked in part through a process of consonantal **mutation**. This means that the word-initial consonant of a noun undergoes morpho-phonological changes. In particular, Welsh feminine nouns undergo 'soft mutation' after the definite article and some numerals, but only in singular forms and for certain word-initial sounds.

For example, the noun *cat* in its citation form is *cath*, with an initial [k]. It changes from *cath* to *y gath* (the cat), [k] > [g], and the same change, [k] > [g], occurs in *dwy gath* (two cats). Masculine nouns do not change after the definite article but also change after certain numerals. For example, the noun *dog* changes from *ci*, again with initial [k], to *dau gi* (two dogs), with initial [g]. Overall, there is no clear form to function mapping, which makes gender marking difficult to learn.

Welsh plurals. The plural forms in Welsh are outlined in Box 9.1. Unlike English, where there is a default form and few irregular plurals, Welsh has eight different patterns of forming the plural. These include the addition of a suffix to the stem (as in *cath-cathod*), the deletion of the singular suffix (as in *mochyn-moch*), an exchange of the singular and plural suffix (as in *blodyn-blodau*), as well as patterns where either one vowel changes in addition to the previous forms, and patterns with more than one vowel change or where the plural form is completely different.

The complexity of the plural system means that even children who only hear Welsh at home do not reach adult levels in any of the different plurals forms up to the age of 11. This means that the acquisition of plural forms continues well into the teenage years.

Bilingual catch-up. Binks (2017) investigated the possibility of a catch-up for vocabulary in both languages, as well as gender and plural in Welsh. She compared a group of teenagers aged 12–13 with teenagers aged 15–16. Each age group included speakers with Welsh as their home language, simultaneous Welsh–English speakers, and L2 Welsh speakers.

Box 9.1: Plural forms in Welsh

1) and 2) the addition of a suffix (with or without vowel change)
   Example: *cath (cat)* becomes *cath**od*** (with the additional suffix *od*).
3) and 4) the deletion of the singular suffix (with or without vowel change)
   Example: the singular noun *mochyn* (pig) becomes *moch* (pigs).
5) and 6) exchange of the singular with a plural suffix (with or without vowel change)
   Example: the singular noun *blodyn* (flower) becomes *blod**au*** (flowers).
7) change of the first and penultimate vowel
   Example: the singular noun *castell* (castle) becomes *cestyll* (castles).
8) a plural form that is different from the singular form
   Example: The singular noun *ci* (dog) becomes *cŵn* (dogs).

For vocabulary, the subjects were tested in both English and Welsh. The tasks included a verbal analogy and verbal categorisation test and included 54 teenagers aged 12–13 and 88 teenagers aged 15–16. She found that both groups of teenagers had similar vocabulary levels for both languages, regardless of home language background. This is in line with the results by Gathercole et al. (2013) and suggests that bilinguals can indeed catch up at this age, provided there is ongoing language input.

To test gender, 154 teenagers aged 12–13 and 15–16, as well as 66 adult controls, were included. The participants were given a set of 30 sentences with masculine and feminine nouns, as well as a further sentence with a pronoun that referred back either to the masculine or the feminine noun. The subjects had to choose one of two pictures that showed the two initial referents. The picture they chose indicated whether or not they took the gender marking of the pronoun into account. The results showed a certain amount of catch-up. The performance of the 12–13-year-old teenagers who were bilingual or only had English at home was similar to that of the adults, but both groups scored below the group with only Welsh at home. These results indicate that the English at home group caught up with the bilingual speakers, but neither group reached the level of the L1 Welsh speakers.

The plural task involved the same participants as for the gender task. Participants were asked to provide the plural forms of a set of 25 different Welsh nouns. The results showed that teenagers in all language groups were below the adults, although the older speakers with only Welsh at home were close to the level of the adults. The bilingual teenagers at both age levels had higher scores than teenagers with only English at home, who performed at only 50–60% accuracy.

The investigation of Welsh by different language groups confirms that the language acquisition process continues up to, and including, the teenage years. A bilingual catch-up is possible, and has been shown here for vocabulary development, and partially for morpho-syntactic development. It seems that a catch-up depends on a variety of factors, including, of course, the amount of time that children and teenagers engage with both languages. Possible further factors that had an influence on the results were found to be language attitude as well as language confidence.

Offline and online tasks

In Chapter 7 we made a distinction between offline and online tasks. The language tests that were outlined in Chapters 5 and 6 are all offline tasks. While offline language tasks allow us to assess a child's level of language, they do not give any information about the mental processes involved during the tasks.

For example, during the Test of Early Grammatical Impairment (TEGI) past tense task, the child either provides correct regular and irregular past tense forms, overregularises irregular verb forms, or does not provide past tense forms for some or all of the items. This gives us some idea of the child's ability to apply rules or retrieve irregular forms, but it does not give us any insights into the child's processing of verbs during the task.

As we saw in Chapter 7, tasks including reaction time measurements, eye tracking and even-related potentials can provide some information about these mental processes. Reaction times give an indication of the amount of processing effort, eye fixations during a task give an indication of the particular stimulus that is processed at a particular point in time, and measurements of brain activity during a task give an indication of the types of processes (syntactic or semantic) that are taking place at a given moment in time.

Combining both offline and online tasks enables us to get information on both children's language level as well as their mental processes. One example where a task includes different measurements was discussed in Chapter 5. Masterson, Druks & Gallienne (2008) measured the accuracy as well as reaction times in a group of 5-year-olds naming noun and verb pictures. While the children were able to name nouns and verbs at similar levels of accuracy, they found that children had higher reaction times for naming verbs in comparison with nouns. They concluded that the semantic representation of verbs is more complex compared to nouns, which is why verb processing takes longer.

A different example involves the production and processing of English tense morphemes. Chondrogianni & Marinis (2012) compared 39 sequentially bilingual Turkish–English learners aged 6–9 with 28 monolingual English children aged 7, using a combination of offline and online tasks. The sequential learners were exposed to English from the age of 3.

Two offline comprehension tasks were the Test of Reception of Grammar task (TROG) (see Chapter 6), and the British Picture Vocabulary Scale (BPVS) (see Chapter 5). The tasks measure grammar and word comprehension respectively. It was found that the sequentially bilingual children had lower scores than the monolinguals on both tasks. This was expected, given that the monolingual children were exposed to English for a longer time than the bilinguals.

The children were also compared in terms of their production of grammar, using the offline TEGI (see Chapter 6). Comparing children's production of present and past tense morphemes, it was also found that the sequentially bilingual children were less accurate in both types of morphemes. This is also in line with the previous results.

In order to gain more information about children's processing of the task items, the participants also completed an online word processing task, where they had to listen out for a critical word and press a button when the word occurred. The task is illustrated in Box 9.2. The critical word always occurred after a verb which was either inflected or uninflected. The time it took the child to press the button at the point where the critical word was heard, is taken as evidence for the processing of the verb ending. The structures included in the task were third person –*s*, past tense –*ed*, progressive –*ing* and possessive –*s*.

The results from the word processing task show that the monolinguals were more accurate and they were also found to be faster at reacting to the critical word than the bilinguals. However, when the reaction times for inflected and uninflected sentences were compared, both groups were faster for the inflected sentences, compared to the uninflected ones. This result shows that both groups were processing the verb ending before the critical word, even if their accuracy levels were different.

Studies like the ones outlined in Box 9.2 clearly show that the inclusion of offline as well as online tasks can lead to new insights about the way language is processed by different groups of subjects.

STUDY ACTIVITY 9.1

1. Welsh bilingual teenagers were similar to speakers with Welsh only at home for vocabulary levels but not for plural and gender marking. Consider possible reasons for this result.
2. What information can be gained by using online tasks together with offline tasks? Consider reaction time measurements, eye tracking and event-related potentials.

Bilingual language processing

Another direction for the study of bilingual development is the application of studies that have addressed adult bilingual processing. We have seen in the models and studies discussed in Chapter 7 that the cognate status of a word was found to have an effect in picture-naming and translation tasks, but that it also plays a role in early bilingual acquisition.

In recent years, one focus of adult bilingual processing has been on the question of whether both languages of the bilingual are always activated when language is processed, even if the context only requires one of the language systems to be active. If a bilingual has no choice as to whether or not both languages are active, this means that there is a constant competition between words and grammatical structures. This could explain the bilingual advantage that was discussed in Chapter 8.

We shall outline some evidence relating to parallel activation in adults and discuss their implications for the study of simultaneous and sequential bilingual children.

Box 9.2: Word processing task

In the word processing task, children are given a critical word (and picture) and hear a sentence. They have to press a button on the keyboard when they hear the critical word. In each case, the target word occurs after a verb that is either inflected or uninflected.

Inflected sentence

> John's mum likes to bake. Most nights she bakes <u>muffins</u> for him and his friends.

Uninflected sentence

> Kerry usually has a snack after school. Most days after school she eat <u>apples</u> and grapes before the evening meal.

The idea behind the task is that there will be a difference in children's reaction time, depending on whether the verb is inflected or not. If children process the ending of the verb unconsciously, then a missing inflection should result in more processing and therefore a longer reaction time.

Bilingual co-activation in adults

In Chapter 7, the distributed lexical/conceptual feature model was outlined. This assumes that both the conceptual as well as the lexical level can be defined in terms of different features. For the lexical level, these are the different phonemes that make up a word. For the conceptual level, it was not so clear what the features represent. The model allows an overlap of features for word forms in both languages at both levels, the conceptual as well as the lexical level. This means that when a particular word is heard, the features of the word that overlap, also partially activate the word form in the other language. We shall consider two different studies that show parallel activation in adults.

A study by Marian, Blumenfeld & Boukrina (2008) used an eye-tracking paradigm to test co-activation of the two languages with 29 bilingual English–German adults aged 25. Half of the bilingual speakers (14) were native speakers of English, the other half (15) were native speakers of German. The methodology is outlined in Box 9.3.

The underlying idea of the paradigm is that the sound overlap between the target and the competitor word results in the activation of the competitor word in the subjects' mental lexicon. As a result, subjects fixate on the picture representing the word. If both languages of the bilingual are co-activated, bilinguals are expected to fixate on the cross-language competitor during the task.

The participants in the study were given 114 panels of four pictures. Half of them included targets and competitor words that were similar within English (*road-rope*, within language competition), the other half were targets and competitor words where the German translation equivalent was similar to the English target (*dove-Dach*, across language competition).

The results showed that in both conditions, the subjects fixated on the target as well as the competitor while processing the spoken form of the stimulus word. There were more fixations to the competitor compared to either of the filler pictures. This confirms that subjects did not look at the competitor picture just by chance, but the competitor fixations occurred as a result of the similar-sounding stimulus. The fact that the bilingual subjects looked at the competitor picture in both conditions (within language and across language) shows that both of their languages were activated when they heard a word.

The effect varied according to the number of similar sounding words of the target. If a word has a high number of so-called **neighbours** within the same language, it is said to have a high-density neighbourhood. For example, a word like *cat* has a larger number of similar sounding words. Those that share the first phoneme include: *can, cab, cap, cut, caught, coat, court, kite, kit, cart, cash, cot.*

On the other hand, if a word has fewer neighbours, it has a low-density neighbourhood. For example, a word like *dove* has fewer neighbours. Those that share the first phoneme include: *dug, duck, done, dumb, does, dull.* In the eye-tracking task, more competitor eye fixations occurred for low-density targets as opposed to high-density targets. It seems that when a bilingual speaker hears the initial sounds of a high-density target, more possible words are activated overall. This reduces the competition with the other words represented in the task.

The findings show that bilingual speakers activate both languages at the same time when they start hearing a word, even if the context only requires one of the languages to be active. This means that bilinguals do not make a language choice beforehand, rather, access to the mental word store is non-selective.

Bilingual co-activation in children

Having established that lexical access is non-selective in adults, is this also the case for bilingual children? Given that simultaneously bilingual children do not initially have translation equivalents for all of their words, co-activation might not be possible.

We shall consider two studies that have investigated this question in children. Von Holzen & Mani (2012) studied a group of 17 bilingual and 17 monolingual toddlers aged 21–43 months. The bilingual children heard German at home and both German and English at their pre-school. The monolingual toddlers only heard German. All children were tested using a preferential looking paradigm.

In the study, children were presented with an English carrier phrase *I saw X*, where the target word, *X*, always occurred at the end of the sentence and was always given in German. While children heard the carrier phrase, they saw a cross in the middle of the screen. Then two pictures appeared on a computer screen. The stimuli consisted of 12 German words that were identified as being acquired by the age of 18 months by both German and English children.

In this task, there were two different conditions: in the target-distractor condition, children were presented with a target and a distractor picture which was completely unrelated to the target, for example *eggs* and *clock*. On the other hand, in the target-prime condition, children were presented with a target and a picture where the word overlapped in sound with the English word of the represented picture (phonological priming) or with the German translation equivalent of the represented picture (phonological priming through translation).

For example, in the phonological priming condition, the target word *Kuh* (cow) was paired with the English word *blue* which overlaps in sound. This is similar to the across language condition in the study by Marian, Blumenfeld & Boukrina (2008).

An example of phonological priming through translation is given in a target like *Tasche* (bag), as the German translation equivalent of the paired picture, *bottle*, is *Flasche*, which rhymes with the target. This is similar to the within language condition in the study outlined in Box 9.3.

Box 9.3: Eye-tracking paradigm

In the eye-tracking paradigm used in this study, participants saw a number of panels consisting of four pictures in the corners of the screen and a cross in the middle of the display. One of the pictures was the target, another picture represented a word that sounds similar to the target word (the competitor). The two remaining pictures were fillers.

In the study, subjects were asked to first click on a particular target picture and then on a particular filler picture.

Example I:

Within language similarity: *road –rope*
The word of the picture of *rope* sounds similar to the word *road*
The task was carried out in English. In the panels, the word shown by the target picture sounded similar to the word shown by one of the other pictures. For example, in the within language display, the first two phonemes of the target word *rope* are the same as the first two phonemes of the word *road*.

Example 2:

Across language similarity: *dove –Dach*
The word of the picture of *dove* sounds similar to the German word *Dach* (roof). On the other hand, the first two phonemes of the target *dove* are similar to the German translation equivalent *Dach* (roof).

The results show a difference between monolingual and bilingual toddlers in recognising the targets in the target-prime condition. While the monolingual toddlers did not show any differences between the different conditions, the bilingual children's results show that it was easier for them to recognise the target when the word overlapped in sound with the English word of the picture displayed alongside the target. At the same time, their recognition of the target was reduced when the German translation of the primed word overlapped in sound with the target. The findings for the bilingual children together with the differences between the monolingual and bilingual toddlers, are seen as evidence that bilingual children are also activating both languages at the same time.

Different evidence for co-activation in children comes from a picture-naming task, where children were asked to produce names of the objects in the pictures. Poarch & van Hell (2012) tested 21 German second language learners of English aged 5–8 who were attending a bilingual pre-school or primary school in the Frankfurt area, 21 early German–English bilingual children aged 4–8, 19 trilingual 5–7-year-old children with either English or German as their third language, 15 monolingual German children aged 7, as well as 20 German–English bilingual adults aged 20–28. Children's language proficiency in English and German was tested using the TROG (see Chapter 6).

The picture-naming task consisted of 84 pictures that were black and white line drawings of different objects (Szekely et al., 2004). The names of 28 of the pictures were cognates between German and English, where the words sounded very similar in both languages (see Chapter 5). For example, the word *anchor* is a cognate between English and German as the German word is *Anker*. On the other hand, 28 words were non-cognates, where the words and their translation equivalents do not sound similar. For example, the word *tree* is a non-cognate as the German translation equivalent, *Baum* is not similar to the English form.

The bilinguals and second language learners were first tested with 56 pictures in German, and then with 28 new non-cognate words in English and 28 cognates that were repeated from the German task. The monolinguals were only tested with the German pictures.

The results showed that there was a cognate facilitation effect for all bilingual speakers in their non-dominant language, including the early bilinguals as well as the later learners and the trilingual children. The effect was not found in the monolingual children. The more balanced bilinguals also showed a cognate facilitation effect in their dominant language, though the effect was smaller. These results provide evidence for parallel activation of both languages in balanced bilinguals. They also show that language learners need to have developed a certain proficiency in their non-dominant language in order for co-activation to occur.

STUDY ACTIVITY 9.2

1. What is co-activation of both languages in bilingual speakers? Was co-activation shown for both adults and children?
2. What facilitates co-activation? Consider the role of phonological neighbourhood within and across the languages of the bilingual.

Bilingual reading

The last aspect to be outlined in terms of further directions of study in bilingualism, is reading. When children enter school, they will be taught to read, mostly in the dominant language, regardless of the language background of the child. For a number of children this means that they are learning to read in their minority language. Does this affect their ability to learn to read? On the other hand, does the exposure to more than one language result in bilingual children being more sound aware?

We shall look more at the acquisition of literacy in the context of a bilingual learner, but also take up the question of whether parallel activation of the two languages of the bilingual, which we saw in the previous section, also extends to the recognition of words that are written (written word recognition).

Literacy development in bilingual children

Bilingual children learn to read at least in one of their languages when they enter school. However, their language level in the majority language, together with other factors, such as the socio-economic status and education levels of the parents, have an influence on children's literacy development (Murphy, 2018).

Reading involves mapping visual words onto spoken words. The process requires phonological awareness skills, as well as letter knowledge, working memory and skills to access words from the mental lexicon. We discussed phonological awareness skills in bilingual children in relation to metalinguistic awareness in Chapter 8. It was found that phonological awareness was not always enhanced in bilingual children, but that this was dependent on the closeness of the two languages.

At the same time, a number of children who grow up with a minority language at home and learn English as an additional language (EAL), have been found to be below the level of monolingual children in terms of literacy development when they enter school.

A study by Bowyer-Crane et al. (2017) investigated the language and literacy skills of 80 monolingual children with language weaknesses and 80 children with EAL. The children were tested when they started school and the tests were repeated after 2 years.

The language tests that were used included tests to assess children's phonological skills, vocabulary and grammar. Children's literacy skills were assessed with the York Assessment of Reading for Comprehension test (YARC) (Hulme et al. (2009). In particular, the study assessed children's ability to match letters and sounds, word reading, spelling and reading comprehension. An example of the relationship between letters and sounds in English is given in Box 9.4.

The study found a difference between the monolingual children and the EAL children in terms of expressive language skills, both at the point of school entry, as well as after two years of schooling. While the initial difference can be explained in terms of the amount of input that children have had (see Chapter 3), the two years of schooling clearly did not provide enough input for the EAL children to close the gap.

On the other hand, the results show that the EAL children were similar to the monolinguals in terms of reading comprehension and better in word reading and spelling at both observation points. This shows that the lower expressive skills have not affected the literacy development of the EAL children.

Box 9.4: Letter-sound relationship in English

| ice | horse | dress | seesaw |

Phonemes map onto letters in different ways. In English, the /s/ sound is represented by the letter s in words like *sun* or *seesaw*, but it maps onto the letters ss in words such as *dress* and *kiss*, the letters se in words like *horse* or *purse* and the letters ce in words such as *ice* and *mice*.

Letter-sound matching is not the same for different languages. For example, in German, the sound /s/ maps onto the letter s in words like *Eis* (ice cream), and the letters ss in words like *Tasse* (cup). Overall, there are fewer mapping options.

In terms of a possible bilingual advantage, the study found that the EAL children were better than the monolingual children at repeating **non-words**, letter strings that are possible but do not have meaning in a language. But there was no difference between the two groups in terms of their phonological skills.

Visual word recognition

The findings of the study on children's literacy development are interesting as they lead on to the question of what processes children engage in during the process of reading and word recognition.

When adults read words, they also activate the phonological representation of the words. This can be compared to reading aloud internally and has been confirmed by tiny movements of the speech organs during reading. Children at school often read aloud when decoding the letters of a word. But does this mean that they automatically activate the sounds of words they read, as adults do?

Are there differences between monolingual and bilingual children in terms of visual word recognition? Do bilingual children activate the other language when reading in the same way as has been shown for auditory word recognition in both adults and children in the previous section?

A study by Sauval et al. (2017) investigated these questions in a group of 78 French–English bilingual children aged between 8 and 10. The children were exposed to both languages from early on. They attended two French schools in London where the teaching was about 70% in French and 30% in English. The children learnt to read in both languages.

The children were given a lexical decision task (see Chapter 7) where they saw a sequence of uppercase letters on a computer screen and were instructed in French to decide whether the letter sequence was a real word or not and press the appropriate button. The children saw 106 different letter strings. Half of them (53) were real words in French, the other half (53) were French pseudowords. Pseudowords are strings that are plausible words in the language, yet they do not have any meaning. For example, the string *brillig* could be an English word, but it does not have an assigned meaning.

Before children saw the target word for the lexical decision, they saw a word segment for 60 milliseconds (masked prime). All primes were fragments of English words and were either similar in sound to the beginning of the French word, or they started with the same letter, or were unrelated.

For example, for the French target word *rouge* (red), the phonological prime was *roo* (where the English phonological form overlapped with the beginning of the French word), the orthographic prime was *roe* (where the first letter overlapped with the French word) and the unrelated prime was *fie* (where there was no overlap).

The results showed that the older group of children had lower reaction times than the younger group. This shows that children are able to react faster as they get older. Both groups of children were found to be equally affected by the presence of a prime that resembled an English word. Their reaction times were significantly lower in the phonological priming condition, compared with the orthographic priming and unrelated conditions. This means that the presence of the phonological prime enabled the children to make the decision faster.

STUDY ACTIVITY 9.3

1. Does bilingualism lead to bilingual literacy? Consider different bilingual learners and different types of schooling (majority language schools, immersion, bilingual schools).
2. Do bilingual children who learn to read in just one language still co-activate both languages when reading words?

This result firstly suggests that children at both ages activated the phonological representation of the written words that they saw in the experiment. This means that the children at both ages processed the written words in a similar way to the adults. Secondly, the fact that the phonological cue was based on the other language suggests that phonological activation during visual word recognition affects both languages, similar to the co-activation of words in both languages when a word is heard.

Bilingual acquisition: Costs and benefits

Research on bilingual language acquisition is in agreement that bilinguals do not acquire their languages later than monolingual children, nor do children get confused by hearing two languages from early on. However, when looking at bilingualism from birth to the teenage years, results show some costs and specific benefits.

Any costs are associated with language skills, in particular word knowledge, but also grammatical language skills. The benefits are in relation to cognitive advantages, particularly in terms of 'executive functions' (see Chapter 8).

We shall look at the costs and benefits of growing up bilingually in relation to both simultaneous as well as sequential bilingual learners.

Simultaneous bilingual learners

Simultaneous bilinguals hear more than one language from very early on, and in most cases they hear them in the home. But this does not necessarily mean that the amount of exposure time to both languages is exactly the same. For example, the child might spend more time with one of the caretakers. Also, the speech rate between caretakers can vary.

We saw in Chapters 5 and 6 that simultaneous bilinguals tend to have lower vocabulary and grammar skills, compared to monolingual children, in at least one of their languages. Gathercole et al. (2016) also found differences between monolinguals and simultaneous bilinguals with regard to development of semantic categories where there is a difference in the application of terms across languages (*tree* including *arbol* and *palmera* in Spanish). These findings, together with possible cross-linguistic influences that we discussed in Chapter 5, can be seen as the 'cost' of growing up with more than one language.

But we need to see these possible costs in perspective. Studies of young children show that, when the concepts are counted (including words from either language), there is no difference between monolingual and bilingual children at an early stage. As was discussed in Chapter 5, rather than looking at language skills as a cost in bilingual acquisition, differentiated norms would enable a more helpful comparison of developing language skills.

Lower language skills are often seen in relation to lower academic achievement. But this is not generally the case for children based on their language status. Bowyer-Crane et al. (2017) found that the EAL children were as good as the monolinguals in reading comprehension.

At the same time, simultaneous bilingual children in particular were found to have enhanced cognitive skills involving executive functioning, such as inhibitory control, non-verbal working memory and shifting (see Chapter 8). Most of the children tested in tasks such as the Simon task and the Flanker task were children who spoke more than one language from birth in the home. They showed enhanced performance in relation to their monolingual peers.

The findings discussed earlier in this chapter also show that bilingual children activate both languages at the same time when engaged in language and reading tasks, similar to adults. This is not surprising. The cognitive functions that are enhanced in bilinguals involve the ability to suppress another stimulus, and the ability to shift from one task to another. These skills are used when selecting one language system over another and thereby suppressing the other system.

Sequential bilingual learners

What about the costs and benefits of learning another language sequentially? Sequential bilingual learners are an even more heterogeneous group, as the onset of another language is different for individual children. Also, the amount of exposure varies for individual children.

In the case of children living in Wales where only English is spoken at home, the results of the Gathercole (2007) study clearly show that sequential learners have lower language skills in Welsh than the monolingual and simultaneous bilingual children, showing that the level of exposure determines the level of language at a given point.

Obviously, the language situation within the community also makes a difference: if a child lives in a community where the home language is the dominant language and the other language is acquired through attending an immersion pre-school, for example, the child's language skills in the dominant language will continue to develop. On the other hand, a child who speaks a minority language at home will pick up the dominant community language over time, but their language skills are lower than those of monolinguals for some time.

Findings from studies using online and offline tasks show that children who have been exposed to another language do not process words or grammar differently, even though the results from offline tasks show a lower level of language.

STUDY ACTIVITY 9.4

1. Do you think that bilingual acquisition can be seen in terms of costs and benefits?
2. Can sequentially bilingual children and second language learners develop the same cognitive advantages as simultaneous bilinguals?

In terms of the cognitive advantage, we have seen in the study by Bialystok & Barac (2012) that this develops gradually with regular exposure to another language. Their findings suggest that the cognitive advantage is not limited to simultaneous bilinguals. This means that learning another language has distinct cognitive advantages, regardless of the age at which the language is learnt.

SUMMARY

In this chapter we have discussed different directions for further study of bilingual acquisition. In the area of language development, it seems that it is possible for bilingual children to catch up with their monolingual peers, provided there is ongoing input in the catch-up language. While language tasks show lower levels of language for bilingual children, a combination of online and offline tasks is useful, not only in measuring language skills but also the processes underlying those language skills.

Studies of bilingual processing in adults have found that bilingual speakers co-activate both languages in language tasks, even when only one of the languages is required, such as picture naming. The studies that have been carried out with children show a similar co-activation for both spoken and written word processing.

Bilingual children do not always learn to read and write in both of their languages. A number of sequentially bilingual children learn to read and write in their subsequent language only. In general, even where language skills are lower compared to monolinguals, this does not seem to affect word comprehension.

Lower language skills in bilinguals can be seen as a cost of being exposed to two languages, however, there is no evidence of lower academic achievement. A comparison with monolingual norms is misleading. Any potential costs need to be seen in relation to the cognitive advantages that have been shown for both simultaneous and sequential bilinguals.

FURTHER READING

The possibility of a bilingual catch-up was first found in Gathercole et al. (2013) and investigated further in Binks (2017). For a comparison of plurals in different child and adult learners see Thomas et al. (2014). For a summary of the literature on adult bilingual language co-activation, see Bobb & Kroll (2018). For an account of vocabulary and reading in the Welsh context, see Rhys & Thomas (2013). Finally, for a summary of bilingualism and executive function see Bialystok (2018).

Data sources

Unless otherwise stated, the examples in the boxes are taken from personal knowledge or constructed.

Chapter 1

Box 1.1, p.2: Examples from personal experience
Box 1.2, p.5: Constructed example
Box 1.3, p.6: Adapted from Redlinger & Park (1980)
Box 1.4, p.7: Louis (Ronjat, 1913), Hildegard (Leopold, 1939–49),
        Eve (Tabouret-Keller, 1969), Lisa and Giulia (Taeschner, 1983),
        Kate (de Houwer, 1990), Siri and Thomas (Lanza, 1997),
        Manuela (Deuchar & Quay, 2001)
Box 1.5, p.14: Eppler (1999)
Box 1.6, p.15: Peter (Stern & Stern, 1907), Douchan (Pavlovitch, 1920),
        Stephen (Burling, 1959), Raivo (Vihman, 1985), Hanna (Bolonyai, 1998)
Box 1.7, p.23: Adapted from Klammler & Schneider (2011)
Box 1.8, p.27: Piaget (1929, pp. 81–83)

Chapter 2

Box 2.1, p.31: Genesee et al. (1995, p. 630)
Box 2.2, p.33: Volterra & Taeschner (1978, pp. 321–323)
Box 2.3, p.38: Chomsky (1995)
Box 2.4, p.41: Example a) is taken from Gawlitzek-Maiwald & Tracy (2005, p. 292)
        Example b) is taken from Döpke (1998, p. 567)
        Example c) is taken from Yip & Matthews (2000, p. 198)
Box 2.5, p.43: The data is taken from the Italian conversations of the Koroschetz corpus,
        CHILDES database (Koroschetz, 2008)
Box 2.6, p.44: The data is taken from the German conversations of the Koroschetz corpus,
        CHILDES database (Koroschetz, 2008)
Box 2.7, p.49: Gathercole (2007, pp. 230–235)

Chapter 3

Box 3.1, p.57: Romaine (1999, pp. 253–255)
Box 3.2, p.61: Granena & Long (2012, p. 321)
Box 3.3, p.62: Granena & Long (2012, p. 324)
Box 3.4, p.64: Granena & Long (2012, p. 325)
Box 3.5, p.65: Naigles & Hoff-Ginsberg (1998)

Box 3.6, p.68: Adapted from the FerFuLice Corpus, CHILDES, bilingual corpus, Liceras et al. (2008)

Box 3.7, p.69: Adapted from the FerFuLice Corpus, CHILDES, bilingual corpus, Liceras et al. (2008)

Box 3.8, p.72: Adapted from the Bangor Miami corpus in Talkbank, https://talkbank. org/access/BilingBank/Bangor/Miami.html

Box 3.9, p.75: Cantone (2007, pp. 178–181)

Chapter 4

Box 4.1, p.80: Werker, Polka & Pegg (1997)

Box 4.2, p.82: Byers-Heinlein et al. (2010)

Box 4.3, p.83: Sundara, Polka & Genesee (2006)

Box 4.4, p.85: Adapted from Boysson-Bardies & Vihman (1991)

Box 4.5, p.87: From Dodd, Holm, Hua & Crosbie (2003)

Chapter 5

Box 5.1, p.93: Example from personal experience

Box 5.2, p.95: Markman (1990)

Box 5.3, p.97: Clark (1987b)

Box 5.4, p.98: Adapted from Deuchar & Quay (2001, p. 59)

Box 5.5, p.99: Schelletter (2002)

Box 5.6, p.103: http://wordbank.stanford.edu/

Box 5.7, p.106: Schelletter (2016)

Box 5.8, p.107: Gathercole et al. (2013)

Box 5.9, p.110: Rohde (2010, p. 56)

Box 5.10, p.112: Szekely et al. (2004)

Chapter 6

Box 6.1, p.117: Brown (1973)

Box 6.2, p.118: Personal knowledge

Box 6.3, p.122: Berko-Gleason (1958)

Box 6.4, p.123: de Houwer (1990)

Box 6.5, p.125: Serratrice (2001)

Box 6.6, p.128: Adapted from Jia & Fuse (2007)

Box 6.7, p.130: Kersten et al. (2012)

Box 6.8, p.131: Rice & Wexler (2001)

Box 6.9, p.132: Paradis et al. (2011)

Box 6.10, p.134: Gagarina et al. (2015)

Chapter 7

Box 7.1, p.141: Meyer & Schvaneveldt (1971)

Box 7.2, p.142: Personal experience

Box 7.3, p.143: Example printout from the BE GAZE Experimental Software, Sensomotoric Instruments (SMI), https://www.smivision.com/

Box 7.4, p.147: Adapted from Collins & Loftus (1975)
Box 7.5, p.148: Miller et al. (1990)
Box 7.6, p.150: Collins & Loftus (1975)
Box 7.7, p.151: Adapted from Paivio & Desrochers (1980)
Box 7.8, p.152: Personal knowledge
Box 7.9, p.153: Adapted from Kroll & Stewart (1994)
Box 7.10, p.154: Constructed example
Box 7.11, p.155: Constructed example
Box 7.12, p.157: Kroll & de Groot (2014)
Box 7.13, p.160: Adapted from Dong et al. (2005)
Box 7.14, p.161: Rosch, Mervis, Gray, Johnson & Boyes-Braem (1976)
Box 7.15, p.163: Gathercole et al. (2016)

Chapter 8

Box 8.1, p.168: Siegler, DeLoache & Eisenberg (2003)
Box 8.2, p.169: Piaget (1936)
Box 8.3, p.170: Baren-Cohen et al. (1985)
Box 8.4, p.171: Karmiloff-Smith (1999, p. 92)
Box 8.5, p.175: Campbell & Sais (1995)
Box 8.6, p.177: Ricciardelli (1993, pp. 361–362)
Box 8.7, p.180: Murphy & Pine (2003, p. 151)
Box 8.8, p.182: Reck & Hund (2011, p. 506)
Box 8.9, p.183: Baddeley (2007)
Box 8.10, p.184: Carle (2002)
Box 8.11, p.185: Miyake et al. (2000)
Box 8.12, p.188: Simon (1969)
Box 8.13, p.189: Eriksen & Eriksen (1974)

Chapter 9

Box 9.1, p.195: Binks (2017, p. 88)
Box 9.2, p.198: Montgomery & Leonard (2006)
Box 9.3, p.200: Marian et al. (2008)
Box 9.4, p.203: Personal knowledge

Bibliography

Aitchison, J. (2012). *Words in the Mind: An Introduction to the Mental Lexicon*. Oxford: Blackwell.

Al-Hindawy, S. (2016). A longitudinal investigation of a sequential Arabic–English bilingual child's vocabulary development. Undergraduate thesis, Missouri State University.

Armstrong, S. & Ainley, M. (2007). *South Tyneside Assessment of Syntactic Structures 2: STASS 2*. Ponteland, Northumberland: STASS Publications.

Baddeley, A. D. (2007). *Working Memory, Thought, and Action* (Vol. 45). Oxford: Oxford University Press.

Balason, D. & Dollaghan, C. (2002). Grammatical morpheme production in 4-year-old children. *Journal of Speech, Language, and Hearing Research, 45*, 961–969.

Barac, R., Bialystok, E., Castro, D. C. & Sanchez, M. (2014). The cognitive development of young dual language learners: A critical review. *Early Childhood Research Quarterly, 29*(4), 699–714.

Baren-Cohen, S. (2001). Theory of mind in normal development and autism. *Prisme, 34*, 174–183.

Baren-Cohen, S., Leslie, A. & Frith, U. (1985). Does the autistic child have a 'theory of mind'?. *Cognition, 21*, 37–46.

Bedore, L. & Peña, E. D. (2008). Assessment of bilingual children for identification of language impairment: Current findings and implications for practice. *International Journal of Bilingual Education and Bilingualism, 11*(1), 1–29.

Benedict, H. (1979). Early lexical development: Comprehension and production. *Journal of Child Language, 6*, 183–200.

Ben-Zeev, S. (1977). The influence of bilingualism on cognitive strategy and cognitive development. *Child Development, 48*(3), 1009.

Berko-Gleason, J. (1958). The child's learning of English morphology. *Word, 14*, 150–177.

Best, J. R. & Miller, P. H. (2010). A developmental perspective on executive function. *Child Development, 81*(6), 1641–1660.

Bialystok, E. (1986). Factors in the growth of linguistic awareness. *Child Development, 57*(2), 498–510.

Bialystok, E. (1988). Levels of bilingualism and levels of linguistic awareness. *Developmental Psychology, 24*(4), 560–567.

Bialystok, E. (2001). *Bilingualism in Development: Language, Literacy and Cognition*. Cambridge: Cambridge University Press.

Bialystok, E. (2009). Bilingualism: The good, the bad, and the indifferent. *Bilingualism: Language and Cognition, 12*(1), 3–11.

Bialystok, E. (2010). Global-local and trail-making tasks by monolingual and bilingual children: Beyond inhibition. *Developmental Psychology, 46*(1), 93–105.

Bialystok, E. (2018). Bilingualism and executive function. In D. Miller, F. Bayram, J. Rothman & L. Serratrice, (Eds.), *Bilingual Cognition and Language* (pp. 283–306). Amsterdam: John Benjamins.

Bialystok, E. & Barac, R. (2012). Emerging bilingualism: Dissociating advantages for metalinguistic awareness and executive control. *Cognition, 122,* 67–73.

Bialystok, E., Luk, G., Peets, K. F. & Yang, S. (2010). Receptive vocabulary differences in monolingual and bilingual children. *Bilingualism: Language and Cognition, 13*(4), 525–531.

Bialystok, E., Majumder, S. & Martin, M. M. (2003). Developing phonological awareness: Is there a bilingual advantage?. *Applied Psycholinguistics, 24*(1), 27–44.

Bialystok, E., Peets, K. F. & Moreno, S. (2014). Producing bilinguals through immersion education: Development of metalinguistic awareness. *Applied Psycholinguistics, 35,* 177–191.

Binks, H. (2017). *Investigating the Bilingual 'Catch-up' in Welsh–English Bilingual Teenagers.* Unpublished PhD thesis., Bangor University, Wales.

Bishop, D. (2003). *Test for Reception of Grammar* (version 2 (TROG 2)). London: Harcourt Assessment.

Bishop, D. (2014). *Uncommon Understanding.* Hove: Psychology Press.

Blom, E. & Unsworth, S. (2010). *Experimental Methods in Language Acquisition Research.* Amsterdam: Benjamins.

Bobb, S. & Kroll, J. F. (2018). Words on the brain: The bilingual mental lexicon. In D. Miller, F. Bayram, J. Rothman & L. Serratrice, (Eds.), *Bilingual Cognition and Language* (pp. 307–324). Amsterdam and Philadelphia: John Benjamins.

Bolonyai, A. (1998). In-between languages: Language shift/maintenance in childhood bilingualism. *The International Journal of Bilingualism, 2*(1), 21–43.

Bosch, L. & Ramon-Casas, M. (2014). First translation equivalents in bilingual toddlers' expressive vocabulary: Does form similarity matter?. *International Journal of Behavioral Development, 38*(4), 317–322.

Bowerman, M. (1980). The structure and origin of semantic categories in the language-learning child. In M. Foster & S. Brandes, (Eds.), *Symbol as Sense* (pp. 277–299). New York: Academic Press.

Bowerman, M. & Levinson, S. C. (2001). *Language Acquisition and Conceptual Development.* Cambridge: Cambridge University Press.

Bowyer-Crane, C., Fricke, S., Schaefer, B., Lervåg, A. & Hulme, C. (2017). Early literacy and comprehension skills in children learning English as an additional language and monolingual children with language weaknesses. *Reading and Writing, 30*(4), 771–790.

Boysson-Bardies, B. D. & Vihman, M. M. (1991). Adaptation to language: Evidence from babbling and first words in four languages. *Language, 67*(2), 297–319.

Brown, R. (1973). *A First Language.* Oxford: Harvard University Press.

Burling, R. (1959). Language development of a Garo- and English-speaking child. *Word, 15,* 45–68.

Bybee, J. (1995). Regular morphology and the lexicon. *Language and Cognitive Processes, 10*(5), 425–455.

Bybee, J. (2006). From usage to grammar: The mind's response to repetition. *Language, 82*(4), 711–733.

Byers-Heinlein, K,. Burns, T. & Werker, J. (2010). The roots of bilingualism in newborns. *Psychological Sciences, 21*(3), 343–348.

Byers-Heinlein, K. (2013). Parental language mixing: Its measurement and the relation of mixed input to young bilingual children's vocabulary size. *Bilingualism: Language and Cognition, 16*(1), 32–48.

Byers-Heinlein, K. (2018). Speech perception. In F. Grosjean & K. Byers-Heinlein, (Eds.), *The Listening Bilingual. Speech Perception, Comprehension, and Bilingualism* (pp. 153–175). Hoboken, NJ: Wiley-Blackwell.

Byers-Heinlein, K., Burns, T. C. & Werker, J. F. (2010). The roots of bilingualism in newborns. *Psychological Science, 21*(3), 343–348.

Campbell, R. & Sais, E. (1995). Accelerated metalinguistic (phonological) awareness in bilingual children. *British Journal of Developmental Psychology, 13*(1), 61–68.

Cantone, K. (2007). *Code-Switching in Bilingual Children* (Vol. 37). Dordrecht: Springer.

Carle, E. (2002). *The Very Hungry Caterpillar.* London: Puffin.

Carroll, S. E. (2017). Exposure and input in bilingual development. *Bilingualism: Language and Cognition, 20*(1), 3–16.

Chomsky, N. (1965). *Aspects of the Theory of Syntax.* Cambridge, MA: MIT Press.

Chomsky, N. (1981). *Lectures on Government and Binding.* Dordrecht: Foris.

Chomsky, N. (1995). *The Minimalist Programme.* Cambridge, MA: MIT Press.

Chondrogianni, V. & Marinis, T. (2012). Production and processing asymmetries in the acquisition of tense morphology by sequential bilingual children. *Bilingualism: Language and Cognition, 15*(1), 5–21.

Clahsen, H. & Felser, C. (2006). Grammatical processing in language learners. *Applied Psycholinguistics, 27,* 3–42.

Clark, E. (1987). The principle of contrast: A constraint on language acquisition. In B. MacWhinney, (Ed.), *Mechanisms of Language Aquisition.* Hillsdale, NJ: Lawrence Erlbaum.

Clark, E. (1995). *The Lexicon in Acquisition.* Cambridge: Cambridge University Press.

Collins, A. M. & Loftus, E. F. (1975). A spreading activation theory of semantic processing. *Psychological Review, 82,* 407–428.

Collins, A. M. & Quillian, M. R. (1969). Retrieval time from semantic memory. *Journal of Verbal Learning and Verbal Behaviour, 8,* 240–247.

Conboy, B. T. & Montanari, S. (2016). Early lexical development in bilingual infants and toddlers. In B. A. Goldstein (Ed.), *Bilingual language development & disorders in Spanish–English speakers* (2nd ed.) (pp. 47–71). Baltimore, MD: Paul H.Brookes.

Costa, A. & Caramazza, A. (2000). The cognate faciliation effect: Implications for models of lexical access. *Journal of Experimental Psychology: Learning, Memory and Cognition, 26*(5), 1283–1296.

Craik, F. I. M., Bialystok, E. & Freedman, M. (2010). Delaying the onset of Alzheimer disease: Bilingualism as a form of cognitive reserve. *Neurology, 75*(19), 1726–1729.

Crystal, D., Fletcher, P. & Garman, M. (1989). *The Grammatical Analysis of Language Disability,* 2nd Edition. London: Cole & Whurr.

Davis, B. & MacNeilage, P. (1995). The articulatory basis of babbling. *Journal of Speech and Hearing Research, 38,* 1199–1211.

de Houwer, A. (1990). *The Acquisition of Two Languages from Birth: A Case Study.* Cambridge: Cambridge University Press.

de Houwer, A. (1995). Bilingual language acquisition. In P. Fletcher & B. MacWhinney, (Eds.), *Handbook of Child Language* (pp. 219–250). Oxford: Blackwell.

de Houwer, A. (2014). The absolute frequency of maternal input to bilingual and monolingual children. In T. Grüter & J. Paradis, (Eds.), *Input and Experience in Bilingual Development* (pp. 37–58). Amsterdam: John Benjamins.

de Houwer, A., Bornstein, M. & Putnik, D. (2014). A bilingual-monolingual comparison of young children's vocabulary size: Evidence from comprehension and production. *Applied Psycholinguistics, 35*(6), 1189–1211.

Deuchar, M. & Quay, S. (2001). *Bilingual Acquisition: Theoretical Implications of a Case Study.* Oxford: Oxford University Press.

Dodd, B., Holm, A., Hua, Z. H. U. & Crosbie, S. (2003). Phonological development: A normative study of British English-speaking children. *Clinical Linguistics & Phonetics, 17*(8), 617–643.

Doherty, M. (2009). *Theory of Mind: How Children Understand Others' Thoughts and Feelings.* Hove: Psychology Press.

Dong, Y., Gui, S. & MacWhinney, B. (2005). Shared and separate meanings in the bilingual mental lexicon. *Bilingualism: Language and Cognition, 8*(3), 221–238.

Döpke, S. (1992). *One Parent One Language: An Interactional Approach.* Amsterdam: John Benjamins.

Döpke, S. (1998). Competing language structures: The acquisition of verb placement by bilingual German–English children. *Journal of Child Language, 25*, 555–584.

Döpke, S. (2000). *Cross-Linguistic Structures in Simultaneous Bilingualism.* Amsterdam: John Benjamins.

Dunn, D. & Dunn, L. (2013). Peabody Picture Vocabulary Test, Fourth Edition (PPVT).

Dunn, D., Dunn, L. & Styles, B. (2009). *The British Picture Vocabulary Scale* (3rd Ed. BPVS3). London: GL Assessment.

Edwards, S., Letts, C. & Sinka, I. (2011). *The New Reynell Developmental Language Scales (NRDLS).* London: GL Assessment.

Eimas, P. D., Siqueland, E. R., Jusczyk, P. & Vigorito, J. (1971). Speech perception in infants. *Science, 171*(3968), 303–306.

Eppler, E. (1999). Word order in German–English mixed discourse. *UCL Working Papers in Linguistics, 11*, 285–309.

Eriksen, B. & Eriksen, C. (1974). Effects of noise letters upon identification of a target letter in a non- search task. *Perception and Psychophysics, 16*, 143–149.

Fabiano-Smith, L. & Goldstein, B. A. (2010). Phonological acquisition in bilingual Spanish–English speaking children. *Journal of Speech, Language, and Hearing Research, 53*(1), 160–178.

Fantini, A. E. (1985). *Language Acquisition of A Bilingual Child: A Sociolinguistic Perspective (To Age Ten).* San Diego, CA: College Hill Press.

Fellbaum, C. (2005). WordNet and wordnets. In A. Barber, *Encyclopedia of Language and Linguistics* (2nd edn, pp. 2–665). Oxford: Elsevier.

Fennell, C., Tsui, A. & Hudon, T. (2016). Speech perception in simultaneously bilingual infants. In E. Nicoladis & S. Montanari, (Eds.), *Bilingualism across the Lifespan: Factors Moderating Language Proficiency* (pp. 43–62). Washington, DC: Mouton de Gruyter.

Fenson, L., Dale, P., Reznick, J., Bates, E. & Thal, D. (1994). Variability in early communicative development. *Monographs of the Society for Research in Child Development, 59.* 242.

Fifer, W. P., Byrd, D. L., Kaku, M., Eigsti, I.-M., Isler, J. R., Grose-Fifer, J., et al. (2010). Newborn infants learn during sleep. *Proceedings of the National Academy of Sciences of the United States of America, 107*(22), 10320–10323.

Foursha-Stevenson, C. & Nicoladis, E. (2011). Early emergence of syntactic awareness and cross-linguistic influence in bilingual children's judgments. *International Journal of Bilingualism, 15*(4), 521–534.

Gagarina, N., Klop, D., Kunnari, S., Tantele, K., Välimaa, T., Balčiūnienė, I., et al. (2015). Assessment of narrative abilities in bilingual children. In S. Armon-Lotem, J. de Jong & N. Meir, (Eds.), *Assessing Multilingual Children: Disentangling Bilingualism from Language Impairment* (pp. 243–276). Bristol: Multilingual Matters.

Ganger, J. & Brent, M. (2004). Reexamining the vocabulary spurt. *Developmental Psychology, 40*(4), 621–632.

Garman, M., Schelletter, C. & Sinka, I. (1999). Three hypotheses on early grammatical development. In M. Perkins & S. Howard, (Eds.), *New Directions in Language Development and Disorders* (pp. 73–84). New York: Kluwer/Plenum.

Gathercole, V. (2007). Miami and North Wales, so far and yet so near: A Constructivist account of morpho-syntactic development in bilingual children. *International Journal of Bilingual Education and Bilingualism, 10*, 22–247.

Gathercole, V. (2013a). *Issues in the Assessment of Bilinguals* (1.), Bristol: Multilingual Matters.

Gathercole, V. (2013b). *Solutions for the Assessment of Bilinguals* (1.), Bristol: Multilingual Matters.

Gathercole, V., Stadthagen-González, H., Pérez-Tattam, R. & Yavaş, F. (2016). Semantic and conceptual factors in Spanish–English bilinguals' processing of lexical categories in their two languages. *Second Language Research, 32*(4), 537–562.

Gathercole, V., Thomas, E. & Hughes, E. (2008). Designing a normed receptive vocabulary test for bilingual populations: A model from Welsh. *International Journal of Bilingual Education and Bilingualism, 11*(6), 678–720.

Gathercole, V., Thomas, E., Roberts, E., Hughes, C. & Hughes, E. (2013). Why assessment needs to take exposure into account: Vocabulary and grammatical abilities in bilingual children. In V. Gathercole, (Ed.), *Issues in the Assessment of Bilinguals*. Bristol: Multilingual Matters.

Gawlitzek-Maiwald, I. & Tracy, R. (2005). The multilingual potential in emerging grammars. *International Journal of Bilingualism, 9*(2), 277–297.

Genesee, F., Nicoladis, E. & Paradis, J. (1995). Language differentiation in early bilingual development. *Journal of Child Language, 22*(3), 611–631.

Gentner, D. (1982). Why nouns are learned before verbs: Linguistic relativity versus natural partitioning. In S. Kuzcaj, (Ed.), *Language Development, Vol. 2, Language, Thought and Culture* (pp. 301–334). New Jersey: Erlbaum.

Gershkoff-Stowe, L. & Hahn, E. R. (2007). Fast mapping skills in the developing lexicon. *Journal of Speech, Language, and Hearing Research, 50*, 682–697.

Gleason, J. B. (1975). Father's and other strangers: Men's speech to young children. In D. P. Dato, (Ed.), *Developmental Psycholinguistics: Theory and Applications* (pp. 289–297). Washington: Georgetown University Press.

Goldfield, B. & Reznick, J. (1990). Early lexical acquisition: Rate, content and the vocabulary spurt. *Journal of Child Language, 17*, 171–184.

Goldstein, B. A. & Bunta, F. (2012). Positive and negative transfer in the phonological systems of bilingual speakers. *International Journal of Bilingualism, 16*(4), 388–401.

Granena, G. & Long, M. (2012). Age of onset, length of residence, language aptitude, and ultimate L2 attainment in three linguistic domains. *Second Language Research, 29*(3), 311–343.

Grosjean, F. (2008). Studying bilinguals: Methodological and conceptual issues. In T. Bhatia & W. Ritchie, (Eds.), *The Handbook of Bilingualism*. Oxford: Blackwell.

Grüter, T. & Paradis, J. (2014). *Trends in Language Acquisition Research: Input and Experience in Bilingual Development*. Amsterdam: John Benjamins.

Hager, M. & Müller, N. (2015). Ultimate attainment in bilingual first language acquisition. *Lingua 164.* 289–308.

Haman, E., Łuniewska, M. & Pomiechowska, B. (2015). Designing cross-linguistic lexical tasks (CLTs) for bilingual preschool children. In S. Armon-Lotem, J. de Jong & N. Meir, (Eds.), *Assessing Multilingual Children: Disentangling Bilingualism from Language Impairment* (pp. 196–242). Bristol: Multilingual Matters.

Hart, B. & Risley, T. R. (1995). *Meaningful Differences in the Everyday Experience of Young American Children*. Baltimore, MD: P.H. Brookes.

Henry, L. (2011). *The Development of Working Memory in Children* (1.), London: SAGE Publications.

Hoek, D., Ingram, D. & Gibson, D. (1986). Some possible causes of children's early word overextensions. *Journal of Child Language, 3*, 477–495.

Hoff, E. & Naigles, L. (2002). How children use input to acquire a lexicon. *Child Development, 73*(2), 418–433.

Hoffmann, C. (1985). Language acquisition in two trilingual children. *Journal of Multilingual and Multicultural Development, 6*, 479–495.

Huettig, F., Rommers, J. & Meyer, A. (2011). Using the visual world paradigm to study language processing: A review and critical evaluation. *Acta Psychologica, 137*, 151–171.

Hulk, A. & Müller, N. (2000). Bilingual first language acquisition at the interface between syntax and pragmatics. *Bilingualism: Language and Cognition, 3*(3), 227–244.

Hulme, C., Stothard, S. E., Clarke, P., Bowyer-Crane, C., Harrington, A., Truelove, E., et al. (2009). *York Assessment of Reading for Comprehension: Early Reading [Measurement Instrument]*. London: GL Assessment.

Huth, A. G., de Heer, W. A., Griffiths, T. L., Theunissen, F. E. & Gallant, J. L. (2016). Natural speech reveals the semantic maps that tile human cerebral cortex. *Nature, 532*, 453–458.

Hyams, N. (1986). *Language Acquisition and the Theory of Parameters*. Norwell, MA: Kluwer Academic Publishers.

Ianco-Worrall, A. (1972). Bilingualism and cognitive development. *Child Development, 43*, 1390–1400.

Jia, G. & Fuse, A. (2007). Acquisition of English grammatical morphology by native Mandarin-speaking children and adolescents: Age-related differences. *Journal of Speech, Language, and Hearing Research, 50*, 1280–1299.

Jørgensen, N., Dale, P., Bleses, D. & Fenson, L. (2010). CLEX: A cross-linguistic lexical norms database. *Journal of Child Language, 37*(2), 419–428.

Jusczyk, P. (1997). *The Discovery of Spoken Language*. Cambridge, MA: MIT Press.

Karmiloff-Smith, A. (1999). *Beyond Modularity: A Developmental Perspective on Cognitive Science*. Cambridge, MA: MIT Press.

Karmiloff-Smith, A., Grant, J., Sims, K., Jones, M.-C. & Cuckle, P. (1996). Rethinking metalinguistic awareness: Representing and accessing knowledge about what counts as a word. *Cognition, 58*, 197–219.

Kay, D. & Anglin, J. (1982). Overextension and underextension in the child's expressive and receptive speech. *Journal of Child Language, 9*(1), 83–98.

Kersten, K., Piske, T., Rohde, A., Steinlen, A., Weitz, M. & Kurth, S. (2012). *ELIAS Grammar Test II*. Unpublished manuscript, Magdeburg.

Kersten, K., Rohde, A., Schelletter, C. & Steinlen, A. (2010). *Bilingual Preschools Volume 1: Learning and Development*. Trier: Wissenschaftlicher Verlag Trier.

Klammler, A. & Schneider, S. (2011). The size and composition of the productive holophrastic lexicon: German–Italian bilingual acquisition vs. Italian monolingual acquisition. *International Journal of Bilingual Education and Bilingualism, 14*(1), 69–88.

Klassert, A., Gagarina, N. & Kauschke, C. (2014). Object and action naming in Russian- and German-speaking monolingual and bilingual children. *Bilingualism: Language and Cognition, 17*(1), 73–88.

Koroschetz, C. (2008). *Sprachentrennung und Spracheinfluss im bilingualen Erstspracherwerb: Strategien der Personenmarkierung eines italienisch-deutsch bilingualen Kindes*. Unpublished master's thesis, University of Graz.

Kroll, J. F. & de Groot, A. M. B. (2014). Lexical and conceptual memory in the bilingual: Mapping form to meaning in two languages. In A. de Groot & J. Kroll, (Eds.), *Tutorials in Bilingualism* (pp. 169–199). Mahwah, NJ: Lawrence Erlbaum.

Kroll, J. F. & De Groot, A. M. B. (2005). *Handbook of Bilingualism: Psycholinguistic Approaches.* Oxford: Oxford University Press.

Kroll, J. F. & Stewart, E. (1994). Category interference in translation and picture naming: Evidence for asymmetric connections between bilingual memory representations. *Journal of Memory and Language, 33,* 149–174.

Lanza, E. (1997). *Language Mixing in Infant Bilingualism: A Sociolinguistic Perspective.* Oxford: Oxford University Press.

Lanza, E. (2008). Multilingualism and the family. In P. Auer & L. Wei, (Eds.), *Handbook of Multilingualism and Multilingual Communication* (pp. 45–68). Berlin and New York: Mouton de Gruyter.

Lenneberg, E. (1967). *Biological Foundations of Language.* New York: Wiley.

Leopold, W. F. (1939). *Speech Development of a Bilingual Child: A Linguist's Record. Vol. 1: Vocabulary growth in the first two years.* Evanston, Illinois: Northwestern University Press.

Leopold, W. F. (1947). *Speech Development of a Bilingual Child: A Linguist's Record. Vol. 2: Sound-learning in the first two years.* Evanston, Illinois: Northwestern University Press.

Leopold, W. F. (1949). *Speech Development of a Bilingual Child: A Linguist's Record. Vol. 3: Grammar and general problems in the first two years.* Evanston, Illinois: Northwestern University Press.

Leopold, W. F. (1949). *Speech Development of a Bilingual Child: A Linguist's Record. Vol. 4: Diary from age 2.* Evanston, Illinois: Northwestern University Press.

Liceras, J. M., Fernández Fuertes, R., Perales, S., Pérez-Tattam, R. & Spradlin, K. T. (2008). Gender and gender agreement in bilingual native and non-native grammars: A view from child and adult functional-lexical mixings. *Lingua, 118*(6), 827–851.

McCarthy, K. M., Mahon, M., Rosen, S. & Evans, B. G. (2014). Speech perception and production by sequential bilingual children: A longitudinal study of voice onset time acquisition. *Child Development, 85*(5), 1965–1980.

McLaughlin, B. (1977). Second language acquisition in childhood. *Psychological Bulletin, 84*(3), 438–459.

McLaughlin, B. (1978). *Second-Language Acquisition in Childhood.* Hillsdale, NJ: Lawrence Erlbaum Associates.

MacWhinney, B. (2000). *The CHILDES Project: Tools for Analyzing Talk. Volume 1: Transcription Format and Programs. Volume 2: The Database.* Mahwah, NJ: Lawrence Erlbaum Associates.

Marchman, V. A. & Bates, E. (1994). Continuity in lexical and morphological development: A test of the critical mass hypothesis. *Journal of Child Language, 21*(2), 339–366.

Marcus, G., Brinkmann, U., Clahsen, H. & Wiese, R. (1995). German inflection: The exception that proves the rule. *Cognitive Psychology, 29,* 189–256.

Marian, V., Blumenfeld, H. & Boukrina, O. (2008). Sensitivity to phonological similarity within and across languages. *Journal of Psycholinguistic Research, 37*(3), 141–170.

Markman, E. M. (1990). Constraints children place on word meanings. *Cognitive Science, 14,* 57–77.

Masterson, J., Druks, J. & Gallienne, D. (2008). Object and action picture naming in three- and five-year-old children. *Journal of Child Language, 35,* 373–402.

Matthews, D. & Tomasello, M. (2009). Grammar. In J. B. Benson & M. M. Haith, (Eds.), *Language, Memory and Cognition in Infancy and Early Childhood* (pp. 192–204). Oxford: Academic Press.

Mehler, J., Jusczyk, P., Lambertz, G., Halsted, N., Bertoncini, J. & Amiel-Tison, C. (1988). A precursor of language acquisition in young infants. *Cognition, 29*(2), 143–178.

Meisel, J. (1989). Early differentiation of languages in bilingual children. In K. Hylten-stam & L. Obler, (Eds.), *Bilingualism across the life span. Aspects of acquisition, maturity, and loss* (pp. 13–40). Cambridge: Cambridge University Press.

Meisel, J. (1994). Code-switching in young bilingual children. The acquisition of grammatical constraints. *Studies in Second Language Acquisition, 16*, 413–439.

Meisel, J. (2004). The bilingual child. In T. Bhatia & W. Ritchie, (Eds.), *The Handbook of Bilingualism* (pp. 91–113). Oxford: Blackwell Publishing.

Meisel, J. (2007). The weaker language in early child bilingualism: Acquiring a first language as a second language?. *Applied Psycholinguistics, 28*(03), 495–514.

Meisel, J. (2011). *First and Second Language Acquisition.* Cambridge: Cambridge University Press.

Meyer, D. E. & Schvaneveldt, R. W. (1971). Facilitation in recognizing pairs of words. *Journal of Experimental Psychology, 90*, 227–234.

Miller, G. (1995). WordNet: A lexical database for English. *Communications of the ACM, 38*(11), 39–41.

Miller, G., A., Beckwith, R., Fellbaum, C., Gross, D. & Miller, K. J. (1990). Introduction to wordNet: An on-line lexical database. *International Journal of Lexicography, 3*(4), 235–244.

Miller, J. & Chapman, R. (1981). The relation between age and mean length of utterance in morphemes. *Journal of Speech and Hearing Research, 24*, 154–161.

Miyake, A., Friedman, N. P., Emerson, M. J., Witzki, A. H., Howerter, A. & Wager, T. D. (2000). The unity and diversity of executive functions and their contributions to complex 'frontal lobe' tasks: A latent variable analysis. *Cognitive Psychology, 41*, 49–100.

Montgomery, J. W. & Leonard, L. B. (2006). Effects of acoustic manipulation on the real-time inflectional processing of children with specific language impairment. *Journal of Speech, Language, and Hearing Research, 49*(6), 1238–1256.

Montrul, S. A. (2008). *Incomplete acquisition in bilingualism: re-examining the age factor.* Amsterdam: John Benjamins.

Morales, J., Calvo, A. & Bialystok, E. (2013). Working memory development in monolingual and bilingual children. *Journal of Experimental Child Psychology, 114*(2), 187–202.

Morrow, A., Goldstein, B. A., Gilhool, A. & Paradis, J. (2014). Phonological skills in English language learners. *Language, Speech, and Hearing Services in Schools, 45*(1), 26–39.

Müller, N. & Cantone, K. (2009). Language mixing in bilingual children. In B. Bullock & A. Toribio, (Eds.), *Linguistic Code-Switching* (pp. 199–220). Cambridge: Cambridge University Press.

Müller, N. & Hulk, A. (2001). Crosslinguistic influence in bilingual language acquisition: Italian and French as recipient languages. *Bilingualism: Language and Cognition, 4*(1), 1–21.

Murphy, V. A. (2018). Literacy development in linguistically diverse pupils. In D. Miller, F. Bayram, J. Rothman & L. Serratrice, (Eds.), *Bilingual Cognition and Language* (pp. 155–182). Amsterdam/Philadephia: John Benjamins.

Murphy, V. A. & Pine, K. J. (2003). L2 influence on L1 linguistic representations. In V. J. Cook, (Ed.), *Effects of the Second Language on the First* (pp. 142–167). Clevedon: Multilingual Matters.

Naigles, L. & Hoff-Ginsberg, E. (1998). Why are some verbs learned before other verbs? Effect of input frequency and structure on children's early verb use. *Journal of Child Language, 25*, 95–120.

Newman, A. J., Ullman, M. T., Roumyana, P., Waligura, D. L. & Neville, H. J. (2007). An ERP study of regular and irregular English past tense inflection. *Neuroimage, 34,* 435–445.

Nguyen, T.-K. & Astington, J. W. (2014). Reassessing the bilingual advantage in theory of mind and its cognitive underpinnings. *Bilingualism, 17*(2), 396–409.

Oller, D. K. & Eilers, R. E. (2002). *Language and Literacy in Bilingual Children.* Clevedon: Multilingual Matters.

Paivio, A. & Desrochers, A. (1980). A dual coding approach to bilingual memory. *Canadian Journal of Psychology/Revue Canadienne De Psychologie, 34*(4), 388–399.

Paradis, J. (2001). Do bilingual two-year-olds have separate phonological systems?. *International Journal of Bilingualism, 5*(1), 19–38.

Paradis, J. (2010). Bilingual children's acquisition of english verb morphology: Effects of language exposure, structure complexity, and task type. *Language Learning, 60*(3), 651–680.

Paradis, J. & Genesee, F. (1996). Syntactic acquisition in bilingual children: Autonomous or interdependent?. *Studies in Second Language Acquisition, 18,* 1–15.

Paradis, J. & Genesee, F. (1997). On continuity and the emergence of functional categories in bilingual first-language acquisition. *Language Acquisition, 6*(2), 91–124.

Paradis, J., Nicoladis, E., Crago, M. & Genesee, F. (2011). Bilingual children's acquisition of the past tense: A usage-based approach. *Journal of Child Language, 38,* 554–578.

Pavlenko, A. (2009). Conceptual representation in the bilingual lexicon and second language vocabulary learning. In A. Pavlenko, (Ed.), *The Bilingual Mental Lexicon* (pp. 125–160). Bristol: Multilingual Matters.

Pavlovitch, M. (1920). *Le langage enfantin; acquisition du serbe et du français par un enfant serbe.* Paris: Librairie Ancienne Hnore Champion.

Piaget, J. (1929). *The Child's Conception of the World.* London: Routledge & Kegan Paul.

Piaget, J. (1936). *Origins of Intelligence in the Child.* London: Routledge & Kegan Paul.

Piaget, J. (1997). *The Language and Thought of the Child* (3rd.), Hoboken, NJ: Taylor & Francis.

Pierce, L., Genesee, F., Gauthier, K. & Dubois, M.-E. (2015). Communication patterns between parents and children: Comparing mothers and fathers in different learner contexts. *Applied Psycholinguistics, 36*(5), 1223–1246.

Pine, K. & Messer, D. (2003). The development of representations as children learn about balancing. *British Journal of Developmental Psychology, 21,* 285–301.

Pine, K., Messer, D. & St. John, K. (2002). Children's learning from contrast modelling. *Cognitive Development, 17*(2), 1249–1263.

Pinker, S. (2015). *Words and Rules: The ingredients of language.* New York: Basic Books.

Pinker, S. & Ullman, M. T. (2002). The past and future of the past tense. *TRENDS in Cognitive Sciences, 6*(1), 456–463.

Pizzuto, E. & Caselli, M. (1992). The acquisition of Italian morphology: Implications for models of language development. *Journal of Child Language, 19,* 491–557.

Poarch, G. J. & van Hell, J. G. (2012). Cross-language activation in children's speech production: Evidence from second language learners, bilinguals, and trilinguals. *Journal of Experimental Child Psychology, 111,* 419–438.

Podesva, R. J. & Sharma, D. (2013). *Research Methods in Linguistics.* Cambridge: Cambridge University Press.

Poulin-Dubois, D. & Goodz, N. (2001). Language differentiation in bilingual infants: Evidence from babbling. In J. Cenoz & F. Genesee, (Eds.), *Trends in Bilingual Acquisition* (Vol. 1, pp. 95–106). Amsterdam: John Benjamins.

Quay, S. (1995). The bilingual lexicon: Implications for studies of language choice. *Journal of Child Language, 22*, 369–387.

Radford, A. (1990). *Syntactic Theory and the Acquisition of English Syntax.* Oxford: Blackwell.

Reck, S. G. & Hund, A. M. (2011). Sustained attention and age predict inhibitory control during early childhood. *Journal of Experimental Child Psychology, 108*(3), 504–512.

Redlinger, W. & Park, T. (1980). Language mixing in young bilinguals. *Journal of Child Language, 7*, 337–352.

Renfrew, C. & Mitchell, P. (2010). *Word Finding Vocabulary Test.* Bicester: Speechmark Publishing.

Rhys, M. & Thomas, E. M. (2013). Bilingual Welsh–English children's acquisition of vocabulary and reading: Implications for bilingual education. *International Journal of Bilingual Education and Bilingualism, 16*(6), 633–656.

Ricciardelli, L. A. (1992). Bilingualism and cognitive development in relation to threshold theory. *Journal of Psycholinguistic Research, 21*(4), 301–316.

Ricciardelli, L. A. (1993). Two components of metalinguistic awareness: Control of linguistic processing and analysis of linguistic knowledge. *Applied Psycholinguistics, 14*(3), 349–367.

Rice, M. & Wexler, K. (2001). *Test of Early Grammatical Impairment: Examiner's Manual.* San Antonio, TX: The Psychological Corporation.

Richards, B. J. (1994). Child-directed speech and influences on language acquisition: Methodology and interpretation. In C. Gallaway & B. J. Richards, (Eds.), *Input and Interaction in Language Acquisition* (pp. 74–106). Cambridge: Cambridge University Press.

Rispens, J. & De Brie, E. (2015). Bilingual children's production of regular and irregular past tense morphology. *Bilingualism: Language and Cognition, 18*(2), 290–303.

Rohde, A. (2010). Receptive L2 lexical knowledge in bilingual preschool children. In K. Kersten, A. Rohde, C. Schelletter & A. Steinlen, (Eds.), *Bilingual Preschools. Volume 1: Learning and Development* (Vol. 1, pp. 45–68). Trier: Wissenschaftlicher Verlag.

Romaine. (1999). Bilingual language development. In M. Barratt. (Ed.), *The Development of Language* (pp. 251–276). Hove: Psychology Press.

Ronjat, J. (1913). *Le Developpement Du Langage Observe Chez Un Enfant Bilingue.* Paris: Champion.

Rosch, E., Mervis, C., Gray, W., Johnson, D. & Boyes-Braem, P. (1976). Basic objects in natural categories. *Cognitive Psychology, 8*, 382–439.

Rueda, M. R., Fan, J., McCandliss, B. D., Halparin, J. D., Gruber, D. B., Lercari, L. P., et al. (2004). Development of attentional networks in childhood. *Neuropsychologia, 42*(8), 1029–1040.

Rumelhart, D. E. & McClelland, J. L. (1986). On learning the past tenses of English verbs. In J. L. McClelland e. al. (Ed.), *Parallel Distributed Processing: Explorations in the Microstructures of Cognition* (Vol. 2, pp. 216–271). Cambridge, MA: MIT Press.

Sauval, K., Perre, L., Duncan, L. G., Marinus, E. & Casalis, S. (2017). Automatic phonological activation during visual word recognition in bilingual children: A cross-language masked priming study in grades 3 and 5. *Journal of Experimental Child Psychology, 154*, 64–77.

Schelletter, C. (2002). The effect of form similarity on bilingual children's lexical development. *Bilingualism: Language and Cognition, 5*(02), 93–107.

Schelletter, C. (2016). Wortschatzlernen in bilingualen Kindertagesstätten. In T. Piske & A. K. Steinlen, (Eds.), *Bilinguale Programme in Kindertageseinrichtungen:*

Umsetzungsbeispiele Und Forschungsergebnisse (pp. 219–238). Tübingen: Gunther Narr Verlag.

Schlyter, S. (1990). The acquisition of tense and aspect. In J. Meisel, (Ed.), *Two First Languages*. Dordrecht: Foris.

Schmitz, K., Patuto, M. & Müller, N. (2012). The null-subject parameter at the interface between syntax and pragmatics: Evidence from bilingual German–Italian, German–French and Italian–French children. *First Language, 32*(1–2), 205–238.

Sekerina, I., Fernández, E. M. & Clahsen, H. (2008). *Developmental psycholinguistics: on-line methods in children's language processing.* Amsterdam: John Benjamins.

Serratrice, L. (2001). The emergence of verbal morphology and the lead-lag pattern issue in bilingual acquisition. In J. Cenoz & F. Genesee (Eds.), *Trends in Bilingual Acquisition* (pp. 43–70). Amsterdam: Benjamins.

Serratrice, L. (2005). The role of discourse pragmatics in the acquisition of subjects in Italian. *Applied Psycholinguistics, 26*, 437–462.

Siegler, R. S., DeLoache, J. S. & Eisenberg, N. (2003). *How Children Develop*. New York: Worth.

Simon, J. (1969). Reactions toward the source of stimulation. *Journal of Experimental Psychology, 81*, 174–176.

Slobin, D. (1985). *The Crosslinguistic Study of Language Acquisition* (Vol. 1). Hillsdale, NJ: Lawrence Erlbaum.

Snodgrass, J. G. (1993). Translating versus picture naming. In R. Schreuder & B. Weltens, (Eds.), *The Bilingual Lexicon*. Amsterdam: John Benjamins.

Snow, C. (1995). Issues in the study of input: Finetuning, universality, individual and developmental differences, and necessary causes. In P. Fletcher & B. MacWhinney, (Eds.), *The Handbook of Child Language*. Oxford: Blackwell.

Stern, C. & Stern, W. (1907). *Die Kindersprache: Eine Psychologische und Sprachtheoretische Unlersuchung.* Leipzig: Earth.

Sundara, M., Polka, L. & Genesee, F. (2006). Language-experience facilitates discrimination of /d/ in monolingual and bilingual acquisition of English. *Cognition, 100*(2), 369–388.

Szekely, A., Jacobsen, T., D'Amico, S., Devescovi, A., Andonova, E., Herron, D., et al. (2004). A new on-line resource for psycholinguistic studies. *Journal of Memory and Language, 51*(2), 247–250.

Tabouret-Keller, A. (1969). *Le bilinguisme de l'enfant avant six ans: Etude en milieu alsacien*. Strasbourg.

Taeschner, T. (1983). *The Sun Is Feminine: A Study on Language*. Berlin: Springer.

Tardif, T. (1996). Nouns are not always learned before verbs: Evidence from Mandarin speakers' early vocabularies. *Developmental Psychology, 32*(3), 492–504.

Thomas, E. M., Williams, N., Jones, L. A., Davies, S. & Binks, H. (2014). Acquiring complex structures under minority language conditions: Bilingual acquisition of plural morphology in Welsh. *Bilingualism, 17*(3), 478–494.

Tomasello, M. (1992). *First Verbs: A Case Study of Early Grammatical Development*. Cambridge: Cambridge University Press.

Tomasello, M. (2003). *Constructing a Language: A Usage-Based Theory of Language Acquisition*. Cambridge, MA and London: Harvard University Press.

Tomasello, M. (2009). The usage-based theory of language acquisition. In E. Bavin, (Ed.), *The Cambridge Handbook of Child Language*. Cambridge: Cambridge University Press.

Unsworth, S. (2014). Comparing the role of input in bilingual acquisition across domains. In T. Grüter & J. Paradis, (Eds.), *Input and Experience in Bilingual Development* (pp. 181–201). Amsterdam: John Benjamins.

Vihman, M. (1985). Language differentiation by the bilingual infant. *Journal of Child Language, 12*, 297–324.

Vihman, M. (2016). Prosodic structures and templates in bilingual phonological development. *Bilingualism, 19*(1), 69–88.

Volterra, V. & Taeschner, T. (1978). The acquisition and development of language by bilingual children. *Journal of Child Language, 5*, 311–326.

Von Holzen, K. & Mani, N. (2012). Language nonselective lexical access in bilingual toddlers. *Journal of Experimental Child Psychology, 113*(4), 569–586.

Weinreich, U. (1953). *Languages in Contact: Findings and Problems.* Linguistic Circle of New York.

Werker, J. F., Polka, L. & Pegg, J. E. (1997). The conditioned head turn procedure as a method for testing infant speech perception. *Early Development and Parenting, 6*(3–4), 171–178.

Wiig, E. H. & Secord, W. (1992). *Test of Word Knowledge.* San Antonio, TX: Pearson.

Williams, K. T. (2007). *The Expressive Vocabulary Test* (2nd Ed.). Circle Pines, MN: AGS Publishing.

Xanthos, A., Laaha, S., Gillis, S., Stephany, U., Aksu-Koç, A., Christofidou, A., et al. (2011). On the role of morphological richness in the early development of noun and verb inflection. *First Language, 31*(4), 461–479.

Yip, V., Mai, Z. & Matthews, S. (2018). CHILDES for bilingualism. In D. Miller, F. Bayram, J. Rothman & L. Serratrice, (Eds.), *Bilingual Cognition and Language* (pp. 183–201). Amsterdam: John Benjamins.

Yip, V. & Matthews, S. (2000). Syntactic transfer in a Cantonese–English bilingual child. *Bilingualism: Language and Cognition, 3*(3), 193–208.

Glossary of Terms

Agglutinative   languages are called agglutinative if the morphological endings map onto a specific meaning and are added to a word.

Analysis of knowledge   knowledge of how language works. For example, the knowledge of what a word is and the boundary between what is a word and what is not a word.

Antonyms   words that are opposite in meaning: *hot* and *cold*.

Accommodation   a process which occurs if a new object or situation does not fit into an existing schema and the schema has to be revised as a result.

Assimilation   a process whereby a new object or situation is adapted into an existing schema.

Bound morpheme   a morpheme that cannot stand alone, i.e. needs to be attached to a word.

Closed class words   closed class words include: articles (a, the), conjunctions (and, because), pronouns (he, she), auxiliaries (have, do) and prepositions (on, under). They are closed because no new words can be added.

Code-switching   conscious use of elements of more than one language in one utterance.

Cognates   word forms that are similar in sound and meaning across two languages.

Collocation   words that frequently occur together are collocated.

Compound Bilingual   a term introduced by Weinreich (1953) to describe a bilingual who has separate language forms but a common conceptual level.

Concept   abstract knowledge that is built up on the basis of experience.

Control of attention   the ability to selectively attend to a particular aspect of a representation or a stimulus.

Co-ordinate Bilingual   a term introduced by Weinreich (1953) to describe a bilingual who has separate language and conceptual systems for both languages.

Critical Mass   this refers to the point in a child's development where they have internalised a particular language form and what the form represents.

Cross-sectional   observation of data at a particular point in time.

Deductive (Top Down)   a way of reasoning where general assumptions are derived first and specific predictions subsequently tested using empirical data.

Embedded Language   the language of the bilingual that is less activated at a given time.

Equilibration   the state in Piaget's theory where there is a balance between the child's schema's and the experiences encountered.

Executive Functions   mental processes that are involved in behaviour to achieve a particular goal. They include inhibitory control, working memory and shifting.

Exposure   the language a child hears at a particular time and in a particular context.

Free morpheme   a morpheme that can stand on its own, i.e. does not need to be attached to a word.

Functional categories   a term from the Universal Grammar. Functional Categories include closed class words and inflections, as well as their phrasal extensions.

223

Grapheme   the written representations of phonemes.

Heritage language   a language that a speaker only hears in the home and that is not spoken in the community.

High Amplitude Sucking paradigm   a method where the sucking rate of infants is measured with an adapted dummy while infants hear different sounds.

Hyponymy   a semantic relationship between words, based on inclusion: *an apple is a type of fruit.*

Inductive (Bottom up)   a way of reasoning where empirical data is observed and assumptions and theories derived from the data.

Inhibitory Control   the ability to stop yourself from acting in a particular way.

Input   the language or languages that are spoken in the environment of the child.

Language Acquisition Device (LAD)   the innate linguistic knowledge that children are assumed to have.

Lemma   a particular word form, including the grammatical information.

Language processing   the mental processes that are involved in understanding and speaking language.

Longitudinal   observation of data over a particular period of time.

Mean Length of Utterans (MLU)   a measure in child language which determines the average number of morphemes of a child's utterance.

Mental Representations   the knowledge that we have about language, the language forms as well as the relations between these forms.

Mental Word Store   the part of the mind that stores knowledge of words and their meanings.

Meronomy   a semantic relationship between words where one is a part of the other: *Feathers are part of a bird.*

Metalinguistic Awareness   the knowledge a speaker has about their language.

Matrix Language   the language of a bilingual that is more activated in a given context.

Mixing   this term is used to describe children's use of elements from both languages in the same utterance.

Morpheme   the smallest grammatical unit that has meaning, for example the plural in *cats.*

Mutual Exclusivity Constraint   this constraint refers to children's tendency not to accept more than one label for a specific object.

Non-cognates   word forms that have a similar meaning across languages but do not overlap in their phonology.

Object Permanence   a state in Piaget's theory where the child has realised that objects exist even if they are not visible to the child.

Offline Task   an experimental task that measures the behaviour that occurs as a result of a particular stimulus, for example picture naming.

Online Task   an experimental method that enable us to get information about the mental processes involved in processing language, such as reaction time measurements or eye tracking.

One person one Language Principle (OPOL)   this was suggested by Ronjat (1913). It refers to a strategy used by parents with different native languages to speak their native language to their child.

Open Class words   open class words include nouns, verbs, adjectives and adverbs. They are open because new items can be added.

Overregularisation   treating an irregular verb form like a regular. Children of a particular age overregularise past tense verbs and plural nouns: *drawed, mouses.*

Parameter Setting   Chomsky assumed that children have a set of innate options. Learning language involves setting the parameters.

Phoneme   the smallest unit of sound that results in changes of meaning: *cat-mat*.

Phonological Processes   systematic error patterns that young children apply in their sound productions.

Priming   the facilitation of a stimulus by a prior, similar stimulus.

Pro(noun)-drop   the characteristic of particular languages (such as Italian) to drop certain pronouns when these can be inferred from the context.

Sensitive Period   a sensitive period (critical period) is a time window when something needs to happen, otherwise it is too late.

Simultaneous Bilingual   someone who grew up with two languages from birth or shortly after birth.

Sequential Bilingual   someone who has grown up with two languages but exposure to the second language started after birth but before the age of 3–4.

Shifting   the ability to change attention from one task to another.

Subordinate Bilingual   a term introduced by Weinreich (1953) to describe a bilingual where the second language word forms are linked to the first language forms for all concepts of a word.

Taxonomic Constraint   an assumed mechanism whereby children know that words refer to a group of objects that share common features.

Visual World Paradigm   an experimental task which involves a visual display consisting of line drawings of objects or semi-realistic scenes and a stimulus relating to the scene.

Vocabulary Spurt   a period of accelerated word growth in children, usually between 18 and 24 months.

Voice Onset Time (VOT)   the interval between the release of the closure of the vocal tract and the vibration of the vocal cords.

Whole Object Constraint   an assumed mechanism whereby children will assign a given label only to the object as a whole, rather than any of the parts.

Working Memory   the ability to hold information in your mind in order to complete a particular task.

Index